LIGHTHEARTED EVERYDAY
COOKING

ANNE LINDSAY

MCM Books
A Division of Canada Publishing Corporation
Toronto, Ontario, Canada

Canadian Cataloguing in Publication Data
Lindsay, Anne, 1943–
    Lighthearted everyday cooking

U.S. ed.
Includes index.
ISBN 0-7715-9061-X

1. Heart — Diseases — Diet therapy — Recipes.   2. Low-fat diet — Recipes.   I. Title.

RC684.D5L55 1994   641.5′638   C94-930550-2

Design by Libby Starke
Food photography by Clive Webster
Illustrations by Bo-Kim Louie
Food styling by Olga Truchan
Photograph of Anne Lindsay by Shane Harvey Productions

Cover photo: Harvest Vegetable Curry (page 171)

MCM Books
A Division of Canada Publishing Corporation
Toronto, Ontario, Canada

Printed in Canada

1 2 3 4 5   BP   98 97 96 95 94

CONTENTS

Author's Acknowledgements

I'd like to thank Nancy Byal and Lorri Fishman for their help with this edition. Also John Lough and the American Institute for Cancer Research for their support, and for providing the excellent introduction to this edition.

Anyone who hasn't been part of writing a healthy eating cookbook could never imagine the large number of people involved. I have the enjoyable task of cooking and writing but that is just a small part in the total work involved to produce this book. A few behind-the-scenes workers whom I would like to thank are:

Shannon Graham, my friend, dietitian and co-worker who has helped with recipe testing for all my cookbooks.

Nancy Williams, my sister-in-law, who researches and keeps my office in order.

Carol Dombrow, nutritionist, Heart and Stroke Foundation of Canada, who has put many hours into reading the manuscript and coordinating the nutritional analysis.

Denise Beatty, for always being available to consult.

Sharyn Joliat at Info Access, for the expert nutritional analysis.

Bev Renahan, for her careful editing of the recipes.

Clive Webster, photographer, Olga Truchan, food stylist, and Diane Hood, props coordinator, for the beautiful photographs.

Everyone involved with the book at the Heart and Stroke Foundation of Ontario and the national office.

Elizabeth Baird, friend and food editor at *Canadian Living* magazine for her help and support.

Susan Pacaud, Claire Arfin and all my friends who knowingly or unknowingly gave me recipes for this book.

Everyone at Macmillan for their commitment to the book, for being so pleasant to work with and special thanks to Philippa Campsie for giving up a few sunny weekends so this book could get out on time.

Many, many thanks to my family, first to my husband, Bob, for his constant support and excellent advice, and for doing the family grocery shopping on Saturday mornings when I worked. Thanks to my daughter Susie, sons Jeff and John, my most honest critics and usually willing dishwashers for all the great dinners we have together.

To everyone who has bought this book, I hope it will help you to have delicious dinners and mealtimes you enjoy every day. Your appreciation and regular use of my cookbooks makes me very happy.

PREFACE

Dear Friend,

For most of us it isn't news. We know a healthier diet can mean a healthier life. But what surprises many people is how interesting, good-tasting and easy healthier cooking can be. That's why the American Institute for Cancer Research is so pleased to be able to be part of *Lighthearted Everyday Cooking*. This cookbook is an absolutely wonderful example of how the principles of good nutrition can be an easy and enjoyable part of everyday meal preparation.

Today there is an overwhelming and still growing body of scientific evidence that our daily food choices play a major role in our health. The link between heart disease and dietary choices is well documented and one with which most of us are already familiar. But an even more important relationship may be the one between diet and cancer risk.

Each year more than one half million lives are lost to cancer, this nation's second leading cause of death. Yet current research indicates a great many of those lives could be saved with simple dietary changes. What that means is making simple changes to a diet that reduce the amount of fat and put much more emphasis on fruits, vegetables and whole grains. They're simple steps to take, but important ones for better health.

Yes, eating for better health does require some additional thinking, planning and effort. But as I think you'll see in *Lighthearted Everyday Cooking*, it does not require special knowledge, and the extra effort required is minimal. And there's no question the results make it all worthwhile. Not only will you be making changes that can mean better health for you and your family, but you will be enjoying delicious meals that are fun and easy to prepare.

Through its research programs and public health education programs, the American Institute for Cancer Research has helped to make an important difference in the fight against cancer. The Institute's proceeds from this cookbook will help further those research and education efforts. That's important. But just as important is the healthy change this cookbook can help bring to your own life.

Start today making changes for a healthier diet and lower cancer risk.

Marilyn Gentry
President
American Institute for Cancer Research

A COMMON-SENSE APPROACH TO EVERYDAY EATING

Today we know that the food choices we make have an important effect on our health. But too often it seems that making the right choices is difficult, inconvenient, expensive or just something too complicated to do. It doesn't have to be that way.

For more than a decade the American Institute for Cancer Research has been helping consumers understand that making dietary choices for lower cancer risk need not be difficult, complicated or time consuming. *Lighthearted Everyday Cooking* is one more example of how easy and good-tasting healthier eating can be.

In this book, best-selling cookbook author Anne Lindsay has put together a collection of more than 200 recipes, from appetizers through desserts, that are healthy and delicious. But just as important for today's busy families, they're foods that can be made quickly and simply and that everyone will truly enjoy.

Although you'll find some special-occasion recipes here, the real focus in *Lighthearted Everyday Cooking* is on everyday meals and cooking for today's active family. You'll also find tips on menu planning, food substitutions, smart shopping and healthy food preparation.

If you've been looking for delicious and easy ways to make some changes for healthier eating, *Lighthearted Everyday Cooking* can help. Enjoy discovering just how easy, interesting and delicious healthy eating can be. *Bon appétit.*

Getting Past the Confusion

"Don't eat that, it's bad for you."
"Careful, those kinds of foods can increase your risk of heart disease and cancer."
Does it often seem as though someone's leaning over your shoulder, wagging a finger and giving a lecture every time you reach for something to eat?
"Eat more of this — it lowers your risk for heart attacks."
"Don't forget to eat these — they offer cancer protection."
Do you feel that you're bombarded with advice from newspapers, magazines, television and radio, all based on the latest research and studies about the healthiest foods?

If all that advice sometimes makes you feel confused, don't worry, you're not alone. It's great that so many people are paying more attention to their health and to making healthy food choices, yet sometimes there just seems to be too much information from too many sources.

That excess of information can be particularly confusing when it comes to reporting all the latest scientific research. Too often the media has time or space for only part of the story. Or what turns out to be only a preliminary research study, perhaps a laboratory study on mice or cells, may be reported as if it's information ready for all of us to be following in our own kitchens.

Important lifestyle changes, such as changing to a healthy diet, should be based on proven research that is generally accepted throughout the medical and health communities, not just on the latest preliminary report headlined on last night's evening news.

That's why the American Institute for Cancer Research, or AICR, has used widely accepted reports and authorities, such as *Diet, Nutrition and Cancer* and *Diet and Health* from the National Academy of Sciences, and the 1990 report of the U.S. Surgeon General. These reports, as well as information from research studies funded by AICR and other organizations, are the basis of the American Institute for Cancer Research's Dietary Guidelines to Lower Cancer Risk, a set of easy-to-follow guidelines that can play a significant role in promoting good health.

AICR Dietary Guidelines to Lower Cancer Risk

1. **Reduce the intake of total dietary fat from the current average of approximately 37% to a level of no more than 30% of total calories and, in particular, reduce the intake of saturated fat to less than 10% of total calories.**
2. **Increase the consumption of fruits, vegetables and whole grains.**
3. **Consume salt-cured, salt-pickled and smoked foods only in moderation.**
4. **Drink alcoholic beverages in moderation, if at all.**

An Easy Way to Healthy Eating

The Dietary Guidelines to Lower Cancer Risk can be the foundation on which to build a healthier diet and a healthier life. But note that they're guidelines, not a set of strict rules that can't be broken or a list of specific foods that must be eaten or must be avoided. Eating for better health can and should be enjoyable. Just a quick look through the recipes in this cookbook should show you how easy that is.

But some people approach healthy eating as if it has to be a complicated chore with lots of rules that must be followed religiously. That's almost a guarantee of failure.

A good starting point in healthier eating is to make simple changes, and to make them one at a time. It isn't necessary to give up all your favorite foods or to totally revise your diet overnight in order to eat healthier. What you are trying for is a basic lifestyle change that includes a focus on healthier foods. Healthy eating should eventually become something you do naturally, without really thinking about it. But it may take some time to get to that point. If you currently have some bad eating habits, remember that it took a lifetime to develop them. You can't expect them all to disappear overnight. So start slowly and make it fun. Eating for good health should be enjoyable.

Good Food vs Bad Food

When it comes to healthy eating, some people make the mistake of thinking that there are certain "bad" foods, which must be avoided at all costs, while there are "good" foods, which if you eat them enough will protect you from all sorts of health problems, including heart disease and cancer. The truth is something quite different.

By themselves, individual foods are just foods. They're not good or bad, and they're not magic. Although considerable research shows that certain kinds of foods appear to help promote cancer and other health problems, and that others appear to offer increased levels of protection, by itself no individual food will cause or prevent cancer.

What does matter is your overall diet. Although we know that a diet high in fat, for example, usually means higher risk for many cancers, heart disease, stroke, obesity and other health problems, eating an occasional serving of a particular high-fat food is certainly not going to cause any of those health problems. But if your diet is one that regularly includes many such high-fat foods, the story is a much different one. In that case the diet you are following is one that will have a direct and negative effect on your overall health.

We also know that many foods appear to play a positive role in helping maintain good health: fruits, vegetables and whole grains, for example. But notice that the emphasis is on groups of foods, not on any one or two particular foods.

The focus of any program of healthier eating is to choose an overall diet that emphasizes foods that can help your body stay healthy. Such a diet is not a guarantee that health problems such as heart attack, stroke or cancer will never occur, but it can do much to stack the odds in your favor. Healthy eating reduces the risk of nutrition-related disease while promoting and maintaining good health in general.

Our Typical American Diet

The "typical American diet" makes for a convenient title, but the truth is that there really isn't any typical diet. Some of us make pasta and pizza a regular part of our diets. Others enjoy an occasional steak, or like fish three times a week, or will eat nothing but chicken, or have given up meat, poultry and fish entirely and want only vegetarian meals.

Although none of us may actually eat the "typical" diet, there is value in looking at the averages that studies have found regarding the foods we consume. It can be a good starting point to see how close our own food choices may be to that "typical" diet, or to the "ideal" diet we should be eating for better health.

Take, for instance, what groups of foods supply the calories in our "typical" current diet. The following is the percentage of calories that come from each of our dietary sources, according to the most recent USDA studies:

> PROTEIN — 16%
> CARBOHYDRATES — 47%
> FAT — 37%

But according to health experts, that typical diet is not an ideal diet, not if we wish to choose foods that will provide the most health benefits. Experts today recommend that the best diet for good health provides percentages of calories from our dietary sources as follows:

> PROTEIN — 9% to 15%
> CARBOHYDRATES — 55% to 70% or more
> FAT — 10% to 30%

Switching to such a diet might at first seem like a drastic change to have to make. But it really isn't, and the health benefits it can supply are extremely important. One easy way to follow this type of diet is simply to put a slightly different emphasis on the foods you choose. It doesn't have to mean giving up all your old favorites or finding totally new kinds of foods to eat. Instead, you just put a much greater focus on fruits, vegetables and grains and less importance on meats, poultry, fish and high-fat dairy products.

How to Refocus Your Diet

The Dietary Guidelines to Lower Cancer Risk are an excellent starting point for refocusing your diet. But a question for many people is how to put them into use in everyday life. It is one thing to say you want to limit fat intake to 10% to 30% of daily calories, but what does that mean when you're sitting in a restaurant, holding a menu that includes a great many high-fat temptations?

Some people think the answer is to keep track of the grams of fat in every serving of food, counting all their calories each day, and doing endless calculations about the percentage of fat in each food they eat. However, there's a great deal of evidence that doing all that work contributes very little toward healthier eating.

A more sensible approach is to begin to understand more about groups of foods — to get a better sense of what types of foods offer the most benefits and what types of foods should be avoided or eaten only in moderation. What you want to do is get a healthy balance to your over-all diet, not worry about whether a single serving of a specific food is too high in fat.

Learning to Limit the Fat

Dietary Fat and Health Concerns

Scientific evidence suggests that dietary fat is one of the most serious health threats that most of us face in our diets. Our bodies require some fat for good health, but most of us eat too much of it. We especially eat too much saturated fat, the type of fat we get primarily from animal sources and that appears to do the most harm to our bodies.

The negative health effects of a diet high in fat are well documented. The relationship between high-fat diets and higher rates of heart disease has been well publicized. Saturated fats tend to raise blood cholesterol, which in turn means a greatly increased risk for heart attacks and stroke.

The link between fat and cancer risk is also a strong one, though not as well known and documented as the fat and heart disease relationship. The type of fat in regard to cancer risk does not appear to be as important as the overall level of fat in the diet. From laboratory studies and observation of people's eating habits, there is considerable evidence that eating too much fat leads to increased risk of colon, rectal, prostate and breast cancers.

The Sources of Fat in Our Diets

Fat is a component of many types of food, and our bodies need it for good health and normal growth. But the current Western diet often provides fat far in excess of that required to maintain good health. For the typical American diet, studies have found the following percentages of fat coming from these food sources:

vegetable oils, margarine, butter and other added fats	— 47%
meat, poultry and fish	— 32%
dairy products (milk, cheese, yogurt, etc., except butter)	— 12%
nuts, legumes and miscellaneous	— 6%
eggs	— 2%
fruits, vegetables and grains	— 1%

On average, the typical American diet gets about 37% of its calories from dietary fat. This number may be down somewhat over the past decade, the result of people becoming more conscious of the positive health benefits of a lower-fat diet. But this number is also only an average, and still too high. Although many people have made an effort to follow a low-fat diet, many of us are still getting far more than 37% of our calories from fat each day.

The Health Effects of Dietary Fat

Both saturated and unsaturated fats play essential roles in the functioning of our bodies, in addition to being a source of calories for energy. Both types of fat function as carriers of the fat-soluble vitamins A, D, E and K. Unsaturated fat also provides linoleic acid, a fatty acid considered essential for good nutrition. And we know that in children under age two, dietary fat plays an important role in the development of the brain and the nervous system.

Therefore, no one is recommending that we cut out all fat from our diets. That wouldn't be healthy or even possible. But we know from numerous studies around the world that there exists a clear link between high-fat diets and higher rates of various health problems.

One of the most common health problems associated with a high-fat diet is obesity. Fat provides, gram for gram, more than twice the calories of carbohydrates or protein. That means that for the same quantity of food, a high-fat food provides you with a great many more calories. And, to compound the problem, your body finds it much easier to turn dietary fat into body fat for storage. So not only do the calories come faster with a high-fat diet but you may find they stay around longer.

Heart disease and other cardiovascular illnesses have a clear association with high-fat diets. Risk for heart attacks and strokes is much higher in people whose diets include a lot of fat, and particularly saturated fat. At least part of the reason for that is the role fat, and especially saturated fat, plays in raising cholesterol levels, which in turn help to clog our arteries.

Scientists are still trying to understand the exact role that dietary fat plays in the cancer process. There is some evidence that excessive fat may weaken the immune system or make certain cells more susceptible to the carcinogens they encounter. There is also some preliminary evidence that excessive dietary fat may make the growth and spread of cancer cells easier, particularly in cancer's earliest stages. Some studies have found that high-fat diets appear to increase breast cancer risk, but there is still considerable controversy regarding that link. One theory is that excess dietary fat appears to affect body hormone levels, and several types of cancer, including breast cancer, seem to be influenced by hormones. There is also considerable evidence that risk for prostate cancer and cancers of the colon and rectum is much higher for those on a high-fat diet.

But even though science may not understand the mechanisms that may be at work in regard to fat and cancer, the message for all of us is clear: we should be eating a diet lower in fat. That means a maximum of 30% of daily calories from fat, according to most health authorities today. And, in fact, a growing body of evidence suggests that an even lower level of fat for adults, perhaps 20% or less of calories, may be a diet that provides the most health benefits, in reducing not only cancer risk but also the risk for heart disease and stroke, and to help fight obesity.

Learning to Cut the Fat

By itself, fat is not a food we normally think about eating. None of us has a big bowl of fat for breakfast or goes to a restaurant and orders fat for dinner. But fat is a component of many foods and especially important in a lot of our favorite foods. That's because we've learned over the years to like the rich, smooth taste and texture that fat brings to foods, and thus have made those foods our favorites.

However, it's important to remember that our taste for fat is acquired. Whether it is the rich smoothness of a bowl of ice cream or the creamy taste of butter spread on a warm roll, our taste for fat is one that we have developed and one that we can change, if we wish to. For example, researchers have done studies in which people have been placed on very low fat diets. In time, sometimes weeks and sometimes months, these people lose their taste for fat. They no longer crave the taste of high-fat foods and, indeed, find them unpleasant to taste and eat.

You should not go so far as to try to eliminate all the fat from your diet. It would be difficult to do and unhealthy for you. A much more sensible and healthful approach is to begin to make small changes that limit some of the higher-fat foods in your diet. Keep in mind that if you currently get about 40% of your calories each day from fat, cutting back to the 30% level means reducing your fat intake by only one-fourth. That's not a massive change. It can often be done by simply eliminating a high-fat dessert, making a few small changes in the snack foods you choose or switching to low-fat dairy products. For many of us it means finding a way to cut out only about 15 to 20 grams of fat each day.

The following are some simple and easy ideas for reducing the fat in your diet:

- use less of high-fat spreads, like butter, margarine and cream cheese, on breads and pastries, or switch to low-fat or nonfat varieties
- read food labels and select foods lower in fat
- bake, broil or boil foods instead of frying them
- limit consumption of foods you know to be very high in fat, such as potato chips, regular cheeses, chocolate, ice cream and nuts
- choose lean cuts of red meat and lower-fat versions of sausage and luncheon meat, and limit serving sizes on the occasions when you do eat them
- limit consumption of meats, poultry and fish to 3 to 6 ounces per day
- use low-fat or nonfat salad dressings
- choose low-fat or nonfat dairy products, including 1% or skim milk and reduced-fat versions of cheeses, ice cream and yogurt
- look for lower-fat menu choices in fast-food restaurants and avoid foods dipped in batter or deep fried
- save snacks extremely high in fat, such as candy bars and potato or taco chips, for "occasional use only," and instead choose a low-fat, crunchy substitute, like popcorn or pretzels, or a no-fat healthier snack such as a piece of fruit
- in baking, use one-half to two-thirds of the fat called for in recipes — applesauce or apple butter can often be used to replace the fat
- use nonstick pans to avoid adding extra fat during cooking, and use cooking sprays when necessary to add the least amount of extra fat to your cooking

How to Figure the Fat

The simplest advice for adults about fat is that the less you have in your diet, the better off you'll be. For good health reasons, you don't want to reduce your fat intake to less than 10% of calories — anyway, that's virtually impossible to do on a normal diet.

Your starting goal should be to limit your total daily fat intake so that fat provides no more than 30% of your total daily calories. By looking at your overall diet in this way, rather than at individual foods, it becomes clear that you can enjoy an occasional high-fat food while still limiting your total daily fat intake to less than 30% of calories. The trick is to balance your overall food intake during the day. If your menu choices are going to include a few foods you know to be high in fat, get a healthy balance by emphasizing foods low in fat for the rest of your food choices for the day.

The new Nutrition Facts box that is required on the label of all packaged foods makes it easier to see how individual foods fit into a healthy, low-fat diet. You'll find that these labels include the amount of total fat and the amount of saturated fat, giving both figures in grams. For each type of fat the label also gives the percentage of the recommended daily value for the item. It is thus easy to judge what effect that particular food will have on your total fat intake for the day.

The basis for the percentages given on these labels is the number of grams of fat that the average person would eat during a day in order to hold his or her consumption of dietary fat to about 30% of total calories. The bottom portion of the Nutrition Facts box explains this information and states that the percentage of daily value for fat shown is based on a 2,000-calorie diet. That amount of calories may be slightly high or low for you, based on your body size and level of activity. If, for example, you are a woman who is not particularly active, you may be consuming less than 2,000 calories each day. In that case you should also be consuming less fat each day. Similarly, a woman who is very active is probably consuming more than 2,000 calories per day, and therefore her consumption of fat could also be higher and still be in the healthy range.

Estimating Fat Intake for Yourself

A starting point for estimating the health impact of your food choices on your diet is to have a general idea of how much fat in total your daily good-health diet should provide. That's the information you are getting, in part, from the Nutrition Facts portion of food labels. But it is also helpful to have a general idea of what your individual maximum fat intake should be for the day.

For example, if you are limiting your fat intake to about 30% of daily calories, the following are approximately the maximum amounts of dietary fat that should be eaten each day:

	daily calories	maximum grams of fat/day
older sedentary women	1,600	53
active women, children, sedentary or older men	2,200	73
men, average activity	2,500	83
active men, teenage boys	2,800	93

These amounts of fat should be adjusted up or down slightly if you are more or less active than average. Your total fat intake should also be slightly less if you are on a diet with a lower than average number of calories, perhaps because you are trying to lose weight. Or, if you are very active and consuming a diet with a greater amount of calories, your fat intake could also be slightly higher.

In any case, the exact number of grams of fat you should be eating each day is not as important as judging individual foods against your approximate total. When you make those judgments, even as approximations, it becomes much easier to see whether a particular food is high in fat and whether you want to eliminate it from your diet, or at least limit how much you eat.

For example, if you know a particular food, say your morning bowl of cereal, is providing you with about 2 to 4 grams of fat, you know that's only a small part of your overall fat total for the day. But when you reach for that container of premium ice cream and see that a single serving may be providing 22 grams of fat, you know that one food is suddenly providing a substantial portion of the recommended amount of daily fat in your diet.

Do you have to think a little more about which foods are high in fat and what effect they're having on your total fat intake for the day? Yes, you do. But think how good you'll feel about gaining more control over your diet and health. And think how extra-good that occasional high-fat food will taste when you know it's a special treat, and when you know it's something that fits into a balanced, healthy diet and not just another food about which to feel guilty.

One More Reason to Limit the Fat

At any given moment, about half of Americans are on a diet of one sort or another. We are a nation obsessed with losing weight. And that is another good reason to pay attention to the fat in your diet!

Cutting back on fat is the most effective change you can make for cutting back on calories and helping to trim a few pounds. That's because fat is such a concentrated source of calories. Each gram of fat contains about 9 calories. On the other hand, each gram of protein or carbohydrate contains only about 4 calories.

Limit the fat, therefore, and you're automatically limiting the calories. In fact, it is possible on a low-fat diet to eat a much greater quantity of food but still be eating fewer calories. And, as we've discussed, limiting the fat is a much healthier approach to your food choices.

It's also a way of ensuring greater success for your diet, an important consideration since studies show that about 90% of those who lose weight on a diet gain most of it back in a short time. But when you make dietary changes to cut out fat, you aren't so much dieting as making basic food choice decisions that can and should be part of your normal eating. You're making healthy choices that you can live with every day of your life.

What's even better is that learning to limit the fat, especially when you're trying to lose weight, means cutting back on high-fat foods, not cutting back on all foods. So when you give up those potato chips for a snack and instead have an apple, you aren't starving yourself, but you are making a no-fat, lower-calorie food choice that can take away that feeling of hunger and help you lose that extra weight as well. And instead of that average serving of one ounce of potato chips (as if any of us has ever eaten just one ounce of chips), you could easily have two apples. You might not save any calories, but you sure would feel a lot fuller and more content, and you would have avoided a whole lot of fat while enjoying the health benefits of all the nutrients in those apples.

There are lots of easy food substitutions that can help you avoid the fat and calories of some common foods but that won't leave you hungry and grumpy like most typical diets:

Instead of:	Try:
whole milk	skim milk or 1% milk
ice cream	ice milk, sherbet or low-fat frozen yogurt
doughnut	bagel with jelly
sour cream	low-fat plain yogurt or low-fat sour cream
regular salad dressing	low-fat or fat-free salad dressing, or lemon juice
potato or taco chips	popcorn or pretzels
candy bar	piece of fresh fruit
nuts	fruit or vegetable snack; dry cereal or popcorn
bologna sandwich	turkey breast, chicken or water-packed tuna sandwich
regular cheese	low-fat or nonfat cheese
regular yogurt	low-fat or nonfat yogurt
ground beef	extra-lean or lean ground beef; ground turkey
chocolate candy	hard candy
Danish or commercial muffin	bagel or English muffin
pepperoni pizza	pizza with veggie toppings or low-fat cheese
breaded fried fish fillet	broiled fish fillet
large serving of beef	small serving of beef with extra veggies
avocado	cucumber or zucchini
fast-food egg muffin breakfast	pancakes or waffles, no butter or margarine
steak	lean beef, skinless chicken, fish
bologna, frankfurter, sausage	chicken, turkey, lean thin sliced beef
bacon	Canadian (pea meal) bacon
regular layer or pan cake	angel food cake
french fries	baked potato

Fruits, Vegetables and a Healthier You

Although we've spent a lot of time talking about foods to avoid or to eat in limited amounts — those high in fat — learning to eat healthier really is much more positive than that. The real fun of a healthier diet is all the delicious, fresh tastes that can come from foods that are good for you.

Again, the emphasis here is not on one or two specific foods but rather on those groups of foods that research has shown provide the most in health benefits. The foods you should focus your diet on are the fruits and vegetables.

There are some very well-documented reasons why these foods are so important to a balanced healthy diet. One important reason is that they are low in fat and calories. Almost all fruits and vegetables (avocados are one of the few exceptions) contain no fat or only small amounts of fat. Another is all the nutrients these foods supply, nutrients essential not only to maintaining good health but also to help protect you from illnesses such as cancer.

Getting More Fruits and Vegetables into Your Diet

Just as cutting back on fat requires you to think about your food choices and to select lower-fat foods, adding more fruits and vegetables to your diet requires you to plan ahead and think about the food decisions that you make each day. But again, it isn't a complicated process or one that requires lots of planning or special knowledge.

The simple fact is that when you choose fruits, vegetables and whole grains as the main part of your diet, you really can't go wrong. Consider how you currently think about your meals. If someone asks you what you want for dinner tonight, or what you had for dinner last night, the odds are pretty good your response will be to name a meat or fish or poultry. But why should the focus of your meals be foods that usually provide more fat, calories and even protein than we need for good health?

One way to get more fruits and vegetables into your diet is to think of them as a more important part of your meals. That doesn't mean that you must consider only vegetarian dishes, but rather that you think of fruits and vegetables as a focus for the meals you eat, rather than just a side dish added to the meat entrée.

Despite all the nutritional benefits that fruits and vegetables have to offer, most of us eat only about half the amount we should of these foods each day. Health experts say that the minimum amount of fruits and vegetables we should be eating for good health is five servings a day. But most adults eat only two to two and a half servings. Our children aren't doing much better. The average consumption for kids is also two and a half servings per day. Some studies have found that large numbers of children will eat no fruit or vegetables on a given day. Those are dietary choices, for adults and children, that put us at a real nutritional disadvantage.

The Health Benefits of Fruits and Vegetables

Fruits and vegetables aren't magic, but they do provide, among other things, a number of critically important micronutrients our bodies require for good health. Vitamins such as A (in the form of beta-carotene), C, E and folate are all essential and obtained from various fruits and vegetables. Other nutrients important to our health and readily available from many fruits and vegetables include potassium, magnesium, iron, manganese and selenium. Without a varied diet that includes a wide variety of foods providing these essential nutrients, it is impossible for our bodies to maintain good health and proper growth and functions.

What surprises many people is the role these and other nutrients can play in disease prevention. Recent research has shown, for example, that beta-carotene, a nutrient converted to vitamin A in our bodies, appears to play a major role in helping reduce cancer risk. An antioxidant, it helps to scavenge free radicals, the unstable products of normal metabolism that appear to play a role in cell damage and the cancer process. Other antioxidants, such as vitamins C and E, appear to perform similar functions.

Research has linked a number of other nutrients found in fruits and vegetables to an active role in cancer prevention. Some foods, such as the cruciferous vegetables, including broccoli, cabbage, kale and Brussels sprouts, provide nutrients that appear to stimulate the production of enzymes that help detoxify some of the carcinogens our bodies encounter.

The role that such nutrients can play in cancer prevention is one of the most complicated areas of research, but also one of the most promising. We are only beginning to understand the mechanisms by which various nutrients affect the cancer process. Even more complicated is the interaction between various nutrients as we eat a varied diet every day.

The complexity of that interaction is a main reason why consuming a diet that includes a variety of fruits, vegetables and grains is so important. We do not yet know how all the compounds within foods work together to provide us with good nutrition and good health. That is also why it does not appear wise to rely on supplements to get the vitamins and minerals needed by your body. Does your body use the beta-carotene provided in a pill the same way it does the beta-carotene provided by a carrot? And what difference is made by all the other nutrients in that carrot as they are absorbed by your body along with the beta-carotene? We don't have answers to those questions yet, which is why the consumption of a diet rich in a variety of fruits, vegetables and whole grains is currently the smartest answer to eating for good health.

Although the science may be complex, the message is simple. The more fruits and vegetables we consume, the more we help our bodies protect themselves against cancer and many other health problems. Your parents knew what they were was talking about when they told you to eat all your vegetables.

Think Quantity and Variety for Good Health

There's nothing complicated about getting adequate amounts of fruits and vegetables into our daily diets. It certainly isn't necessary to understand all the biochemistry involving your body and the foods you eat. All you need to know is that eating adequate amounts of a variety of fruits and vegetables will provide you with the nutrients you need to maintain good health and to lower your risk for diseases such as cancer.

Just five servings a day of most fruits and vegetables will provide a good basic intake of many essential vitamins and minerals. Just half a carrot, for example, provides the recommended daily intake of beta-carotene. One glass of orange juice meets the daily minimum for vitamin C.

Is eating five servings of fruits and vegetables a lot to ask of us? Not really. The servings are small and easy to fit comfortably into any diet. When we say one serving of fruits and vegetables, we mean:

for fruits like apples, bananas, pears, oranges,
    etc. .... one serving equals one whole fruit
for small, solid vegetables and fruits like peas,
    corn, berries, beans, etc. .... one serving equals 1/2 cup
for loose, leafy vegetables like raw spinach,
    lettuce, cabbage .... one serving equals 1 cup
for juices .... one serving equals 3/4 cup

Equally important as eating five servings a day is getting a variety of fruits and vegetables into your diet. Too often we become stuck in the rut of eating the same few favorites over and over. That's certainly better than not eating any fruits or vegetables, but there's a lot more to be gained by trying new foods and getting a real variety into your menu planning. Not only will that help assure a balance to the vitamins and minerals you're adding to your diet but it will help make your overall menu more interesting and enjoyable, which is what healthy eating should be.

One test of how much variety you're getting is to think back over the past two weeks. Did your diet include at least 10 varieties of fruits and vegetables? If so, you're probably getting a good mix of nutrients and have a good start on a healthy diet, if you're eating at least five servings each day.

But whether you are already eating a good variety of fruits and vegetables, or whether it's a change that you still have to make, remember that there can be a lot of pleasure in experimenting with new foods. Make it a point to try at least one new or different fruit or vegetable each week. That's especially important if you have children in your family. Giving them a chance to try new foods helps widen the range of foods that they like and eat. And we know that a key to good health is eating a variety of foods.

Don't Forget the Legumes

"What are legumes?" many people ask. They're actually familiar foods we all know. Legumes are the family of vegetables that produce seeds in pods. If that doesn't sound any more familiar, then start thinking peas and beans.

Legumes are one of the most nutritious and economical foods we have. They contain complex carbohydrates, a variety of nutrients, lots of dietary fibre and considerable amounts of good protein. And they're economical because they're easy to grow and store, particularly in their dried form.

This family of high-nutrition foods includes kidney beans, garbanzo beans or chick peas, black-eyed peas, lentils, pinto beans, navy beans, black beans, split peas, lima beans and lots more. Legumes are such nutritional powerhouses that they should be an essential part of the vegetable content of your menu planning on a regular basis. And since many varieties of beans are now available canned and ready to use, there's no excuse for not finding more ways to include these foods in your diet.

Adding More Fruits and Vegetables to Your Diet

If getting your daily intake of fruits and vegetables up to five servings seems like a lot to do, try some of these suggestions for simple ways to eat more of these foods essential for good health:

- include a glass of juice or an orange with breakfast
- top your breakfast cereal with fresh berries or a sliced banana
- grab a bagel and a piece or two of fresh fruit for a breakfast on the run
- include some vegetable sticks (carrots, celery, green peppers) in that packed lunch
- toss in a piece of fresh fruit for dessert with a packed lunch
- include lettuce and tomato on your lunchtime sandwich
- keep a piece or two of fresh fruit in your briefcase for that morning or afternoon snack
- take advantage of salad bars at grocery stores and delis, just skip the high-fat creamy salad items and the regular salad dressings
- have a bowl of fresh fruit available for the kids' after-school snack
- keep some vegetable sticks in the fridge for the kids to snack on
- let the kids snack and dip with vegetable sticks and a low-fat yogurt dip
- offer fruit juice instead of soda pop for an after-school drink
- add extra nutrition to commercial soups by tossing in additional fresh or frozen chopped vegetables
- include two vegetables with dinner and a smaller portion of meat
- for casseroles and stews, increase the amounts of vegetables and decrease the meat
- try one, two or more meatless meals every week
- when you choose pizza, load up on vegetable toppings
- make a small salad a regular part of your dinner menu
- have fresh, in-season fruit for a great dessert, or use canned or frozen fruit when fresh varieties aren't available or affordable
- eat desserts that include fruits (poached pears, peach cobbler, chopped or puréed fruit topping for low-fat frozen yogurt)

There isn't any big secret to getting more fruits and vegetables into your diet, just a little planning to have these foods available and to include more of them in the meals you serve. Studies have found that one of the biggest factors determining how much fruit and vegetables people eat is simply availability. If your kids come home from school and there's only a bag of chips available, you know that's what they're going to snack on. But if they have a choice between a bowl of fresh fruit, some vegetable sticks and low-fat dip, and that bag of chips, you have a much better chance of encouraging healthier food choices. And if you get rid of that bag of chips, you can really stack the odds in favor of a healthier diet.

Dietary Fibre — A Key to Good Health

Dietary fibre has received a great deal of attention in recent years, and deservedly so. It's an important part of a healthy diet, but most of us eat far too little of it. Yet adding more fibre to our diets is easy to do and can pay real health benefits.

Studies show the average American consumes 11 to 12 grams of fibre daily. The problem is most health experts advise that we should be eating at least 20 to 35 grams of fibre daily, especially if we want to lower our risk for heart disease and cancer. Diets rich in dietary fibre have been associated with lower risk for colon and rectal cancers, diverticulosis, hemorrhoids, gallstones, various intestinal diseases, as well as heart disease.

We get fibre in our diet from plant products — fruits, vegetables and grains. Fibre is found in every type of plant that we use for food. Dietary fibre is composed of a complex variety of different kinds of fibrous, relatively indigestible, complex carbohydrates. But even though we don't digest it very easily, fibre plays an important role in our nutrition.

A primary purpose of fibre in our diet is to help the foods we eat pass smoothly and quickly through our digestive system. Studies have found that with a low-fibre diet, food material can take two to three times longer to pass through the body than with a diet containing an adequate amount of fibre. Just as important is the role the two types of fibre seem to play in health protection.

Soluble Dietary Fibre

One form of dietary fibre is soluble fibre. This type of fibre seems to help in the fight against heart disease. It appears to help control blood sugar and has been found to help lower blood cholesterol, especially in cases where it's unusually high.

Soluble fibre is found in a variety of foods, but oat products are the best-known sources. Some common sources are:

- oat bran
- oatmeal
- barley
- apples
- strawberries
- citrus fruits
- legumes, such as dried peas, and beans and lentils

Insoluble Dietary Fibre

This is the type of fibre that people used to call roughage. Wheat bran is the most common form of insoluble fibre. This is the fibre that appears to play the biggest role in helping move food materials efficiently through our bodies. It thus plays a big role in preventing and controlling bowel problems.

Insoluble fibre has also been linked in various studies to reduced risk for some forms of cancer, particularly colorectal cancers. This form of fibre, by moving foods more quickly though the intestines, helps to decrease the amount of time that potential carcinogens are in our bodies and in contact with our intestines.

Insoluble fibre also appears to help in diluting bile acids, some of which are believed to promote colon cancer. Bile acids, which are part of the bile secreted by our livers, are necessary for our bodies to digest and absorb fat. Research indicates that a diet rich in insoluble dietary fibre helps produce more bulk in the intestines, thus helping to dilute these acids and reduce the risk of colon cancer.

Some good sources for insoluble fibre include:

- wheat bran
- wheat bran cereals
- whole grain breads
- other whole grain foods, such as muffins, cereals, pasta
- fruits and vegetables, including skins and seeds when practical
- legumes, such as dried peas, beans and lentils

Getting More Fibre into Your Daily Diet

Following the AICR Dietary Guidelines to Lower Cancer Risk is a good starting point for adding more fibre to your diet. The second guideline advises, "Increase the consumption of fruits, vegetables and whole grains." Something as simple as raising your fruit and vegetable consumption to five servings a day will do a great deal toward getting more fibre in your diet.

Remember that only plant foods can provide fibre. There is no fibre in foods of animal origin, such as meat, fish, poultry, dairy products or eggs. A diet rich in fruits, vegetables and whole grain foods is therefore essential to a good supply of fibre.

It is also important to start early in getting the daily recommended amount of fibre. Breakfast, for example, is an excellent place to get a head start on fibre for the day. A bowl of whole grain, high-fibre cereal, topped with some sliced fruit, can help you get your day started right. Studies show that people who skip breakfast seldom catch up during the day on needed amounts of fibre.

One important piece of advice is not to add too much fibre too quickly. If you are now eating a diet low in fibre, you may experience some minor discomfort or gas as you begin to add more fibre to your daily diet. One way to avoid that is to add fibre slowly. Start by adding an extra piece or two of fruit to your daily menu. Once your body adjusts to that, then try that bowl of high-fibre cereal at breakfast as well. You'll soon find that the extra fibre causes no problems at all, once your body becomes used to it.

Another essential of a high-fibre diet is to drink plenty of fluids. In order for fibre to work at its best in your body, you must drink plenty of water or other liquids every day. You should be drinking at least two quarts — that's eight 8-ounce glasses — of liquids each day.

Here are some ideas on easy ways to add more daily fibre, both soluble and insoluble:

- begin the day with a high-fibre cereal at breakfast
- sprinkle your favorite morning cereal with some oat or
- wheat bran
- top your cereal with some sliced fruit or dried fruit to add
- even more fibre and other important nutrients
- reach for a piece of fruit or some vegetable sticks when the urge to snack strikes

- choose whole grain breads — check the ingredients label and make sure that the first ingredient listed is a whole grain, such as whole wheat
- choose whole grain muffins, but make sure they're also low fat
- have a second helping of vegetables at dinner, rather than a second helping of meat, fish or poultry
- add extra fibre to casseroles or stews by adding some oat bran, wheat bran or even a handful of a crunchy high-fibre cereal
- make your salads high fibre by adding crunchy extras such as carrots, raw broccoli, cauliflower pieces, garbanzo beans (chick peas), kidney beans or even apple slices
- instead of regular white rice, use brown rice — even the quick-cooking versions of brown rice provide more fibre and other nutrients
- start your day with an orange instead of a glass of orange juice
- for a low-calorie, high-fibre snack, try popcorn, but skip the high-fat buttered toppings
- look for new recipes that include beans, a great source of fibre and other important nutrients
- make green peas, a good fibre source, a regular vegetable in your meals
- think fruit — fresh, frozen or canned — for dessert
- add extra vegetables to stews, soups and casseroles and you'll add extra fibre

One of the best ways to add more fibre to your diet is to include one or more servings of grain products at every meal. The recommendation is that we should eat at least six small servings of grain products each day (one slice of bread, for example, is one serving). It isn't necessary that every serving be made from whole grains, though you should try to have at least four servings per day of whole grain foods. These provide not only a great deal more fibre but also lots of important nutrients.

Many types of high-fibre supplements are available in health food stores. But unless a doctor recommends taking such supplements, the best advice is to avoid them and instead increase your fibre intake by eating foods that are good fibre sources.

Eating a diet that includes a variety of high-fibre foods offers a number of advantages over any supplements. An important one is all the other essential nutrients supplied by those foods. A half-cup serving of broccoli, for example, will provide you with 2.7 grams of dietary fibre. Yet it also provides large amounts of vitamins A and C and potassium, as well as smaller amounts of other vitamins and minerals. And since we still don't fully understand how many nutrients work within our bodies, or how they work in combination with other nutrients, you may be missing out on a lot of important health benefits by just chewing on a fibre supplement. Eating a variety of good sources of fibre also means you'll get a good balance of soluble and insoluble fibres each day, another essential of good health.

Putting It All Together

Less fat ... more fruits and vegetables ... choose whole grains whenever possible. The formula for a healthier diet, a diet that can mean reduced risk for cancer and heart disease, is not complicated. But it does take a little extra effort to make the right food choices throughout your day.

And don't make the mistake of pretending that the principles of healthy eating don't apply just because you're at a restaurant or party or in some other situation where you don't have control over the food choices and preparation methods. The truth is that you are always the one in final control.

If the only food choices available are those high in fat, then limit the amount you eat. If you're being served a meal in which the emphasis is on a large portion of meat, ask for a smaller serving and make your own choice to eat some extra vegetables instead. Taking control of your food can be especially important in restaurants. Most establishments are more than happy to meet your requests, but it's up to you to first make those requests. If you prefer something broiled instead of fried, ask. If you want a sauce or dressing on the side so you can control how much is used, make that request. You'll find that people today are very understanding of healthy eating and usually are willing to help you.

And don't give up on healthy eating just because you may sometimes make a mistake or give in to the temptations of a high-fat meal. One bad day should not sink your entire plan for healthier eating. If you face a meal or day in which you have nothing but high-fat choices, then plan to balance things out later on. Make the next day's meals lower in fat and you'll balance things out to a healthy level.

Also remember that the foods you choose are only one part, although an important one, of your overall health picture. Regular exercise, maintaining the proper weight, getting regular medical checkups and responding quickly to any health problem are all important ingredients in living a long and healthy life. Avoiding tobacco is also one of the most important things you can do for good health and lower risk for heart disease and cancer.

The secret to a healthier diet and a healthier you is you! You are the one who has to make the decisions for better health and then follow through with action. It isn't difficult to do, and the rewards are a healthier and more enjoyable life. Who of us doesn't want that?

About the American Institute for Cancer Research

The American Institute for Cancer Research is the only national cancer charity focusing exclusively in the area of diet and cancer. Researchers have estimated that as many as 40% of cancers in men and 60% of cancers in women may be directly linked to our dietary choices. Some scientists have estimated that 35% of cancer deaths are diet related.

The area of diet, nutrition and cancer offers an enormous potential for reducing the terrible price that we currently pay to cancer. Cancer is still this nation's second leading cause of death, claiming well over a half million lives each year and causing immeasurable amounts of pain and suffering.

The American Institute for Cancer Research has been a leader in research and education programs on diet and cancer. The Institute has provided more than $25 million for research into the role that diet and nutrition play in both cancer prevention and cancer treatment. At universities, hospitals and research centers throughout the United States, AICR has provided grants to support many of the most innovative research efforts in this important area.

The Institute has also been a leader in cancer education programs, helping millions of Americans learn how to make changes that can reduce cancer risk for themselves and their families. Through newsletters, numerous booklets and leaflets, a Nutrition Hotline, seminars, newspaper columns, radio and TV shows, health professional support programs and a variety of other types of education programs, AICR has helped make cancer prevention a more visible and viable part of the fight against cancer.

AICR is a 501 (c)(3) charity supported by the donations of more than 5 million Americans. All gifts in support of AICR's programs are fully tax deductible. For more information about the Institute and its research and education programs, or to provide financial support for AICR's cancer research and education efforts, please contact:

American Institute for Cancer Research
Washington, D.C. 20069
or call
1-800-843-8114

Thank you for your purchase and use of *Lighthearted Everyday Cooking*. A portion of the price of this book is being donated in support of AICR research and education programs.

— American Institute for Cancer Research, 1994

Guidelines for Nutrient Ratings of Recipes

Nutrient analysis of the recipes was performed by Info Access (1988) Inc. using the nutritional accounting component of the CBORD Menu Management System. The nutrient database was the 1988 Canadian Nutrient File supplemented when necessary with documented data from reliable sources.

Unless otherwise stated, all recipes in this book were tested and analyzed using 1.5% yogurt, 2% cottage cheese, soft margarine and canola oil. Since the majority of the population consumes 2% milk, the recipes have been analyzed using 2% milk; however, you can save even more on fat and calories by substituting either 1% or skim milk. As well, most of the recipes in the book do not add salt, or include salt to taste, therefore they have been analyzed without any or using a minimum of salt.

Our rating system is based on the *Guide for Food Manufacturers and Advertisers*, 1988, which states that if a food (in this case a recipe) meets 15% RDI (Recommended Daily Intake (30% for Vitamin C) it can be said to be a "good source of" that nutrient and if it meets 25% of the RDI (50% for Vitamin C) it is an "excellent source of" that nutrient. For dietary fibre, if a food contains 2 grams it may be described as a "source", 4 grams may be described as containing high amounts of dietary fibre. Percent of Recommended Daily Intake is based on the highest recommended intake for each nutrient. This is the most current data available at time of printing.

Nutrient analysis is based on the first ingredient listed when a choice is given and does not include any optional ingredients. The numbers have been rounded off.

Following criteria outlined in the *Guide for Food Manufacturers and Advertisers, Revised Edition 1988* (Consumer and Corporate Affairs Canada), recipes that are good or excellent sources of vitamins A and C, thiamine, riboflavin, niacin, calcium and iron have been identified. In the U.S. there are similar criteria based on Daily Values (Reference Daily Intakes). In some instances the ratings in this book are different from those that would be calculated using U.S. criteria.

The table below displays the percentages of U.S. Daily Values that are equivalent to the good and excellent ratings in this book.

	Ratings	
	Good	**Excellent**
	% U.S. Daily Value	
Vitamin C	30	50
Thiamin	13	22
Riboflavin	14	24
Calcium	17	28
Iron	12	19

Note: It is not possible to calculate the percentages of U.S. Daily Values for vitamin A and niacin because of incompatible units of measurement.

Fibre

It is recommended that we have about 25 to 35 grams of fibre each day (see pages 14 to 17 for more fibre information).

Sodium

Many of us consume too much sodium and lower levels of intake are recommended. Most of the recipes in this book are relatively low in sodium; where the levels are high, suggestions for reducing the sodium have been given to help those on sodium-restricted diets.

Potassium

Potassium is thought to have a positive effect on hypertension and strokes. A diet promoting foods high in potassium, emphasizing fruits and vegetables is recommended.

Daily Total Protein, Fat and Carbohydrate Intake (based on 15% of calories from protein, 30% of calories from fat and 55% of calories from carbohydrate)

calorie intake	grams protein per day	grams fat per day	grams carbohydrate per day
1800	68	60	248
2100	79	70	289
2300	86	77	316
2600	98	87	357
2900	109	97	399
3200	120	107	440

Where to Go for Nutrition Information

In many states, anyone can claim to be a nutritionist. In order to be a dietitian, and use the initials R.D. (Registered Dietitian), a person must meet standards set by the American Dietetic Association. Before receiving nutrition information or counseling, check for qualifications and be wary of quacks.

Local hospitals or health departments, nutrition departments at universities or colleges or dietitians are reliable sources of information.

For more information on healthy eating and nutrition, write or call:

American Institute for Cancer Research
Washington, D.C. 20069
1-800-843-8114

or

The American Dietetic Association
The National Center for Nutrition and Dietetics
216 West Jackson Blvd.
Chicago, Illinois 60606-6995
Consumer Nutrition Hot Line 1-800-366-1655

Consumer Nutrition Hot Line

The National Center for Nutrition and Dietetics provides consumers with direct and immediate access to reliable food and nutrition information. Funding for the hot line is provided through educational grants to The American Dietetic Association Foundation.

- Registered dietitians answer your food or nutrition questions
- You can listen to recorded nutrition messages from registered dietitians
- You can locate registered dietitians in your area for nutrition counseling
- Registered dietitians are available from 9:00 a.m. to 4:00 p.m. (Central Time) Monday through Friday
- Callers can select nutrition messages in English or Spanish from 8:00 a.m. to 8:00 p.m. (Central Time) Monday through Friday
- TDD Service for the hearing impaired is available from 9:00 a.m. to 4:00 p.m. (Central Time) Monday through Friday

About Project LEAN

Project LEAN (Low-fat Eating for America Now) is a national public awareness campaign to promote low-fat eating sponsored by the National Center for Nutrition and Dietetics of The American Dietetic Association.

APPETIZERS AND SNACKS

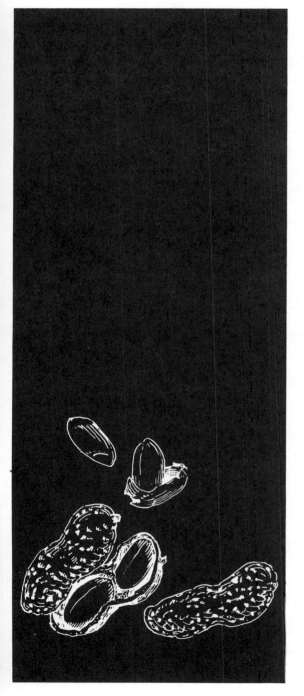

Oriental Salad Rolls

Skewered Tortellini

Spinach and Artichoke Dip

Tomato Bruschetta with
Fresh Basil

Endive with Chèvre and
Shrimp

Light and Easy Guacamole

Green Onion Dip

Smoked Salmon Spread

Mexican Bean Dip

Tomato and Cucumber Salsa

Spicy Chicken Skewers

Thai Peanut Sauce

Cheesy Chili Quesadillas

Jiffy Mexican Burritos

Quick Tomato, Broccoli and
Red Onion Pizza

Citrus Sangria

Gazpacho Cooler

ORIENTAL SALAD ROLLS

Perfect for a first course, because they can be prepared in advance, these wonderfully flavored rolls look and taste terrific. Rice paper wrappers (usually from Thailand) are available at some specialty food stores and at Chinese grocery stores. Add more red pepper flakes to taste depending on how hot you like your food.

Sauce:

1/2 cup	rice vinegar	125 mL
2 tbsp	soy sauce	25 mL
2 tbsp	hoisin sauce	25 mL
1 tbsp	peanut butter	15 mL
2 tsp	granulated sugar	10 mL
1 tsp	grated gingerroot	5 mL
1/8 tsp	crushed red pepper flakes	0.5 mL

Rolls:

2 oz	rice noodles (rice vermicelli)	60 g
8	shiitake mushrooms (fresh or dried)	8
1/4 cup	chicken OR vegetable stock	50 mL
8	small scallions, trimmed	8
16	rice paper wrappers (8-inch/20 cm rounds)	16
8	leaves Boston OR leaf lettuce, halved	8
1 1/4 cups	bean sprouts	300 mL
2	small carrots, coarsely grated	2
2 tbsp	each fresh mint and coriander leaves	25 mL

Sauce: In small bowl, combine rice vinegar, soy sauce, hoisin sauce, peanut butter, sugar, ginger and red pepper flakes.

Rolls: In pot of boiling water, cook noodles for 2 minutes; drain and cool under cold water. Drain and transfer to bowl. Pour 1/4 cup (50 mL) of the sauce over noodles and mix well; set aside.

Soak dried mushrooms (if using) in hot water until soft; cut into thin strips. In small saucepan, cook mushrooms in chicken stock for 3 minutes or until tender. Cut scallions lengthwise into thin strips; cut into 3-inch (8 cm) lengths.

In large bowl of hot water, soak 1 round of rice paper wrapper for 2 minutes or until softened. Remove from water, place on work surface and fold in half.

PER SERVING	
(of 2 each)	
Calories	77
g total fat	1
g saturated fat	trace
g fibre	1

EXCELLENT: Vitamin A

g protein	3
g carbohydrate	16
mg cholesterol	0
mg sodium	187
mg potassium	162

Place lettuce leaf on wrapper with top of lettuce extending slightly over folded half of wrapper. Place a few slices of green onion on top to extend over wrapper slightly. Top with spoonful of noodles, then 2 mushroom pieces, a few bean sprouts, carrots and mint and coriander.

Fold up rounded edge of wrapper, then roll wrapper around filling. Repeat with remaining wrappers. (Rolls can be covered and refrigerated for up to 6 hours.)

Serve 2 rolls per person on individual plates. Pass remaining sauce (for dipping) separately.

Makes 8 servings.

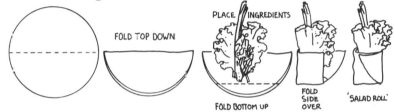

SKEWERED TORTELLINI

Tortellini or capeletti filled with meat or cheese fillings are easy to skewer and make a fabulous appetizer. Buy different colors of the pasta to thread onto wooden skewers, then arrange them on a platter along with crudités and a dip such as Spinach and Artichoke on page 26. (Pictured opposite page 26.)

1/2 lb	tortellini OR capeletti*	250 g
1 tbsp	olive oil	15 mL

In large pot of boiling water, cook tortellini according to package directions or until pasta is tender but firm. Drain and return to pot; toss with oil to prevent sticking.

Thread 2 tortellini, 1 of each color, onto each skewer. (Skewers can be covered and refrigerated for up to 1 day.) To serve, bring tortellini to room temperature or reheat by dipping into boiling water.

PER SKEWER	
Calories	35
g total fat	2
g saturated fat	trace
g fibre	trace

g protein	1
g carbohydrate	4
mg cholesterol	2
mg sodium	22
mg potassium	16

Makes about 25 skewers.

*Available in frozen food and dairy sections of most supermarkets.

SPINACH AND ARTICHOKE DIP

Serve this tasty dip with fresh vegetables or with the Tortellini Skewers on page 25. Or halve the amount of yogurt and use as a stuffing for mushrooms, cherry tomatoes, celery or Belgian endive leaves and garnish with a strip of sun-dried tomatoes. (Pictured opposite.)

1	pkg (10 oz/300 g) frozen chopped spinach	1
1	can (14 oz) artichoke hearts, drained	1
1/2 cup	light mayonnaise	125 mL
1 tbsp	minced fresh dill OR basil OR 1/2 tsp (2 mL) dried	15 mL
1	small clove garlic, minced	1
1 1/4 cup	low-fat yogurt	300 mL
	Salt and pepper	

Thaw spinach and squeeze dry. In food processor, process spinach and artichokes until coarsely chopped. Add mayonnaise, dill or basil, and garlic; process until mixed.

Stir in yogurt. Season with salt and pepper to taste. (Dip can be covered and refrigerated for up to 24 hours.) If too thick add more yogurt.

Makes about 3 cups (750 mL).

Stuffed cherry tomatoes
Slice tops off cherry tomatoes and scoop out seeds; fill with Smoked Salmon Spread p. 34 or with Spinach and Artichoke Dip.

I don't add yogurt before combining the ingredients in the food processor because when processed, the yogurt breaks down and becomes less thick.

PER TABLESPOON
(15 mL)

Calories		14
g	total fat	1
g	saturated fat	trace
g	fibre	trace
g	protein	1
g	carbohydrate	1
mg	cholesterol	2
mg	sodium	32
mg	potassium	42

Endive with Chèvre and Shrimp (p. 31), Skewered Tortellini (p. 25), Smoked Salmon Spread (p. 34), Spinach and Artichoke Dip (above)

TOMATO BRUSCHETTA WITH FRESH BASIL

We make this often for lunch or a snack, especially on the weekends in August or September when tomatoes are sweet and juicy. If fresh basil isn't available, use 1 tsp (5 mL) dried and sprinkle with 2 tbsp (25 mL) grated Parmesan, or dot with soft chèvre and broil for 1 minute. (Pictured opposite.)

2	large tomatoes, diced (about 2 cups/ 500 mL)	2
1/4 cup	chopped fresh basil, lightly packed	50 mL
1	clove garlic, minced	1
	Salt and pepper	
Half	loaf French OR Italian bread OR 1 French baguette	Half
1	large clove garlic, halved	1
1 tbsp	olive oil	15 mL
2 tbsp	freshly grated Parmesan cheese (optional)	25 mL

In bowl, combine tomatoes, basil, minced garlic, and salt and pepper to taste; let stand for 15 minutes or cover and refrigerate for up to 4 hours.

Slice bread in 1-inch (2.5 cm) thick slices. Place on baking sheet and broil until lightly browned on each side. Rub cut side of garlic clove over one side of bread; brush with olive oil. Spoon tomato mixture over top. Sprinkle with Parmesan (if using). If tomato mixture has been refrigerated, broil bruschetta for 1 minute.

Makes about 16 slices.

PER SLICE	
Calories	64
g total fat	1
g saturated fat	**trace**
g fibre	1
g protein	2
g carbohydrate	11
mg cholesterol	1
mg sodium	105
mg potassium	70

Tomato Bruschetta with Fresh Basil (above), Quick Tomato, Broccoli and Red Onion Pizza (p. 40)

KIDS AND HEALTHY EATING

Parents, it's up to you to lay the foundation for good eating habits: your children will follow your example. To make it easier, here are some tips and techniques on feeding your kids right. And, best of all, good nutrition also means delicious-tasting food — please, enjoy your dinnertimes together.

Tips to help establish good eating habits in children:

- Set a good example yourself and children will likely follow.
- Remember,you are in control: preschoolers don't usually go shopping by themselves; if the junk food isn't in the house, you have solved half the problem.
- Be positive at mealtimes. Don't give any attention to children who are fussing over their food or not eating. Do give attention to the child who eats a variety of foods. Usually this works best when handled subtly. For instance, talk about how good a certain food tastes, rather than pointing out the child who is eating it. The child who isn't eating it not only doesn't get any attention but is left out of the conversation.
- Serve food that tastes good. Young children usually like their food quite plain and not overly seasoned or sauced.
- Don't bribe, plead or let the children think they have a hold on you by what they eat — they will quickly take advantage of it.
- Be sensible. If you give small children cookies 15 minutes before dinner, of course they won't be as hungry at dinner. If they are screaming with hunger, consider feeding them earlier or at least give them a nutritious snack of raw carrots, apple wedges, or half a slice of whole wheat bread.
- Don't try to sell food to children by telling them it is good for them — they don't care. Sell it because it tastes good. Discuss good eating habits and point out that we need a variety of foods when children are enjoying their food, not when they're fussing.
- Don't give up when introducing new foods to children. They might not like the food the first time they eat it, but often children like the food by the second or third try. It's best to introduce new foods one at a time along with familiar foods, such as a new vegetable in a stew or vegetable soup.
- Serve small portions to small children — although you're responsible for serving the right kinds of food, let the children decide how much they can eat. Just as adults are hungrier some days, so are children.
- Find out what snacks or meals are served and eaten at school or daycare; keep this in mind when planning your meals.

Tips for packing a nutritious lunch children will love.

- Involve children in making lunches instead of giving them money to spend on chips and pop. Now that my children are teenagers I often give them money to grocery shop for lunch makings and boxed juices. This way they can choose foods they like.
- Tell children that a good lunch has a choice from each of the four food groups:
     dairy (yogurt, milk, cheese)
     fruits and vegetables
     whole grains and bread
     meats or alternates
  If kids choose foods they like from these groups, it is more likely the lunch will be eaten and not thrown away.

- Choose whole grain, rye or pumpernickel instead of white bread. And choose bran muffins or whole wheat pita or buns, not only for extra fibre but also for taste.

- Vary sandwich fillings; include sliced cold meat leftovers from dinner, sliced turkey or chicken, part skim or skim milk cheese, salmon or peanut butter. Choose tuna that has been packed in water, not oil.

- Omit butter or margarine or use as little as possible; choose light mayonnaise over regular and add lettuce, alfalfa sprouts, grated carrots, sliced cucumber or tomato for flavor and to keep the sandwich from drying out. (Pack the juicier items like cucumber, tomato or lettuce separately to add at the last minute or the result may be too soggy to eat.)

- Pack raw vegetables along with a dip (one of the easiest ways to get children to eat vegetables). See the Mexican Bean Dip recipe on page 35 or the Green Onion dip on page 33.

- Pack a safe lunch. My kids freeze the small juice boxes (if your freezer is very cold, put the frozen boxes in the refrigerator the night before). By lunchtime they will be thawed but still cold and will have kept the rest of the lunch cool. If you have a soft insulated lunch bag and a frozen juice box, you can safely pack yogurt or cottage cheese.

- Choose foods that keep safely at room temperature. In warm weather, cheese and peanut butter are good choices; avoid eggs, fish and poultry.

- Don't reuse lunch box wrappings; they may contain bacteria.

- Use leftovers for lunch. Pizza, stir frys, pasta dishes, meatloaf, bean salad and coleslaw make good lunch (or breakfast) choices.

- Pack a hot lunch by using a wide-mouthed thermos to hold chili, baked beans, spaghetti with meat sauce, soups or stew.

- Include a nutritious sweet such as Easy Date and Walnut Squares (recipe page 205), Pineapple Carrot Bars (recipe page 204), oatmeal cookies, Cinnamon Carrot Bread (recipe page 194), pudding or applesauce.

Snacks

Snacks are an important part of children's diet and need to be chosen carefully. Whether a snack is bought or homemade, avoid ones that are high in fat and sugar. This doesn't mean children never have a bag of chips, but they shouldn't be eaten daily. Try to keep on hand a supply of good-for-you foods that children can eat plain such as fruit, raw vegetables or yogurt.

- Toast half a whole wheat English muffin, top with a tomato slice or spread with tomato sauce and low-fat Mozzarella cheese. Sprinkle with oregano and microwave until the cheese melts.

- Use whole wheat pita bread as a base for mini pizzas or tear a pita into pieces and dip into hummus (chick-pea dip) or the Mexican Bean Dip (recipe page 35).

- Top half a whole grain bagel with ricotta cheese and chopped fresh dill or apple slices; or peanut butter and sliced banana; or light cream cheese and sliced cucumber.

- Keep regular or fruit-flavored yogurt on hand, mix with fresh fruit or chopped dried fruits or low-sugar cereals.

- Spread small flour tortillas with refried beans or chopped tomato or chopped cooked chicken; add grated low-fat cheese; roll up and microwave until cheese melts.

Comparisons of Snack Foods

	calories	g fat	sodium
Popcorn, 1 cup/250 mL, plain	23	trace	0
Popcorn, 1 cup/250 mL with 1 tsp/15 mL oil, plus salt	68	5	233
Popcorn, 1 cup/250 mL with sugar coating	142	1	0
Mixed nuts, 1/4 cup/50 mL dry roasted	197	17	4
oil roasted plus salt	210	19	222
Potato chips (10)	105	7	94
Pretzels, bread stick (5)	59	trace	252
Doughnut, yeast type	174	11	98
Chocolate Chip cookies (2)	103	6	70
Milk chocolate bar (30 g)	156	10	28
Ice Cream, 1/2 cup/125 mL — 10% b.f.	142	8	61
Frozen fruit yogurt — 4 oz/125 g; 6.3% b.f.	148	5	63
Fruit yogurt, 4 oz/125 g — 1.4% b.f.	131	2	81
Apple	84	0	0
Banana	105	0	1

Comparing Hamburgers

Healthy eating doesn't necessarily mean giving up your favorite foods but making choices. All burgers are not equal: the beef we buy, how we cook it, and what we put on them can make a big difference in the amount of fat.

Standard fare:
Regular ground 3 oz beef patty, pan fried with regular white bun, 2 tsp (10 mL) butter or margarine, 1 tbsp (15 mL) relish or ketchup and 1 slice (1 oz/28 g) processed cheese = 56% calories from fat

Healthier choice (less fat, higher fibre):
Extra lean ground 3 oz beef patty, grilled or broiled with whole wheat bun, 1 slice tomato, 1 piece lettuce, chopped onion and 1 tbsp (15 mL) relish = 34% calories from fat

ENDIVE WITH CHÈVRE AND SHRIMP

This easy-to-prepare appetizer looks very fancy and tastes terrific. It's my daughter Susie's favorite. Serve on a large platter along with cherry tomatoes. (Pictured opposite page 26.)

4	Belgian endive	4
5 oz	soft chèvre (goat) cheese	140 g
1/3 cup	low-fat ricotta cheese	75 mL
	Pepper	
1/4 lb	small cooked shrimp	125 g
	Small sprigs fresh dill (optional)	

Divide endive into individual leaves; wash under cold running water and drain well.

In small bowl, combine chèvre, ricotta, and pepper to taste; mix well.

Fill wide end of each endive leaf with cheese mixture; top with shrimp. Garnish with sprig of dill (if using).

Makes about 30 appetizers.

PER ENDIVE		
Calories		23
g	total fat	1
g	saturated fat	1
g	fibre	trace
g	protein	2
g	carbohydrate	1
mg	cholesterol	10
mg	sodium	64
mg	potassium	19

LIGHT AND EASY GUACAMOLE

Because avocado is high in fat, I use a mixture of green peas and avocado and still have the authentic flavor of a traditional Mexican dip. Serve with crudités, Belgian endive wedges or baked tortilla chips.

Avocado and asparagus guacamole
In asparagus season try this delicious variation: Instead of peas, substitute 1/2 lb (250 g) cooked asparagus.

1 2/3 cups	frozen peas (1/2 lb/250 g), thawed	400 mL
1	avocado, peeled	1
2	large tomatoes, peeled, seeded and chopped	2
2	small cloves garlic, minced	2
1/4 cup	minced red onion	50 mL
2 tbsp	fresh lemon juice	25 mL
1 tsp	chili powder	5 mL
1/2 tsp	each salt and ground cumin	2 mL
Pinch	cayenne pepper	Pinch

In food processor, purée peas until smooth. In bowl, mash avocado with fork; add peas, tomatoes, garlic, onion, lemon juice, chili powder, salt, cumin and cayenne pepper; mix until blended.

Makes 2 cups (500 mL).

PER 2 TBSP (25 ML)	
Calories	41
g total fat	2
g saturated fat	**trace**
g fibre	1
g protein	1
g carbohydrate	5
mg cholesterol	0
mg sodium	99
mg potassium	166

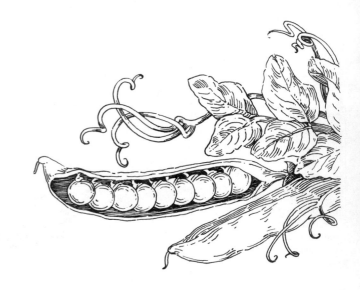

SCALLION DIP

My kids love this dip with fresh vegetables. I like to add fresh basil or any other fresh herbs that I have on hand.

1 cup	low-fat cottage cheese	250 mL
1/4 cup	chopped scallions	50 mL
1/4 cup	chopped fresh parsley	50 mL
1/2 cup	low-fat yogurt	125 mL
	Salt and pepper	

In blender or food processor, process cottage cheese, scallions and parsley. Transfer to bowl and stir in yogurt. Season with salt and pepper to taste. Cover and refrigerate for 1 hour or up to 2 days.

Makes 1 1/2 cups (375 mL).

Fresh Basil Dip
Prepare Green Onion Dip, but add 1/2 cup (125 mL) chopped fresh basil to blender.

PER 2 TBSP (25 ML)	
Calories	**24**
g total fat	**trace**
g saturated fat	**trace**
g fibre	**trace**
g protein	**3**
g carbohydrate	**2**
mg cholesterol	**2**
mg sodium	**84**
mg potassium	**54**

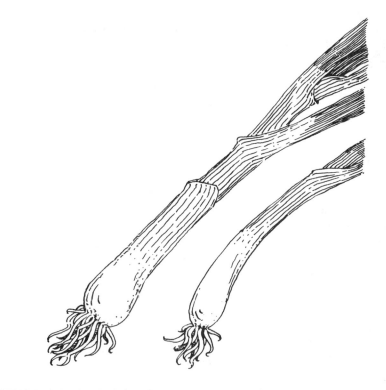

SMOKED SALMON SPREAD

Spread this creamy mixture on melba toast or use it to stuff mushrooms, cherry tomatoes or Belgian endives. Smoked trout can be used instead of salmon. (Pictured opposite page 26.)

Choose carefully when you buy cheese and crackers for a snack. Better choices for crackers are melba toast, rice cakes, crisp breads and soda crackers. Crackers made with fat or cheese are much higher in fat. Compare: 2 Ryvita crackers with 4 tbsp (60 mL) 2% cottage cheese have 2 g fat; 4 Ritz crackers with 2 tbsp (25 mL) cream cheese have 15 g fat.

1 cup	ricotta cheese	250 mL
2 oz	smoked salmon, chopped (about 1/3 cup/75 mL)	60 g
2 tbsp	chopped fresh dill	25 mL
2 tbsp	drained capers	25 mL
2 tsp	lemon juice	10 mL
2 tsp	ketchup	10 mL
1 tsp	prepared horseradish	5 mL
	Salt and pepper	

In food processor or blender, purée ricotta until smooth. Add smoked salmon, dill, capers, lemon juice, ketchup and horseradish; using on/off motion, process until lightly mixed. Season with salt and pepper to taste.

Makes 1 1/3 cups (325 mL).

PER TBSP (15 ML)	
Calories	22
g total fat	1
g saturated fat	1
g fibre	0
g protein	2
g carbohydrate	1
mg cholesterol	5
mg sodium	189
mg potassium	24

*Mexican Bean Dip with
Raw Carrots, Celery
and Green Peppers*
Whole Wheat Crackers
Slice of Cheese
Orange Sections
Oatmeal Cookie

*Canned refried beans
can be found in the
Mexican food section of
most supermarkets. Or,
you can use canned
pinto beans, drained
and rinsed, then
mashed with a chopped
tomato and 1 tsp (5 mL)
of cumin.*

PER 2 TBSP (25 ML)	
Calories	35
g total fat	trace
g saturated fat	trace
g fibre	2
g protein	2
g carbohydrate	6
mg cholesterol	0
mg sodium	126
mg potassium	137

PER 2 TBSP (25 ML)	
Calories	4
g total fat	trace
g saturated fat	0
g fibre	trace
g protein	trace
g carbohydrate	1
mg cholesterol	0
mg sodium	1
mg potassium	42

MEXICAN BEAN DIP

*Kids love this as a filling for celery, as a dip with vegetables, or as a
sandwich spread along with lettuce, sliced tomato or cucumber inside pita
rounds. Fresh or canned chilies (hot or mild) are also delicious in this
dip. For a party, sprinkle it with shredded Cheddar cheese.*

1	can (16 oz) refried beans	1
1/3 cup	low-fat yogurt	75 mL
2	scallions, chopped	2
1	clove garlic, minced	1
1 tsp	each cumin and chili powder	5 mL
2 tbsp	chopped fresh coriander OR parsley	25 mL

In bowl, combine beans, yogurt, onions, garlic, cumin and chili
powder; mix well. Cover and refrigerate for up to 2 days. Just
before serving, sprinkle with parsley or coriander.

Makes about 2 cups (500 mL).

TOMATO AND CUCUMBER SALSA

Serve this with tacos or burritos or as a dip.

1	large tomato, finely diced	1
1 cup	finely diced cucumber	250 mL
1	small green chili pepper (canned or fresh), chopped OR 1/4 tsp (1 mL) hot pepper flakes	1
2 tbsp	minced onion	25 mL
1 tbsp	wine vinegar	15 mL
1 tbsp	chopped fresh coriander (optional)	15 mL
Half	clove garlic, minced	Half

In bowl, combine tomato, cucumber, chili pepper, onion, vinegar,
coriander (if using) and garlic; mix well.
   Transfer 1 cup (250 mL) of the tomato mixture to food
processor or blender and purée; return to remaining mixture in
bowl. Serve at room temperature within 3 hours or cover and
refrigerate for up to 3 days.

Makes about 2 cups (500 mL).

Spicy Chicken Skewers

Nice for a summer barbecue or a winter cocktail party, serve these mouthfuls of spicy tender chicken as an hors d'oeuvre, or cut into long strips as a main course. For a satay, serve with Thai Peanut Sauce (recipe follows). For a less spicy version, reduce or omit hot pepper flakes.

1 lb	boneless skinless chicken fillets OR breasts	500 g

Marinade:

2 tbsp	cider vinegar	25 mL
2 tbsp	dry sherry	25 mL
2 tbsp	liquid honey	25 mL
2 tbsp	reduced-sodium soy sauce	25 mL
2 tbsp	minced gingerroot	25 mL
1 tbsp	sesame oil	15 mL
1 tsp	ground coriander	5 mL
1	large clove garlic, minced	1
1/2 tsp	crushed red pepper flakes	2 mL

Cut chicken into very thin 1/2-inch (1 cm) wide strips about 2 inches (5 cm) long (for appetizers) or 5 inches (12 cm) long for main course.

Marinade: In bowl, combine vinegar, sherry, honey, soy sauce, gingerroot, sesame oil, coriander, garlic and hot pepper flakes; mix well. Add chicken and stir to coat. Cover and refrigerate for 2 hours or up to 24 hours.

Meanwhile, soak 48 toothpicks or 24 wooden skewers in water for 30 minutes. Remove chicken from marinade and thread onto toothpicks or skewers.

Place on baking sheet or grill; broil or grill for 2 minutes on each side or until no longer pink inside.

Makes 48 hors d'oeuvres or 4 main-course servings.

PER SKEWER

Calories		15
g	total fat	trace
g	saturated fat	trace
g	fibre	0

g	protein	2
g	carbohydrate	trace
mg	cholesterol	6
mg	sodium	15
mg	potassium	20

PER SERVING
(main course)

Calories		175
g	total fat	5
g	saturated fat	1
g	fibre	trace

EXCELLENT: Niacin

g	protein	26
g	carbohydrate	6
mg	cholesterol	70
mg	sodium	183
mg	potassium	242

THAI PEANUT SAUCE

*Use this hot Thai sauce for dipping Spicy Chicken Skewers (facing page)
or with your favorite satay recipe. This isn't a low-fat recipe; however, it is
lower in fat than most peanut sauces. Because it's hot and spicy, you'll
probably want just a little.*

1 cup	dry-roasted unsalted peanuts*	250 mL
1 1/3 cups	water	325 mL
3	cloves garlic	3
2 tbsp	packed brown sugar	25 mL
2 tbsp	lime juice	25 mL
1 tbsp	reduced-sodium soy sauce	15 mL
1/4 tsp	crushed red pepper flakes	1 mL
1	piece (1 inch/2.5 cm) gingerroot, peeled and thinly sliced	1

In blender or food processor, combine peanuts, water, garlic,
sugar, lime juice, soy sauce, hot pepper flakes and gingerroot;
process for 2 minutes. Pour into top of double boiler over boiling
water; cook for 30 minutes, stirring occasionally. (Sauce can be
covered and refrigerated for up to 2 weeks.) Serve warm.

Makes about 2 cups (500 mL).

*To roast peanuts: place on baking sheet and roast in 350°F
(180°C) oven for 12 minutes.

PER TBSP (15 ML)	
Calories	30
g total fat	2
g saturated fat	**trace**
g fibre	0
g protein	1
g carbohydrate	2
mg cholesterol	0
mg sodium	16
mg potassium	37

CHEESY CHILI QUESADILLAS

A quesadilla (pronounced Kay-sa-dee-a) is a turnover made with a Mexican tortilla and usually filled with cheese plus other optional fillings such as ham, cooked chicken or sausage, green chilies or refried beans. It's then topped with salsa or taco sauce to make a great snack, lunch or light supper.

Baked quesadillas
Prepare as above except bake on baking sheet in 375°F (190°C) oven for 10 minutes or until crisp.

4	soft 8-inch (20 cm) flour OR corn tortillas	4
1 cup	shredded reduced-fat mozzarella cheese	250 mL
1/4 cup	chopped canned green chilies	50 mL
1/4 cup	chopped scallions	50 mL
2 tsp	soft margarine OR vegetable oil	10 mL
	Tomato and Cucumber Salsa (page 35)	
	Shredded lettuce	

Sprinkle half of each tortilla with cheese, chilies and onions. Fold tortillas in half and press edges together.

Brush griddle or nonstick skillet with 1 tsp (5 mL) of the margarine or oil; heat over medium-high heat. Cook 2 of the tortillas for about 4 minutes on each side or until golden and cheese melts. Remove from heat; cut into 3 wedges. Repeat with remaining tortillas. Top with Tomato and Cucumber Salsa and shredded lettuce.

Makes 4 servings.

PER SERVING
(of 1 tortilla)

Calories		198
g	total fat	8
g	saturated fat	3
g	fibre	1

GOOD: Vitamin C, Niacin, Calcium
EXCELLENT: Vitamin A

g	protein	10
g	carbohydrate	21
mg	cholesterol	17
mg	sodium	330
mg	potassium	129

JIFFY MEXICAN BURRITOS

This is the way my kids make burritos. They spread the tortillas with mashed beans, top with grated cheese and chopped vegetables or salsa, then roll up to bake or microwave.

When shopping for cheeses, look for those with the lowest b.f. (butter fat) or m.f. (milk fat) content. Cheese that is "low fat" will have 15% b.f. or less, about 4.5 g fat per oz (25 g). Skim milk cheese has 7% b.f. or less, or about 2.1 g fat per oz (25 g). By comparison, regular cheddar cheese has 32% b.f., or about 9.6 g fat per oz (25 g).

In recipes that call for grated, chopped, or crumbled cheddar or other hard cheese, remember that 1 oz (25 g) solid cheese equals about 1/4 cup (50 mL) grated cheese.

1	can (16 oz) refried beans	1
1/3 cup	salsa or water	75 mL
4	9-inch (23 cm) soft flour tortillas	4
1	medium tomato, chopped	1
4	small green onions, chopped	4
Half	sweet green pepper, chopped (optional)	Half
1 cup	shredded reduced-fat mozzarella cheese	250 mL
	Shredded lettuce	
	Salsa (pages 35 or 190) OR taco sauce	
	low-fat dairy sour cream OR low-fat	

Combine beans and salsa or water; mix well.

Thinly spread about 1/3 cup (75 mL) bean mixture over each tortilla, leaving 1-inch (2.5 cm) border. Sprinkle tomato, green onions, green pepper (if using) and half the cheese over tortillas.

Roll up each tortilla and place, seam side down, in lightly greased baking dish. Bake in 400°F (200°C) oven for 10 minutes. Sprinkle with remaining cheese; bake for 5 minutes longer or until heated through and cheese melts. (Alternatively, cover with waxed paper and microwave on Medium-high (70%) power for 2 to 4 minutes or until heated through.)

Serve each burrito on a bed of shredded lettuce. Pass salsa or taco sauce and sour cream or yogurt separately.

Makes 4 servings.

PER SERVING	
Calories	308
g total fat	8
g saturated fat	3
g fibre	8

GOOD: Vitamin A, Riboflavin
EXCELLENT: Vitamin C, Calcium, Iron, Niacin

g	protein	17
g	carbohydrate	43
mg	cholesterol	17
mg	sodium	655
mg	potassium	699

Pizza:

Pizza makes a great snack or a quick supper. You can make your own great-tasting pizza in less time than it takes to have one delivered. You'll save money as well!

Pick up ready-made pizza crusts at any supermarket or keep them on hand in the refrigerator or freezer. Or, buy ready-made pizza dough, either fresh or frozen, for when you have the time to roll it out. For other quick crusts, you could also use pita bread rounds or English muffins, or make pizza subs using French bread halved lengthwise.

Use your favorite toppings or the ones suggested here; they take only seconds to prepare. Vegetable toppings add fibre, vitamins and minerals. Avoid salty or higher fat toppings, such as anchovies, olives, bacon, pepperoni and high-fat cheese.

PER SERVING	
Calories	**205**
g total fat	**7**
g saturated fat	**3**
g fibre	**3**

GOOD: Vitamin A, Riboflavin, Calcium, Iron, Niacin
EXCELLENT: Vitamin C

g protein	**12**
g carbohydrate	**25**
mg cholesterol	**18**
mg sodium	**417**
mg potassium	**294**

QUICK TOMATO, BROCCOLI AND RED ONION PIZZA

Juicy vegetable toppings make a pleasing combination of flavors. (Pictured opposite page 27.)

1	12-inch (30 cm) pizza crust	1
1/4 cup	tomato sauce*	50 mL
1 1/2 tsp	dried oregano	7 mL
Half	sweet green pepper, chopped	Half
1	medium tomato, sliced	1
1 cup	small broccoli florets	250 ml
1/2 cup	thinly sliced red onion rings	125 mL
2 tbsp	chopped fresh basil OR 1/4 tsp (1 mL) dried	25 mL
1 cup	shredded reduced-fat mozzarella cheese	250 mL
Pinch	crushed red pepper flakes	Pinch

Place pizza crust on nonstick baking sheet or pizza pan. Spread tomato sauce over crust; sprinkle with oregano.

Arrange green pepper, tomato, broccoli, onion and basil over sauce. Sprinkle with cheese, then hot pepper flakes (if using). Bake in 450°F (230°C) oven for 10 minutes or until cheese is bubbly.

Makes 4 servings.

*To reduce sodium: Instead of tomato sauce, use 2 tbsp (25 mL) tomato paste mixed with 1/4 cup (50 mL) water.

Citrus Sangria

White grape juice and citrus fruit make an elegant drink. Sparkling white grape juice is also nice to use instead of the grape juice and soda water.

1	lime	1
1	lemon	1
1	orange	1
4 cups	white grape juice	1
1	bottle (28 oz) carbonated water	1
	Crushed ice cubes	

Cut lime, lemon and orange in half. Squeeze juice from one half of each; cut remaining halves into thin slices.

In large pitcher, combine grape juice, soda water, lime, lemon and orange slices and juice. Fill wine glasses one-quarter full with crushed ice. Pour in sangria and a slice of citrus.

Makes 8 servings (1 cup/250 mL each).

Easy Holiday Punch
In punch bowl, combine 1 bottle (750 mL each) ginger ale and cranberry juice and 1 small container frozen orange juice concentrate. Stir well and add ice cubes before serving.

PER SERVING		
Calories		85
g	total fat	trace
g	saturated fat	0
g	fibre	trace
g	protein	1
g	carbohydrate	21
mg	cholesterol	0
mg	sodium	24
mg	potassium	194

Gazpacho Cooler

Serve this at a brunch instead of Bloody Marys or as an alternative to an alcoholic drink. It tastes great and is packed with vitamin C.

Quarter	English cucumber, peeled	Quarter
Half	small onion	Half
2	small tomatoes	2
1/4	sweet green pepper, seeded	1/4
1	small clove garlic, minced	1
2 cups	tomato juice	500 mL
2 tbsp	red wine vinegar OR cider vinegar	25 mL
1/4 tsp	dried dillweed	1 mL
Dash	hot pepper sauce	Dash
	Pepper	
	Lemon OR lime slices	

Coarsely chop cucumber, onion, tomatoes and green pepper; transfer to blender. Add garlic and blend until smooth. Stir in tomato juice, vinegar, dillweed, hot pepper sauce, and pepper to taste.

Refrigerate for at least 1 hour or until chilled. Stir to mix well before pouring into glasses. Garnish with lemon or lime slice.

Makes 6 servings (3/4 cup/175 mL each).

PER SERVING		
Calories		27
g	total fat	trace
g	saturated fat	0
g	fibre	1
GOOD: Vitamin C		
g	protein	1
g	carbohydrate	6
mg	cholesterol	0
mg	sodium	297
mg	potassium	300

SOUPS

OLD-FASHIONED QUEBEC PEA SOUP

Most recipes for this soup call for salt pork or a ham bone. In order to reduce fat, I don't use salt pork. I always make it when I have a ham bone, but you can make it without one. In Quebec, this soup is usually made with dried yellow soup peas. If they are not available, use yellow split peas. Try to use leaf savory, not ground.

2 cups	dried yellow soup peas OR split peas	500 mL
10 cups	water	2.5 L
1	ham bone OR 1/4 lb (125 g) ham, chopped	1
5	medium onions, chopped	5
3	medium carrots, peeled and chopped	3
2	stalks celery (including leaves), chopped	2
1 tsp	summer savory	5 mL
1	bay leaf	1
	Salt and pepper	

A pea soup is one of the most nourishing soups you can make. Dried peas are an excellent source of soluble fibre (the kind that research has shown helps lower blood cholesterol) and potassium and a good source of iron and protein.

Rinse peas. In large soup pot, combine peas, water, ham bone or ham, onions, carrots, celery, summer savory and bay leaf; bring to boil. Skim off any scum. Cover and simmer for 3 hours or until peas are softened and soup has thickened. If soup is too thin, uncover and simmer 30 minutes longer. Season with salt and pepper to taste. Discard bay leaf and ham bone.

Makes 8 servings, about 1 1/4 cups (300 mL) each.

PER SERVING	
Calories	203
g total fat	2
g saturated fat	trace
g fibre	8

GOOD: Niacin, Iron
EXCELLENT: Vitamin A, Thiamin

g	protein	14
g	carbohydrate	34
mg	cholesterol	8
mg	sodium	249
mg	potassium	699

SUMMER TOMATO AND GREEN BEAN SOUP

Make this light soup in the summer when both green beans and tomatoes have the best flavor and fresh basil is readily available.

If you are on a sodium-restricted diet, use water, homemade Chicken Stock (page 60) or a low-sodium chicken or vegetable stock. Sodium value given is for canned stock plus water.

2 tsp	soft margarine	10 mL
2	medium onions OR leeks, chopped	2
3	medium carrots, chopped	3
1	large clove garlic, minced	1
1 lb	green beans, cut in 1-inch (2.5 cm) lengths	500 g
6 cups	chicken stock	1.5 L
3 cups	diced tomatoes	750 mL
1/4 cup	chopped fresh basil OR 1 tbsp (15 mL) dried	50 mL
	Salt and pepper	

In large pot, heat margarine over medium heat; cook onions and carrots for 5 minutes. Add garlic, beans and stock; simmer for 20 minutes. Add tomatoes and simmer for 5 minutes. Add basil; season with salt and pepper to taste. Serve hot.

Makes 8 servings, about 1 cup (250 mL) each.

PER SERVING

Calories		87
g	total fat	2
g	saturated fat	1
g	fibre	3

GOOD: Vitamin C, Niacin
EXCELLENT: Vitamin A

g	protein	6
g	carbohydrate	12
mg	cholesterol	0
mg	sodium	616
mg	potassium	554

REHEAT DINNER

*Smoky Sausage Lentil
  Soup
Coleslaw
Whole Wheat Buns
Oranges
Cookies
Milk*

*If you are on a sodium-
restricted diet, use
8 cups (2 L) water
instead of 4 cups each
stock and water, or use
low-sodium stock.
Sodium content per
serving will then be
359 mg. If you omit the
sausage as well, sodium
content will be 54 mg
per serving. Omitting
the sausage will also
reduce the fat content to
4 g per serving.*

PER SERVING	
Calories	**408**
g total fat	**12**
g saturated fat	**3**
g fibre	**9**

GOOD: Riboflavin
EXCELLENT: Vitamin A,
Thiamin, Niacin, Iron

g	protein	**25**
g	carbohydrate	**52**
mg	cholesterol	**19**
mg	sodium	**871**
mg	potassium	**1222**

SMOKY SAUSAGE LENTIL SOUP

*Lentils are an excellent source of fibre and are packed with nutrients —
vegetable protein, iron, some calcium, and B-vitamins. If possible, make
this main-course soup on the weekend or while you are cooking dinner one
night to have a make-ahead dinner ready and waiting just to be reheated.
We aren't supposed to have a lot of sausage because of its high fat content,
so this is a good way to use a little for flavor.*

1 tbsp	olive oil	15 mL
1	onion, chopped	1
4	celery stalks, sliced	4
6 oz	smoked sausage (such as kielbasa), coarsely chopped	170 g
4 cups	chicken OR vegetable stock	1 L
4 cups	water	1 L
2 cups	dried green lentils	500 mL
1	strip (3 inches/8 cm long) orange rind	1
1 tsp	crumbled dried marjoram	5 mL
1 tsp	crumbled dried savory	5 mL
3	carrots, peeled and sliced	3
2	potatoes, peeled and diced	2
	Salt and pepper	

In large heavy saucepan, heat oil over medium heat; add onion and
cook for 5 minutes, stirring occasionally. Add celery and sausage;
cook for 5 minutes, stirring occasionally.

Add stock, water, lentils, orange rind, marjoram and savory;
bring to boil. Reduce heat, cover partially and simmer for 30
minutes.

Add carrots and potatoes; cover partially and simmer, stirring
occasionally, for 35 minutes or until lentils are tender. Discard
orange rind. Season with salt and pepper to taste.

Makes 6 main-course servings, about 1 1/4 cups (300 mL) each.

LENTIL SPINACH SOUP WITH CURRIED YOGURT

This soup is easy to make using either canned or dried lentils. (If using dried brown lentils, see information in margin.) The soup is packed with nutrients and along with toast and a salad makes a satisfying quick meal.

4 cups	chicken OR vegetable stock	1 L
1	can (15 oz) lentils, drained, OR 2 cups (500 mL) cooked	1
2	stalks celery, chopped	2
2	small onions, minced	2
2	small cloves garlic, minced	2
4 cups	chopped fresh spinach, packed (10 oz bag)	1 L
1 tbsp	lemon juice	15 mL
	Salt and pepper	

Curried Yogurt:

1/4 cup	low-fat yogurt	50 mL
1 tsp	curry powder	5 mL

In saucepan, bring stock, lentils, celery, onions and garlic to boil; reduce heat, cover and simmer for 5 minutes. Add spinach and simmer for 3 minutes. Add lemon juice; season with salt and pepper to taste. (If thicker soup is desired, remove half and purée in food processor or blender; return to saucepan and heat through.)

Curried Yogurt: Mix yogurt with curry. Ladle soup into bowls; swirl dollop of curried yogurt into each.

Makes 5 servings, about 1 cup (250 mL) each.

Margin notes

Dried lentils

If using dried lentils, follow lentil soup recipe except substitute 2/3 cup (150 mL) dried brown or green lentils for canned lentils and add 4 cups (1 L) water with lentils. Cover and cook for 25 minutes or until lentils are tender, complete as in recipe.

Inexpensive lentils are a nutrient bargain — packed with all the good things we need such as protein, iron, the B vitamin niacin, complex carbohydrates and soluble fibre. They contain no cholesterol and very little fat. Dried lentils don't need to be soaked before cooking; red lentils cook in about 10 minutes, green in about 30 minutes.

PER SERVING	
Calories	**136**
g total fat	**2**
g saturated fat	**trace**
g fibre	**4**

GOOD: Thiamin, Riboflavin
EXCELLENT: Vitamin A, Niacin, Iron

g protein	**12**
g carbohydrate	**19**
mg cholesterol	**1**
mg sodium	**825**
mg potassium	**773**

Chunky Leek and Cabbage Soup

Because this is one of my favorite winter soups, I try to make enough to last for two nights. The first night, I enjoy the vegetables in pieces; the second night I purée the soup. If I don't have leeks on hand, I use 2 medium onions instead. If I have any fresh herbs — dill or thyme or basil — I add a tablespoon or two (15–25 mL) just before serving.

1	medium onion, chopped	1
3 cups	chicken stock	750 mL
2 cups	chopped leeks (white part mainly)	500 mL
1 1/2 cups	peeled, diced potatoes	375 mL
2 cups	chopped green cabbage	500 mL
1 cup	low-fat milk	250 mL
	Salt and pepper	
	Chopped fresh dill, parsley OR green onions	

To reduce sodium and for a creamier soup, use 1 cup (250 mL) chicken stock and 3 cups (750 mL) milk.

In large saucepan, bring chicken stock, onion, leeks and potatoes to boil. Cover and reduce heat; simmer for about 20 minutes or until vegetables are tender.

Add cabbage; cook for 5 to 8 minutes or until tender. Stir in milk; season with salt and pepper to taste. Sprinkle each serving with dill, parsley or onions.

Makes 6 servings, about 1 cup (250 mL) each.

PER SERVING	
Calories	97
g total fat	2
g saturated fat	1
g fibre	2
GOOD: Niacin	
g protein	5
g carbohydrate	16
mg cholesterol	3
mg sodium	420
mg potassium	406

BLACK BEAN AND HAM SOUP

This is a great way to use up the end of a ham. Just leave a little meat on the bone and don't add any extra ham. Perfect for a casual supper along with toast and a green salad, I like to top each serving with light sour cream or yogurt and chopped tomato and green onion.

2 cups	dried black (turtle) beans	500 mL
2 tbsp	vegetable oil	25 mL
3	cloves garlic, minced	3
4	onions, chopped	4
1	ham bone (optional)	1
1/2 lb	cooked ham chopped (about 1 1/2 cups/ 375 mL)	250 g
1	stalk celery and leaves, chopped	1
1	bay leaf	1
1 tsp	each dried thyme, oregano and ground coriander	5 mL
8 cups	water OR beef stock	2 L

Place beans in strainer and wash. Transfer to large pot and cover with 8 cups (2 L) water. Bring to boil; boil for 2 minutes. Remove from heat and cover; let stand for 1 hour, then drain.

In large heavy saucepan, heat oil over medium heat. Stir in garlic and onions; cook for 3 to 5 minutes or until softened.

Add beans, ham bone (if using), ham, celery, bay leaf, thyme, oregano and coriander. Pour in water or beef stock and bring to boil.

Reduce heat to medium-low; cover and simmer, stirring occasionally, for 1 1/2 hours or until beans are tender. Discard bay leaf and bone.

Transfer about 4 cups (1 L) to food processor or blender and purée; return to saucepan and stir to mix.

Makes 10 servings, about 3/4 cups (175 mL) each.

PER SERVING
(made with water)

Calories		**189**
g	total fat	**5**
g	saturated fat	**1**
g	fibre	**6**

GOOD: Niacin, Iron
EXCELLENT: Thiamin

g	protein	**13**
g	carbohydrate	**24**
mg	cholesterol	**13**
mg	sodium	**327**
mg	potassium	**535**

QUICK AND EASY FISH CHOWDER

If you keep a package of fish fillets in your freezer, you can always make a meal at the last minute. Any fresh or frozen fillets can be used in this recipe. If I have bacon on hand, I'll use it for its smoky flavor. Sometimes I add chopped carrot or celery, and I always add fresh dill when I have it.

1 tbsp	soft margarine OR 4 slices bacon, chopped	15 mL
1	onion, chopped	1
3	potatoes,* diced	3
2 cups	water	500 mL
1 lb	fresh or frozen fish fillets, cut in chunks	500 g
2 cups	low-fat milk	500 mL
1 cup	corn kernels (frozen OR canned)	250 mL
1/4 cup	coarsely chopped fresh parsley OR dill	50 mL
	Salt and pepper	

In heavy saucepan, heat margarine over medium heat (or cook bacon and drain off fat). Add onion and cook for 5 minutes or until tender. Add potatoes and water; cover and simmer until vegetables are nearly tender, about 15 minutes.

Add fish; cover and cook until opaque, about 2 minutes for fresh, 10 minutes for frozen.

Stir in milk and corn; simmer until hot. Add parsley or dill. Season with salt and pepper to taste.

Makes 4 main-course servings, about 1 1/2 cups (375 mL) each.

*I only peel potatoes if the skin is tough. Unpeeled potatoes have twice as much fibre.

PER SERVING
(without bacon)

Calories		301
g	total fat	6
g	saturated fat	2
g	fibre	3

GOOD: Thiamin, Riboflavin, Calcium
EXCELLENT: Niacin

g	protein	27
g	carbohydrate	36
mg	cholesterol	66
mg	sodium	179
mg	potassium	1065

HEARTY SALMON CHOWDER

I first had this delicious soup when it was served to a group of food writers on a boat off British Columbia's Vancouver Island. We all asked for the recipe, which was from the Lopez Island Cookbook. Here it is adapted slightly. You could also use 2% milk instead of evaporated milk; however, I like the flavor with evaporated milk. It is a good recipe to remember when planning a camping or boat trip.

When using canned salmon, be sure to crush bones and include in soup. The bones are an excellent source of calcium.

1	can (7 1/2 oz) salmon	1
2 tsp	soft margarine	10 mL
1/2 cup	each chopped onion and celery	125 mL
1/4 cup	chopped sweet green pepper	50 mL
1	clove garlic, minced	1
3 cups	diced potatoes	750 mL
1 cup	diced carrots	250 mL
1 cup	each chicken stock and water	250 mL
1/2 tsp	each coarse pepper and dill seed	2 mL
1 cup	diced zucchini	250 mL
1	can (12 oz) 2% evaporated milk	1
1	can (8 3/4 oz) cream-style corn	1
	Pepper	
1/2 cup	chopped fresh parsley (optional)	125 mL

Drain and flake salmon, reserving liquid.

In large nonstick saucepan, melt margarine over medium heat; cook onion, celery, green pepper and garlic, stirring often, for 5 minutes or until vegetables are tender.

Add potatoes, carrots. chicken stock, water, pepper and dill seed; bring to boil. Reduce heat, cover and simmer for 20 minutes or until vegetables are tender. Add zucchini; simmer, covered, for 5 minutes.

Add salmon, reserved liquid, evaporated milk, corn, and pepper to taste. Cook over low heat just until heated through. Just before serving, add parsley.

Makes 4 main-course servings (1 3/4 cups/425 mL each) or 8 appetizer servings (3/4 cup/ 175 mL each).

PER MAIN-COURSE SERVING	
Calories	359
g total fat	8
g saturated fat	3
g fibre	5

GOOD: Thiamin
EXCELLENT: Vitamins A and C, Riboflavin, Niacin, Calcium

g	protein	20
g	carbohydrate	54
mg	cholesterol	20
mg	sodium	758
mg	potassium	1194

CREAMY OYSTER CHOWDER

This is a favorite of mine for an easy supper, but it also makes a wonderful appetizer course on its own. (Pictured opposite page 58.)

1 tbsp	soft margarine	15 mL
1	small onion, diced	1
1	stalk celery, diced	1
1	carrot, diced	1
2 tbsp	all-purpose flour	25 mL
1/2 cup	fish stock OR white wine	125 mL
1	can (8 oz) oysters	1
1 cup	diced peeled potatoes	250 mL
1 tsp	dried thyme OR 1 tbsp (15 mL) fresh	5 mL
2 1/4 cups	low-fat milk	550 mL
2 tbsp	chopped fresh parsley	25 mL
	Salt and pepper	

In large saucepan, melt margarine over medium heat; cook onion, celery and carrot, covered, for 5 minutes. Blend in flour. Stirring constantly, gradually pour in stock or white wine. Drain liquid from oysters into pan; set oysters aside. Add potatoes and thyme; stir and bring to boil. Reduce heat and simmer, uncovered, until potatoes are tender, about 10 minutes.

Add oysters, milk and parsley; cook just until heated through. Season with salt and pepper to taste.

Makes 3 main-course servings of 1 1/3 cups (325 mL) each or 6 appetizer servings of 2/3 cup (150 mL) each.

SIMPLE SUPPER FOR TWO
*Tomato Slices with
    Chèvre and Basil
    (p. 78)
Toasted Whole Wheat
    Bread
Creamy Oyster
    Chowder
Fresh Berries and Ice
    Cream*

**PER MAIN-COURSE
SERVING**

Calories		**276**
g	total fat	**9**
g	saturated fat	**3**
g	fibre	**2**

GOOD: Thiamin, Niacin
EXCELLENT: Vitamin A,
Vitamin C, Riboflavin,
Calcium, Iron

g	protein	**15**
g	carbohydrate	**32**
mg	cholesterol	**48**
mg	sodium	**441**
mg	potassium	**675**

Beef 'n' Bean Minestrone

Packed with nutrients, this easy main-course soup is great to have on hand for those nights when everyone is on the run. The soup keeps well in the refrigerator for up to three days, ready and waiting for anyone to warm up a bowlful in the microwave. This version is lighter than many recipes because the vegetables aren't sautéed in oil.

1/2 lb	lean ground beef	250 g
1	large onion, diced	1
1	carrot, diced	1
1	stalk celery, diced	1
1	small zucchini (6-inch/15 cm), diced	1
2	tomatoes OR 1 can (14 oz), undrained, chopped	2
1	potato, peeled and diced	1
3	cloves garlic, minced	3
8 cups	water	2 L
3/4 cup	small pasta	175 mL
1 tsp	each dried oregano and basil OR 2 tbsp (25 mL) each fresh*	5 mL
1	can (19 oz) white kidney beans, drained	1
1/4 cup	freshly grated Parmesan cheese	50 mL
1/2 cup	chopped fresh parsley	125 mL
	Salt and pepper	

In large saucepan, cook meat over medium heat until brown, breaking up with fork; drain off fat. Add onion; cook, stirring, for 3 minutes.

Add carrot, celery, zucchini, tomatoes, potato and garlic; cook, stirring, for 3 minutes. Add water; bring to boil.

Add pasta, oregano and basil; cook, uncovered, until pasta is tender but firm and vegetables are cooked, 10 to 12 minutes.

Add kidney beans, Parmesan and parsley; season with salt and pepper to taste.

Makes 8 servings, about 1 1/4 cup (300 mL) each.

*If using fresh herbs, add just before serving.

PER SERVING	
Calories	203
g total fat	4
g saturated fat	2
g fibre	7

GOOD: Niacin, Iron
EXCELLENT: Viamin A

g	protein	13
g	carbohydrate	29
mg	cholesterol	16
mg	sodium	337
mg	potassium	589

Purée of Carrot and Parsnip

Parsnips add a sweet flavor to this easy-to-make soup. It can be prepared in advance and refrigerated up to 3 days or frozen for up to 2 months. If you make it ahead of time, add the milk just before serving.

1 tsp	vegetable oil	5 mL
2 cups	chopped carrots (about 4 medium)	500 mL
1 cup	chopped, peeled parsnips (about 2 medium)	250 mL
1	small onion, chopped	1
1	medium potato, peeled and chopped	1
3 cups	vegetable OR chicken stock	750 mL
1 1/2 cups	low-fat milk	375 mL
	Chives OR chopped scallion	

In large saucepan or microwaveable dish, toss oil with carrots, parsnips, onion and potato; cover and cook over low heat for 20 minutes or microwave at High power for 10 minutes or until vegetables are tender.

Stir in stock; bring to boil. Reduce heat and simmer, covered, for 30 minutes or microwave, covered, at High power for 15 minutes.

In food processor or blender, process mixture in batches until smooth; return soup to pan. Stir in milk; reheat without boiling.

When serving, sprinkle each bowlful with chives or chopped scallion.

Makes 8 servings, about 3/4 cup (175 mL) each.

PER SERVING

Calories	95
g total fat	2
g saturated fat	1
g fibre	2

EXCELLENT: Vitamin A

g protein	4
g carbohydrate	15
mg cholesterol	3
mg sodium	336
mg potassium	385

CURRIED PUMPKIN SOUP

This wonderful fall soup is a recipe from my friends and good cooks Peter and Penny White. It has only a hint of curry flavor so as not to mask the pumpkin, and is best made ahead so that the flavors develop.

1 tbsp	soft margarine	15 mL
1/2 cup	finely chopped onion	125 mL
1	clove garlic, minced	1
1/2 lb	fresh mushrooms, sliced	250 g
2 tbsp	all-purpose flour	25 mL
1 tsp	curry powder	5 mL
2 cups	Chicken Stock (page 60)	500 mL
1	can (16 oz) pumpkin OR 2 cups (500 mL) cooked fresh pumpkin	1 1
1 tbsp	liquid honey	15 mL
	Freshly grated nutmeg	
2 cups	low-fat milk	500 mL

In large saucepan, melt margarine over medium heat; cook onion, garlic and mushrooms for 8 to 10 minutes or until softened. Stir in flour and curry powder; cook for 1 minute over low heat, stirring, until well blended.

Gradually add stock, whisking until smooth. Stir in pumpkin and honey; season with nutmeg to taste. Cook over low heat for 15 minutes, stirring occasionally. (Soup can be prepared to this point, covered and refrigerated for up to 2 days.)

Add milk and heat until hot.

Makes 8 servings, about 3/4 cup (175 mL) each.

Most canned stocks or stocks made from a cube are high in sodium. If you are on a sodium-restricted diet, you might want to make your own stock.

Easiest chicken stock: Pour all the pan drippings from a roast chicken into a jar; cover and refrigerate. Discard fat from top. Use remaining gelatinous mixture to flavor soups or dilute with water for stock.

Stock from a cube: Because these are high in sodium, use double the amount of water that is called for on the package.

PER SERVING

Calories		94
g	total fat	3
g	saturated fat	1
g	fibre	1

EXCELLENT: Vitamin A

g	protein	5
g	carbohydrate	13
mg	cholesterol	5
mg	sodium	241
mg	potassium	342

Old-Fashioned Mushroom Barley Soup

If possible, make this soup a day in advance, cover and refrigerate. Any fat from soup bone will harden on top and can be easily removed.

Barley makes an excellent base for soups: it's inexpensive, filling and nutritious. Many butchers are delighted to cut up soup bones and give them away. This is a basic recipe: add other vegetables such as leeks, green beans, cabbage, turnip, sweet potato or squash.

8 cups	water	2 L
1/2 cup	pot OR pearl barley	125 mL
1	large soup bone (beef OR lamb)	1
1	bay leaf	1
3	large carrots, chopped	3
1	celery stalk (including leaves), chopped	1
1	large onion, chopped	1
1	large potato, peeled and diced	1
1	clove garlic, minced	1
1/4 tsp	dried thyme	1 mL
1 1/2 cups	coarsely chopped mushrooms	375 mL
	Salt and pepper	

In large pot, combine water, barley, soup bone and bay leaf; bring to boil. Reduce heat, cover and simmer for 1 hour.

Add carrots, celery, onion, potato, garlic and thyme; simmer, covered, for 25 minutes. Add mushrooms and simmer for 5 minutes or until tender. Season with salt and pepper to taste. Remove bay leaf and soup bone.

Makes 8 hearty servings, 1 1/4 cups (300 mL) each.

Barley is high in soluble fibre, which is the kind of fibre that research has shown lowers blood cholesterol.

PER SERVING		
Calories		**83**
g	total fat	**trace**
g	saturated fat	**0**
g	fibre	**3**

EXCELLENT: Vitamin A

g	protein	**2**
g	carbohydrate	**19**
mg	cholesterol	**0**
mg	sodium	**30**
mg	potassium	**243**

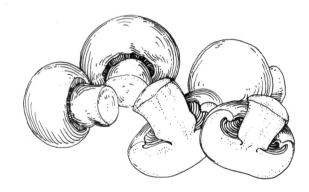

If you are on a sodium-restricted diet, use homemade beef stock, water, or a low-sodium stock. The nutrient values given are based on using canned stock or stock made from a cube. Using water instead will reduce sodium to 252 mg per serving.

FRENCH ONION SOUP

I try (when I'm organized) to make this comforting soup for the next evening's supper while I'm cooking one night. I vary the amount of cheese, using only half if the soup will be a first course. For vegetarians, use vegetable stock instead of beef.

1 tbsp	soft margarine OR vegetable oil	15 mL
6	medium onions, thinly sliced (about 8 cups/2 L lightly packed)	6
1 tsp	granulated sugar	5 mL
1 tbsp	all-purpose flour	15 mL
6 cups	beef stock	1.5 L
1/2 cup	white wine OR water	125 mL
	Pepper	
4 to 8	thick slices day-old French bread, toasted	4 to 8
2 cups	shredded reduced-fat Swiss or Jarlsberg cheese	500 mL
2 tbsp	freshly grated Parmesan cheese	25 mL

In large heavy saucepan, melt margarine or oil over medium-low heat. Add onions and sugar; cover and cook, stirring occasionally, for 30 minutes or until onions are tender. Increase heat slightly and cook, uncovered and stirring often, for about 10 minutes or until onions are rich golden brown.

Sprinkle flour over onions and stir well. Add beef stock and wine or water; cook, stirring often, until boiling. Reduce heat, cover and simmer for 20 minutes. Season with pepper to taste.

Arrange toast on baking sheet. Combine Swiss and Parmesan cheese; sprinkle over toast and broil until cheese melts. Ladle soup into bowls; top with toast.

Makes 4 main-course servings, about 1 1/2 cups (375 mL) each; or 8 appetizer servings.

PER SERVING	
(as appetizer)	
Calories	202
g total fat	8
g saturated fat	4
g fibre	2

GOOD: Niacin, Calcium

g	protein	13
g	carbohydrate	20
mg	cholesterol	19
mg	sodium	904
mg	potassium	253

CHINESE NOODLE AND MUSHROOM SOUP

You can make this soup in less than ten minutes using the packaged cooked chow-mein-type noodles, available in supermarkets in B.C. and some Chinese grocery stores. Otherwise, use the Oriental-style instant noodles and discard the seasoning packets because they are very high in salt or use any thin, cooked noodles. I use this as a base recipe and add whatever vegetables or cooked meats I have on hand. (Pictured opposite.)

1 tbsp	vegetable oil	15 mL
2 cups	sliced mushrooms (6 oz/170 g)	500 mL
1 tsp	minced garlic	5 mL
4 cups	chicken OR vegetable stock	1 L
2 cups	fresh chow mein noodles OR 2 packets (3 oz/85 g each) namen noodles	500 mL
2 tbsp	sherry OR rice wine	25 mL
1 tbsp	lemon juice OR rice vinegar	15 mL
1 tsp	sesame oil	5 mL
Dash	hot pepper sauce OR hot chili oil	Dash
1/2 cup	chopped scallions	125 mL

In large saucepan, heat oil over medium heat; cook mushrooms and garlic for 2 minutes.

Add stock and 2 cups (500 mL) water; bring to boil. Add noodles, sherry, lemon juice or rice vinegar, sesame oil and hot pepper sauce; reduce heat, cover and simmer for 3 minutes. Stir in scallions.

Makes 4 servings, about 1 1/4 cups (300 mL) each.

PER SERVING	
Calories	246
g total fat	7
g saturated fat	1
g fibre	2

GOOD: Thiamin
EXCELLENT: Riboflavin, Niacin

g	protein	9
g	carbohydrate	34
mg	cholesterol	41
mg	sodium	396
mg	potassium	314

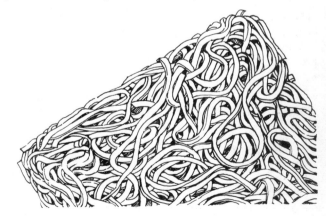

Chinese Noodle and Mushroom Soup (above), Jiffy Bean, Broccoli and Tomato (p. 59), Creamy Oyster Chowder (p. 52)

Jiffy Bean, Broccoli and Tomato Chowder

MENU
Jiffy Bean, Broccoli and
Tomato Chowder
Toasted Bagels
Tossed Green Salad

For a quick supper, try this easy soup. I like to use white kidney beans for their texture and color, though red kidney beans or chick-peas are fine. Broccoli goes into the chowder because I always seem to have it in my refrigerator, but I'm sure zucchini, green beans or spinach would be good, too. (Pictured opposite page 58.)

Vegetable stock: Save vegetable scraps like onion skins, tomato, carrot, parsley stems, potato peelings, green bean strings, beet parts, (except brassica vegetables: cabbage, broccoli, turnip and eggplant) in a plastic bag in the refrigerator. When you have about a half a saucepan full, cover with water; bring to a boil and simmer for 25 minutes. Strain stock, cool, cover and refrigerate.

2	medium onions, chopped	2
1 cup	beef OR vegetable stock	250 mL
1	can (19 oz/540 mL) tomatoes (undrained)	1
2 cups	chopped broccoli	500 mL
1	can (16 oz) tomatoes drained and rinsed	1
1/2 tsp	dried basil	2 mL
Dash	hot pepper sauce	Dash
	Salt and pepper	

In large saucepan, combine onions and 1/2 cup (125 mL) of the stock; cover and simmer for 5 minutes or until onion is tender. Add tomatoes, breaking up with back of spoon. Add remaining stock, 1 cup (250 mL) water and broccoli; bring to boil. Reduce heat and simmer for 5 minutes or until broccoli is tender-crisp.

Add beans, basil, hot pepper sauce, and salt and pepper to taste; heat until hot.

Microwave Method: In large bowl, combine onions and 1/2 cup (125 mL) of stock; cover and microwave at High power for 3 minutes. Add tomatoes, remaining stock, 1 cup (250 mL) water and broccoli; cover and microwave at High power for 5 minutes. Add beans, basil and hot pepper sauce; cover and microwave at High power for 3 minutes or until heated through. Season with salt and pepper to taste.

Makes 5 servings, about 1 1/4 cups (300 mL) each.

PER SERVING

Calories		150
g	total fat	1
g	saturated fat	trace
g	fibre	11

GOOD: Vitamin A, Thiamin, Riboflavin, Niacin, Iron
EXCELLENT: Vitamin C

g	protein	10
g	carbohydrate	28
mg	cholesterol	0
mg	sodium	622
mg	potassium	736

Green Bean and Carrot Salad (p. 70), Red Bean Salad with Feta and Peppers (p. 65), Thai Noodle Salad (p. 63)

When Making Stock
After chicken is cooked, remove meat from bones and use in salads, sandwiches, pasta dishes, casseroles or add to soups. Freeze homemade chicken stock in ice-cube trays or 1/2 cup/125 mL container and use in cooking whenever you want extra flavor without added salt.

Turkey Stock
Use turkey bones or carcass instead of chicken.

Beef, Veal or Lamb Stock
Use beef, veal or lamb bones instead of chicken. For added flavor, roast bones before simmering in water. Spread bones in roasting pan and bake in 400°F/200°C oven for 1 hour or until browned; transfer to stock-pot and continue as in Basic Chicken Stock recipe.

PER CUP		
Calories		3
g	total fat	trace
g	saturated fat	trace
g	fibre	0
g	protein	trace
g	carbohydrate	trace
mg	cholesterol	3
mg	sodium	4
mg	potassium	11

BASIC CHICKEN STOCK

If you are on a sodium-restricted diet you should avoid using cubes or canned stock. Instead make your own stock or use water or a low-sodium vegetable stock cube. Any pieces of chicken can be used, even a whole chicken (giblets removed). Backs and necks are least expensive.

4 lb	chicken, whole or pieces	2 kg
12 cups	cold water	3 L
2	carrots, chopped	2
2	onions, chopped	2
2	stalks celery, chopped	2
2	bay leaves	2
6	black peppercorns	6
2	sprigs fresh thyme (OR pinch each dried thyme, basil and marjoram)	2

In stockpot, combine chicken and water; bring to boil. Skim off any scum. Add carrots, onions, celery, bay leaves, peppercorns and thyme; simmer, uncovered, for 4 hours.

Remove from heat and strain; cover and refrigerate stock until any fat congeals on surface. Remove fat layer. Refrigerate for up to 2 days or freeze for longer storage.

Makes about 8 cups (2L).

Note: This recipe has 4 mg sodium per 1 cup/250 mL. Compare this to 746 mg of sodium in a cup of canned chicken broth or 762 mg of sodium in chicken broth from a cube.

SALADS

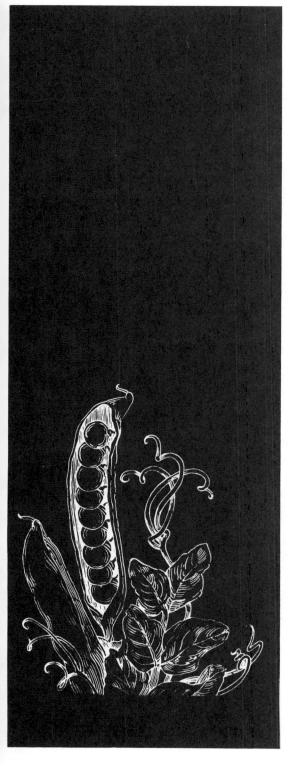

Lighthearted Caesar Salad

Thai Noodle Salad

Curried Rice and Salmon Salad

Red Bean Salad with Feta and
Peppers

French Potato Salad with
Tarragon Vinaigrette

Broccoli Buffet Salad

Oriental Chicken Pasta Salad

Greek Salad

Green Bean and Carrot Salad

Lunchtime Lentil Salad

Low-Cal Coleslaw

Southwest Rice and Bean Salad

Wild Rice and Bulgur Salad

Citrus Quinoa Salad

Garden Pasta Salad with
Basil Dressing

Orange and Fennel Salad

Quick Spinach Salad with Sprouts

Tomato Slices with Chèvre
and Basil

Everyday Vinaigrette

Creamy Garlic Dressing

Cucumber-Basil Buttermilk
Dressing

Arugula and Boston Lettuce Salad
with Walnut Oil Vinaigrette

LIGHTHEARTED CAESAR SALAD

You can make this very popular salad with less oil than usual and without the egg.

2	slices bread (whole wheat is best)	2
1	large clove garlic, halved	1
1	large head romaine lettuce	1
3 tbsp	freshly grated Parmesan cheese	45 mL

Dressing:

2 tbsp	lemon juice	25 mL
2 tbsp	olive oil	25 mL
1 tbsp	water	15 mL
1 tbsp	freshly grated Parmesan cheese	15 mL
1/2 tsp	dry mustard	2 mL
1 tsp	Worcestershire sauce	1 tsp
1	anchovy fillet, minced OR 1 tsp (5 mL) anchovy paste	1
	Salt and pepper	

Toast bread until browned and crisp. Rub cut side of garlic over both sides of bread; cut bread into cubes. Mince garlic and use in dressing.

Dressing: In small bowl, combine garlic, lemon juice, oil, water, Parmesan cheese, mustard, Worcestershire and anchovy; mix well.

Just before serving, tear romaine into salad bowl. Pour dressing over and toss to mix. Add croutons and cheese; toss again.

Makes 5 servings.

PER SERVING	
Calories	115
g total fat	7
g saturated fat	2
g fibre	2

GOOD: Vitamin A, Vitamin C

g	protein	4
g	carbohydrate	9
mg	cholesterol	4
mg	sodium	161
mg	potassium	321

THAI NOODLE SALAD

Keep a package of cellophane noodles or Chinese rice noodles (vermicelli) on hand to make this quick salad. Instead of spinach and red pepper, you could use grated carrot, chopped celery and frozen peas. If you don't like hot dishes, you may want to reduce the hot pepper flakes. (Pictured opposite page 59.)

QUICK DINNER MENU
Grilled Garlic-Ginger
  Chicken Breasts
  (p. 84)
Steamed Broccoli
Thai Noodle Salad

8 oz	Chinese rice vermicelli OR mung bean thread noodles	250 g
2 cups	packed spinach leaves, cut in strips	500 mL
1	sweet red pepper, cut in thin strips	1
1/4 cup	chopped fresh coriander OR cilantro (optional)	50 mL

Thai Dressing:

1/4 cup	unsalted peanuts	50 mL
3 tbsp	minced gingerroot	45 mL
1/4 cup	lemon OR lime juice	50 mL
1/4 cup	water	50 mL
2 tbsp	reduced-sodium soy sauce	25 mL
1 tbsp	granulated sugar	15 mL
1 tbsp	vegetable oil	15 mL
1 tsp	sesame oil	5 mL
1/4 tsp	crushed red pepper flakes	1 mL

Prepare noodles according to package directions or cook in boiling water for 3 minutes or until tender. Drain and rinse under cold running water; drain again.

In a salad bowl, toss noodles with spinach and red pepper.

Thai Dressing: In food processor or blender, process peanuts and ginger until finely chopped. Add lemon juice, water, soy sauce, sugar, vegetable and sesame oils and hot pepper flakes; process to mix.

Pour dressing over noodle mixture; toss to mix. Sprinkle with chopped coriander (if using).

Makes 6 servings.

PER SERVING	
Calories	219
g total fat	6
g saturated fat	1
g fibre	2

GOOD: Vitamin C

g protein	3
g carbohydrate	39
mg cholesterol	0
mg sodium	298
mg potassium	225

CURRIED RICE AND SALMON SALAD

Bright red sockeye salmon looks pretty in this salad, though tuna or cooked chicken also works well. Serve in hollowed-out tomato halves for lunch or summer supper, or spoon into a pita for a packed lunch.

3 cups	boiling water	750 mL
1 cup	long-grain brown rice	250 mL
2 tsp	curry powder	10 mL
1 tsp	ground cumin	5 mL
1 cup	frozen peas, thawed	250 mL
1/2 cup	chopped scallions	125 mL
1/2 cup	raisins	125 mL
1/4 cup	chopped fresh parsley	50 mL
1	can (7 1/2 oz/213 g) salmon, drained and flaked	1

Dressing:

1/4 cup	white wine vinegar	50 mL
2 tbsp	olive oil	25 mL
2 tbsp	water	25 mL
2 tsp	curry powder	10 mL
	Salt and pepper	

Bring water to boil; add rice, curry powder and cumin. Reduce heat to medium-low, cover and simmer for 40 minutes or until rice is tender and water absorbed. Fluff with fork. Let cool. Add peas, onions, raisins and parsley; stir to mix. Set aside.

Dressing: In bowl or screw-top jar, combine vinegar, oil, water and curry powder; mix well. Pour over salad and toss to mix.

Gently stir in salmon. Season with salt and pepper to taste. Serve or cover and refrigerate.

Microwave Method: In 8-cup (2 L) microwaveable casserole, combine rice, boiling water, curry powder and cumin; cover and microwave at Medium-low (30%) power for 45 minutes, stirring once midway through cooking. Remove from microwave and let stand, covered, for 5 minutes. Fluff with fork and continue as in above recipe.

Makes 6 servings, about 1 cup (250 mL) each.

PER SERVING	
Calories	298
g total fat	9
g saturated fat	2
g fibre	3

GOOD: Thiamin, Iron
EXCELLENT: Niacin

g	protein	12
g	carbohydrate	44
mg	cholesterol	12
mg	sodium	220
mg	potassium	408

RED BEAN SALAD WITH FETA AND PEPPERS

My aim for this recipe was to create an easy-to-make, nutrient-packed dish that would keep for a few days in the refrigerator and still taste terrific. I picked the beans because of their fibre, protein and iron content; red pepper for Vitamin C; cabbage for Vitamin C, fibre and because it is a brassica vegetable; feta cheese for protein, calcium and because it is a lower fat cheese than many.

Serve this salad for lunch with whole wheat bread — it's perfect for a packed lunch or for a quick supper with a soup, sandwich or omelette. (Pictured opposite page 59.)

Brassica vegetables include cabbage, broccoli, cauliflower, turnips and rutabaga, collard greens, kale, kohlrabi, bok choy and brussels sprouts.

Some studies have suggested that consumption of these vegetables may reduce the risk of certain cancers.

1	can (19 oz) kidney beans	1
1	sweet red pepper, chopped	1
2 cups	finely chopped cabbage	500 mL
2	scallions, chopped	2
4 oz	feta cheese,* cubed (1 cup/250 mL)	125 g
1/4 cup	chopped fresh parsley	50 mL
1	clove garlic, minced	1
2 tbsp	lemon juice	25 mL
1 tbsp	vegetable oil	15 mL

Drain kidney beans and rinse under cold water. In salad bowl, combine beans, red pepper, cabbage, onions, cheese, parsley, garlic, lemon juice and oil; toss to mix. Cover and refrigerate for up to 3 days.

Makes 6 servings, 1 cup (250 mL) each.

*Or reduced-fat mozzarella

PER SERVING

Calories		165
g	total fat	7
g	saturated fat	3
g	fibre	7

GOOD: Riboflavin
EXCELLENT: Vitamin C

g	protein	8
g	carbohydrate	19
mg	cholesterol	17
mg	sodium	455
mg	potassium	394

French Potato Salad with Tarragon Vinaigrette

Red potatoes look attractive; however, you can use any potatoes in this salad. For variety, add chopped chives, sliced celery or radish, niblet corn, blanched snow peas or green beans.

2 1/2 lb	small red potatoes (unpeeled)	1.25 kg
1 cup	chopped fresh parsley	250 mL
1/2 cup	chopped red onion	125 mL
	Pepper	

Tarragon Vinaigrette:

1/3 cup	wine vinegar	75 mL
2 tbsp	olive oil	25 mL
1 tbsp	grainy OR Dijon mustard	15 mL
1/2 tsp	dried tarragon	2 mL
	Pepper	

Instead of Tarragon Vinaigrette, you can use 1 cup (250 mL) low-fat yogurt, 1/4 cup (50 mL) light mayonnaise and 1/2 tsp (2 mL) dried tarragon.

Scrub potatoes. In large pot of boiling water, cook potatoes until fork-tender; drain. Shake pan over medium heat for a minute to dry potatoes. Cut into 1/4-inch (5 mm) thick slices. In salad bowl, combine potatoes, parsley and onion.

Tarragon Vinaigrette: In small bowl, whisk together vinegar, oil, mustard and tarragon; mix well. Pour over warm potatoes and toss to mix. Season with pepper to taste. Cover and let stand at room temperature for at least 1 hour or refrigerate for up to 3 days.

Makes 8 servings, 1 cup (250 mL) each.

PER SERVING

Calories		162
g	total fat	4
g	saturated fat	**trace**
g	fibre	2

GOOD: Vitamin C

g	protein	3
g	carbohydrate	30
mg	cholesterol	0
mg	sodium	34
mg	potassium	609

Broccoli Buffet Salad

Broccoli is packed with nutrients and is a good source of fibre. It contains calcium, iron, magnesium and Vitamins A, B and C. The Vitamin C helps our bodies utilize the iron.

Our best sources of calcium are dairy products. If you don't drink milk regularly, try to have dairy products in other ways such as the feta cheese and yogurt in this salad.

The fat in this salad comes equally from the sunflower seeds, feta cheese and light mayonnaise. To reduce the fat use half the amount of each.

My sister-in-law Ann Braden makes this salad for our summer cottage family reunions. (She sometimes adds cooked, crumbled bacon.) If you have a cold pack or refrigerator at work, this is a great salad for packed lunches.

3 cups	broccoli florets (about 1 bunch)	750 mL
1/2 cup	chopped red onion	125 mL
1/4 cup	sunflower seeds	50 mL
1/2 cup	raisins	125 mL
1/2 cup	feta cheese, crumbled	125 mL

Dressing:

1/2 cup	low-fat yogurt	125 mL
1/4 cup	reduced-fat mayonnaise	50 mL
2 tbsp	granulated sugar	25 mL
1 tbsp	lemon juice	15 mL
	Salt and pepper	

In salad bowl, combine broccoli, onion, sunflower seeds, raisins and cheese.

Dressing: In measuring cup, stir together yogurt, mayonnaise, sugar and lemon juice; pour over salad and toss to mix. Season with salt and pepper to taste. Cover and refrigerate for 2 hours or up to 2 days.

Makes 6 servings.

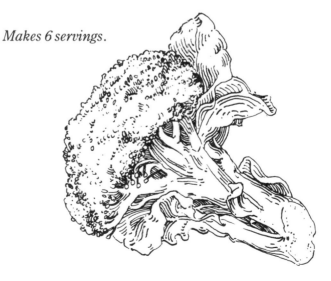

PER SERVING	
Calories	**192**
g total fat	**9**
g saturated fat	**2**
g fibre	**3**

GOOD: Riboflavin
EXCELLENT: Vitamin C, Thiamin

g protein	**7**
g carbohydrate	**24**
mg cholesterol	**17**
mg sodium	**255**
mg potassium	**483**

ORIENTAL CHICKEN PASTA SALAD

This is a wonderful salad for a luncheon, buffet or summer supper. Use corkscrew-shaped pasta or rice or egg noodles broken into 4-inch (10 cm) pieces.

1 1/2 lb	boneless skinless chicken breasts	750 g
1/2 cup	rice vinegar	125 mL
1/4 cup	reduced-sodium soy sauce	50 mL
3 tbsp	minced gingerroot	45 mL
2	cloves garlic, minced	2
1 tsp	granulated sugar	5 mL
1 lb	pasta OR rice noodles	500 g
4	medium carrots	4
2	sweet green peppers	2
1/2 lb	snow peas (optional)	250 g
2 tbsp	sesame oil	25 mL

Cut chicken into 2-inch (5 cm) julienne strips. In bowl, combine vinegar, soy sauce, gingerroot, garlic and sugar; stir in chicken. Cover and let stand for 30 minutes.

Meanwhile, in large pot of boiling water, cook pasta until tender but firm; drain. Rinse thoroughly under cold running water; drain and place in large salad bowl.

Cut carrots and green peppers into julienne strips; set aside.

Using slotted spoon, remove chicken from marinade, reserving marinade. In large nonstick skillet, cook chicken over medium-high heat, stirring often, for 3 minutes or until no longer pink; add to pasta.

Add carrots and green pepper to skillet; stir-fry for 3 minutes. Transfer to bowl with pasta.

Add reserved marinade plus 1/2 cup (125 mL) water to skillet; bring to boil and boil gently for 5 minutes. Add snow peas (if using) to skillet; cover and cook for 1 minute. Pour over pasta; add sesame oil and toss to mix. Serve warm or refrigerate for up to 2 days.

Makes 10 servings, 1 cup (250 mL) each.

Sesame oil

I like to use a little sesame oil in stir-frys and some salads because of its wonderful flavor. Do try it. A little added at the end of a stir-fry or to a salad gives a sensation of richness with only a small amount of oil. It's available at most supermarkets and will keep on your shelf for about a year.

Rice vinegar

Rice vinegar is available in most supermarkets. I like to use it in salad dressings and stir-frys because it isn't too acidic and has a lovely, mild, slightly sweet taste.

PER SERVING	
Calories	297
g total fat	5
g saturated fat	1
g fibre	3

GOOD: Vitamin C
EXCELLENT: Vitamin A, Niacin

g protein	22
g carbohydrate	40
mg cholesterol	42
mg sodium	250
mg potassium	328

Greek Salad

We have this salad at least once a week in the summer. It's perfect for lunch on the weekend or for dinner with grilled chicken or lamb. Sometimes I add artichokes, capers or chopped red onion, but never lettuce. When you have ripe, juicy tomatoes, you'll be surprised at how little dressing you need.

4	large tomatoes, cut in chunks	4
2	medium cucumbers, cut in chunks (or 1 English cucumber)	2
4 oz	feta cheese, crumbled (1 cup/250 mL)	125 g
2 tbsp	crumbled dried oregano	25 mL
2 tbsp	lemon juice	25 mL
1 tbsp	olive oil	15 mL
	Salt and pepper	
10	black olives (Greek type)	10

If you are on a low-fat diet, omit the olives and olive oil and omit or reduce the amount of cheese. Salad prepared without oil or olives and half the amount of cheese has 2.5 g fat per serving.

In shallow salad bowl or platter, combine tomatoes, cucumbers, cheese, oregano, lemon juice and olive oil. Season with salt and pepper to taste. Toss gently to mix; sprinkle with olives. Serve at room temperature.

Makes 6 servings.

PER SERVING	
Calories	130
g total fat	9
g saturated fat	3
g fibre	2

GOOD: Vitamins A and C, Riboflavin

g	protein	5
g	carbohydrate	10
mg	cholesterol	17
mg	sodium	411
mg	potassium	422

GREEN BEAN AND CARROT SALAD

Serve this colorful make-ahead salad in the summer instead of a cooked green vegetable, or pack for picnics or lunches. (Pictured opposite page 59.)

(Pictured opposite page 59.)

1/4 lb	small new carrots, halved lengthwise	125 g
1 lb	green beans, halved crosswise	500 g
1/2 cup	chopped radish	125 mL
1/2 cup	chopped red onion	125 mL
1 tbsp	sesame seeds	15 mL

Dressing:

2 tbsp	lemon juice	25 mL
1 tbsp	olive oil	15 mL
1 tsp	Dijon mustard	5 mL
1 tsp	granulated sugar	5 mL
1/4 tsp	cumin (optional)	1 mL
1/4 tsp	salt	1 mL
1	clove garlic, minced	1

In large pot of boiling water, cook carrots for 4 minutes. Add beans and cook for 4 minutes or until tender-crisp. Drain and cool under cold water; drain again and place in salad bowl. Add radish and onion.

Dressing: In small bowl, whisk together lemon juice, oil, mustard, sugar, cumin (if using), salt and garlic; pour over salad and toss to mix. Cover and refrigerate for up to 3 days. Just before serving, sprinkle with sesame seeds; toss to mix.

Makes 8 servings.

Hidden fat:
Salads are one of the key dishes where we can be fooled into thinking they might be better for us than they actually are.

Iceberg lettuce and cucumber aren't brimming with nutrients, and the salad dressings you add may be very high in fat. A tablespoon (15 mL) of a traditional French dressing can have more fat than a serving of beef or equal the fat in one or two pats of margarine or butter.

PER SERVING

Calories		52
g	total fat	2
g	saturated fat	**trace**
g	fibre	2

EXCELLENT: Vitamin A

g	protein	1
g	carbohydrate	7
mg	cholesterol	0
mg	sodium	87
mg	potassium	215

LUNCHTIME LENTIL SALAD

Because lentils are small, I think this salad looks best if you cut the accompanying vegetables into small 1/4-inch (5 mm) pieces. Serve this salad as part of a salad plate along with sliced tomatoes and cucumbers and marinated asparagus or green beans. It looks attractive on a bed of lettuce for a buffet, and is perfect for a healthy packed lunch.

1/2 cup	long grain rice	125 mL
1/2 cup	dried green lentils	125 mL
3 tbsp	vegetable oil	45 mL
1/2 cup	diced red onion	125 mL
1 cup	diced celery	250 mL
1/2 cup	diced carrots	125 mL
1/2 cup	diced sweet red pepper	125 mL
1/4 cup	lemon juice	50 mL
2 tsp	dried basil OR 3 tbsp (45 mL) chopped fresh	10 mL
1/2 tsp	salt	2 mL
1/2 cup	diced reduced-fat mozzarella cheese	125 mL
1/2 cup	chopped fresh parsley	125 mL
	Pepper	

Bring 2 cups (500 mL) water to boil. Add rice and lentils, cook for 20 minutes or until tender but not mushy; drain and rinse under cold water. Drain again and place in salad bowl.

In skillet, heat 1 tbsp (15 mL) of the oil over medium heat; add onions and cook for 3 minutes.

Add celery and carrots; cook for 3 minutes. Add red pepper; cook for 2 minutes. Add vegetables to lentils in bowl.

Add lemon juice, basil, salt, cheese, parsley and remaining oil to lentil mixture; toss well to mix. Season with pepper to taste. Cover and refrigerate for up to 2 days. Best if served at room temperature.

Makes 8 servings, about 1/2 cup (125 mL) each.

PER SERVING

Calories		171
g	total fat	7
g	saturated fat	1
g	fibre	2

GOOD: Vitamin A

g	protein	7
g	carbohydrate	20
mg	cholesterol	7
mg	sodium	224
mg	potassium	277

Low-Cal Coleslaw

For an attractive salad, use a combination of red and green cabbage, then garnish with toasted caraway seeds, or regular or black sesame seeds.

2 cups	shredded cabbage	500 mL
1/2 cup	shredded carrot	125 mL
1/4 cup	chopped red onion or scallion	50 mL
1/2 cup	chopped sweet red OR yellow OR green pepper (optional)	125 mL

Dressing:

1	clove garlic, minced	1
1/4 cup	water	50 mL
2 tbsp	lemon juice	25 mL
1 tbsp	granulated sugar	15 mL
1 tbsp	olive oil	15 mL
1 tsp	Dijon mustard	5 mL
	Salt and pepper	

In salad bowl, combine cabbage, carrot and onion; add sweet pepper (if using).

Dressing: Combine garlic, water, lemon juice, sugar, oil and mustard; mix until sugar dissolves. Add salt and pepper to taste. Pour over salad and toss to mix.

Makes 4 servings.

PER SERVING	
Calories	64
g total fat	4
g saturated fat	**trace**
g fibre	1

GOOD: Vitamin C
EXCELLENT: Vitamin A

g	protein	1
g	carbohydrate	8
mg	cholesterol	0
mg	sodium	28
mg	potassium	160

SOUTHWEST RICE AND BEAN SALAD

This great-tasting salad is perfect for picnics, ski lunches or to have on hand in the refrigerator for a fast meal. If you have leftover cooked rice, use about 3 cups (750 mL). This salad is particularly nutritious: the combination of rice and beans makes a complete protein, it's high in complex carbohydrates and an excellent source of fibre.

1 tsp	vegetable oil	5 mL
1 cup	long-grain rice	250 mL
1	can (15 oz) red kidney beans	1
1	can (15 oz) black beans OR pinto OR romano beans	1
1 1/2 cups	frozen peas, thawed	375 mL
1 cup	sliced celery	250 mL
1	can (4 oz) green chili peppers, drained and chopped	1
1/2 cup	chopped onion	125 mL
1/4 cup	chopped fresh coriander OR parsley	50 mL

Vinaigrette:

1/3 cup	red wine vinegar	75 mL
1/4 cup	vegetable oil	50 mL
1/4 cup	water	50 mL
1 tsp	minced garlic	5 mL
1/2 tsp	salt	2 mL
1/4 tsp	pepper	1 mL

In saucepan, heat oil over medium heat; add rice and stir to coat well. Add 2 cups (500 mL) boiling water; cover and simmer for 20 minutes or until water is absorbed and rice is tender. Transfer to salad bowl and let cool.

Drain and rinse red kidney and black beans; add to salad bowl. Add peas, celery, chili peppers, onion and coriander. Set aside.

Vinaigrette: In food processor or bowl, combine vinegar, oil, water, garlic, salt and pepper; mix well. Pour over salad and toss to mix. Cover and refrigerate for up to 2 days.

Makes 12 servings, about 3/4 cup (175 mL) each.

Pasta and Bean Salad

Instead of rice, substitute 3 cups (750 mL) cooked orzo (pasta the size of large rice grains) in this recipe.

PER SERVING

Calories		193
g	total fat	5
g	saturated fat	trace
g	fibre	6
g	protein	7
g	carbohydrate	30
mg	cholesterol	0
mg	sodium	433
mg	potassium	367

CANADA DAY DINNER
*Flank Steak with
    Citrus and Pepper
    Marinade (p. 122)
Wild Rice and Bulgur
    Salad
Asparagus
Tossed Green Salad
Lighthearted
    Strawberry Shortcake
    (p. 218)*

WILD RICE AND BULGUR SALAD

Ever since my friend and terrific cook Susan Pacaud brought this salad to our gourmet club dinner, I have made it often for summer barbecues or buffet dinners. (Pictured opposite page 186.)

3/4 cup	bulgur	175 mL
1 1/2 cups	chicken stock	375 mL
3/4 cup	wild rice, rinsed and drained	175 mL
2	large tomatoes, diced	2
1 cup	chopped fresh parsley	250 mL
1/4 cup	finely chopped scallion	50 mL

Lemon Vinaigrette:

1/4 cup	lemon juice	50 mL
2	cloves garlic, minced	2
1/2 tsp	salt	2 mL
1/4 cup	olive oil	50 mL
	Pepper	

**Tomatoes stuffed
with bulgur salad**
*Cut tomatoes in half;
scoop out seeds and
some pulp. Fill hollow
with bulgur salad.
Serve for lunch or as
part of a salad plate.*

Soak bulgur in 6 cups (1.5 L) hot water for 1 hour; drain well.

Meanwhile, in saucepan, bring stock and rice to boil; cover, reduce heat and simmer for 40 to 45 minutes or until rice splays, is tender-crisp and not soft, and most of the liquid is absorbed. Drain if necessary; let cool.

In salad bowl, combine bulgur, rice, tomatoes, parsley and scallion.

Lemon Vinaigrette: In food processor or bowl, combine lemon juice, garlic and salt; blend well. Add oil and process or whisk until mixed. Season with pepper to taste. Pour over salad; stir to mix. Cover and refrigerate until serving time or for up to 2 days.

Makes 10 servings, 1/2 cup (125 mL) each.

PER SERVING		
Calories		153
g	total fat	6
g	saturated fat	1
g	fibre	2
g	protein	4
g	carbohydrate	22
mg	cholesterol	0
mg	sodium	246
mg	potassium	211

Citrus Quinoa Salad

Pronounced keen-wah, this South American grain, or tiny seed, is available at health food stores. It's high in calcium, vitamins, protein and fibre. Its crunchy texture makes an interesting and pleasing base for a salad. (Pictured opposite page 122.)

1 cup	quinoa	250 mL
1 cup	diced (unpeeled) cucumber	250 mL
1/2 cup	diced figs OR dried apricots OR raisins	125 mL
1/2 cup	drained canned mandarin orange sections, halved	125 mL
1/4 cup	sunflower seeds OR toasted almonds	50 mL
2	scallions, diced	2
2 tbsp	chopped fresh coriander OR parsley	25 mL

Dressing:

1 tsp	grated lemon OR lime rind	5 mL
3 tbsp	lemon OR lime juice	45 mL
1 tbsp	sesame oil	15 mL
1 tsp	granulated sugar	5 mL
1/4 tsp	each ground cumin and coriander	1 mL

Rinse quinoa under cold running water; drain. In saucepan, bring 2 cups (500 mL) water to boil; stir in quinoa. Reduce heat, cover and simmer for 15 minutes or until water is absorbed and quinoa is transparent; drain and let cool.

In salad bowl, combine quinoa, cucumber, figs, orange sections, sunflower seeds, onions and coriander.

Dressing: In small bowl, mix lemon rind and juice, sesame oil, sugar, cumin and coriander; pour over salad and toss to mix. Serve immediately or cover and refrigerate for up to 3 days.

Makes 8 servings, about 1/2 cup (125 mL) each.

Use these high-fat ingredients sparingly in your salads: nuts, avocadoes, bacon-bits, high-fat cheese, olives, croutons prepared with added fat, and, of course, high-fat salad dressings.

PER SERVING		
Calories		182
g	total fat	5
g	saturated fat	**trace**
g	fibre	3
g	protein	5
g	carbohydrate	32
mg	cholesterol	0
mg	sodium	6
mg	potassium	183

GARDEN PASTA SALAD WITH BASIL DRESSING

Pasta salads are wonderful on hot summer nights either as a main course or along with grilled meats. Use any vegetables you have on hand. For special occasions, I like to add artichokes, shrimp and capers. For a main-course salad, add cooked chicken, turkey, beef, fish, shrimp, pine nuts or low-fat cheeses.

If you are going to eat the salad soon after adding the dressing, blanch green vegetables in boiling water for 2 to 3 minutes or until tender-crisp — they will be a bright green color and a pleasing texture. If you want to keep it in the refrigerator for a few days, don't blanch green vegetables such as beans, broccoli or snow peas because when cooked they tend to lose color or become yellow after eight hours or so.

3/4 cup	chopped green OR yellow beans	175 mL
1/2 lb	pasta (bow tie, corkscrew OR penne)	250 g
2 cups	thinly sliced yellow OR green zucchini	500 mL
2	medium carrots, diagonally sliced	2
Half	sweet red pepper, cut in thin strips	Half
1	large tomato, chopped	1
1/4 cup	finely chopped scallions OR chives	50 mL
1/4 cup	black olives (preferably Kalamata)	50 mL
2 tbsp	minced fresh basil OR 1 tsp (5 mL) dried	25 mL

Basil Dressing:

3 tbsp	wine vinegar OR cider vinegar	45 mL
2 tbsp	vegetable OR olive oil	25 mL
2 tbsp	water	25 mL
2 tbsp	chopped fresh basil OR 1/2 tsp (2 mL) dried	25 mL
1 tsp	Dijon mustard	5 mL
1 tsp	minced garlic	5 mL
1/8 tsp	crushed red pepper flakes	0.5 mL

In pot of boiling water, blanch beans for 3 minutes; drain and cool under cold water. In large pot of boiling water, cook pasta until tender but firm; drain and rinse well under cold water. Drain again and place in large salad bowl. Add beans, zucchini, carrots, red pepper, tomato, scallions or chives, olives and basil.

Dressing: In small bowl, whisk together vinegar, oil, water, basil, mustard, garlic and hot pepper flakes until well mixed. Pour over salad and toss to mix.

Makes 10 servings, about 1 cup (250 mL) each.

PER SERVING	
Calories	135
g total fat	4
g saturated fat	trace
g fibre	2

GOOD: Vitamin C
EXCELLENT: Vitamin A

g	protein	4
g	carbohydrate	22
mg	cholesterol	0
mg	sodium	40
mg	potassium	231

Orange and Fennel Salad

This crunchy, juicy salad is a good choice for a buffet or a meal with strong flavors. (Pictured after page 122.)

1	small bulb fennel (about 3/4 lb/375 g)	1
4	oranges	4
2	scallions, chopped	2
2 tbsp	chopped fresh parsley (preferably Italian)	25 mL
	Salt and pepper	
	Boston lettuce OR spinach leaves OR Belgian endive	

Garlic Vinaigrette:

1 tbsp	lemon juice	15 mL
1/4 tsp	minced garlic	1 mL
1/4 tsp	Dijon mustard	1 mL
2 tbsp	olive oil	25 mL

Trim base and top of fennel; discard outer leaves. Cut in 1/4-inch (5 mm) thick slices.

Cut a slice from top and bottom of each orange and discard. Cut away peel from oranges so no white part remains. Slice oranges. In bowl, combine fennel, oranges, onions and parsley.

Garlic Vinaigrette: In small bowl, whisk together lemon juice, garlic and mustard; whisk in oil. Pour over orange mixture; toss to coat. Season with salt and pepper to taste. (Salad can be covered and refrigerated for up to 6 hours.) Serve on a bed of lettuce or spinach or with Belgian endive spears.

Makes 8 servings.

PER SERVING	
Calories	**74**
g total fat	**4**
g saturated fat	**trace**
g fibre	**2**

GOOD: Vitamin A
EXCELLENT: Vitamin C

g	protein	**2**
g	carbohydrate	**10**
mg	cholesterol	**0**
mg	sodium	**7**
mg	potassium	**305**

QUICK SPINACH SALAD WITH SPROUTS

It's easy to keep the ingredients for this salad on hand. I sometimes add croutons, chopped red or green onion, celery, mushrooms, grapefruit, apple, orange, regular or cherry tomatoes, kidney beans or chick-peas. I also like the Creamy Dressing (Caesar variation, page 80) with this salad.

1 lb	spinach	500 g
1/2 cup	alfalfa sprouts	125 mL
1/4 cup	crumbled feta cheese OR cubed reduced-fat mozzarella cheese	50 mL
2 tbsp	sunflower seeds	25 mL
1/3 cup	Everyday Vinaigrette (recipe opposite)	75 mL

Trim, wash and dry spinach; tear into bite-sized pieces to make about 10 cups (2.5 L), lightly packed. Place in salad bowl. Add alfalfa sprouts, cheese and sunflower seeds. Pour Everyday Vinaigrette over and toss lightly.

Makes 8 servings.

PER SERVING

Calories		68
g	total fat	6
g	saturated fat	1
g	fibre	2

EXCELLENT: Vitamin A

g	protein	3
g	carbohydrate	3
mg	cholesterol	4
mg	sodium	99
mg	potassium	318

TOMATO SLICES WITH CHÈVRE AND BASIL

Thick slices of ripe, juicy tomatoes topped with fresh herbs is the perfect salad for summer meals. Serve as a separate course or on a large platter. If fresh basil isn't available, use parsley, oregano, coriander or dill.

It's best to chop basil just before serving; chopped basil will darken upon standing for too long.

3	large tomatoes (at room temperature)	3
3 tbsp	crumbled feta OR chèvre cheese	45 mL
2 tsp	balsamic vinegar OR lemon juice	10 mL
	Pepper	
3 tbsp	chopped fresh basil	45 mL
	Watercress (optional)	

Cut tomatoes into thick slices; arrange on individual plates or large platter. Sprinkle with cheese, then vinegar or lemon juice; season with pepper to taste. Just before serving, chop basil, sprinkle over tomatoes. Garnish plate with watercress (if using).

Makes 6 servings.

PER SERVING

Calories		30
g	total fat	1
g	saturated fat	1
g	fibre	1

g	protein	1
g	carbohydrate	4
mg	cholesterol	4
mg	sodium	58
mg	potassium	203

EVERYDAY VINAIGRETTE

Salad dressings are very easy to make, taste much better and are less expensive than store bought. I often add one of the variations below — especially the fresh herbs.

2 tbsp	olive OR vegetable oil	25 mL
2 tbsp	either lemon juice, rice vinegar, cider vinegar OR balsamic vinegar	25 mL
2 tbsp	water	25 mL
1	small clove garlic, minced	1
1 tsp	Dijon mustard	5 mL
Pinch	each salt and pepper	Pinch

This vinaigrette has half the fat of a traditional recipe. However, if you are on a therapeutic low-fat diet, add 2 or 3 tbsp (25–45 mL) water to this vinaigrette or use one of the other dressings in this book.

In small measuring cup, bowl or jar with screw top, combine oil, lemon juice, water, garlic, mustard, salt and pepper; mix well.

Variations: Add one of the following to the dressing:
1 tsp (5 mL) sesame oil
1/4 tsp (1 mL) cumin
1 tbsp (15 mL) freshly grated Parmesan cheese
Herb Dressing: Add 2 tbsp (25 mL) chopped fresh herbs (basil, dill or parsley or a combination).
Poppyseed Dressing: Omit mustard and garlic. Add 1 tbsp (15 mL) poppy seeds and 1 tsp (5 mL) granulated sugar.
Ginger-Garlic Dressing: Use 1 tbsp (15 mL) each of vegetable oil and sesame oil; add 1 tsp (5 mL) finely minced fresh gingerroot, omit mustard.

Makes about 6 tbsp (90 mL).

PER TBSP (15 ML)		
Calories		42
g	total fat	5
g	saturated fat	1
g	fibre	0
g	protein	trace
g	carbohydrate	1
mg	cholesterol	0
mg	sodium	11
mg	potassium	9

CREAMY GARLIC DRESSING

Use this tasty, versatile dressing in pasta or potato salads, with any cooked, cooled leftover vegetables, or with spinach or lettuce salads.

1/2 cup	low-fat yogurt	125 mL
1/4 cup	chopped fresh parsley	50 mL
2 tbsp	low-fat yogurt	25 mL
1 tsp	Dijon mustard	5 mL
1	clove garlic, minced	1
	Salt and pepper	

In small bowl, mix yogurt, parsley, mayonnaise, mustard, garlic, and salt and pepper to taste.

Makes about 2/3 cup (150 mL).

Variations: Add any of the following to the dressing:
Basil: Add 2 tbsp (25 mL) chopped fresh basil.
Dill: Add 3 tbsp (45 mL) chopped fresh dill.
Curry: Add 1 to 2 tsp (5 to 10 mL) curry powder.
Cumin: Add 2 tsp (10 mL) cumin.
Tarragon: Add 1 tsp (5 mL) dried tarragon or 1 tbsp (15 mL) fresh.
Coriander: Add 2 tbsp (25 mL) chopped fresh coriander.
Caesar: Add 1 to 2 tbsp (15 to 25 mL) freshly grated Parmesan cheese.
Blue Cheese: Add 1 to 2 tbsp (15 to 25 mL) crumbled blue cheese.
Cucumber: Add 1/2 cup (125 mL) diced cucumber and 1/2 tsp (2 mL) dried dillweed.

For less fat and more flavor, blend your own salad dressing (it takes less than a minute) using very little oil — there are a number of easy recipes in this section.

If you prefer the convenience of a store-bought dressing, there are now a number of low-fat, even fat-free, ones to choose and it is worth spending some time reading the labels. Concentrate on the light, calorie or fat reduced dressings and read the nutrition information, not just the claims in large type.

Choose dressings that have 3 grams of fat or less per tablespoon, and if possible less than 200 mg of sodium per tablespoon. See Appendix page 240 for clarification of label claims.

PER TBSP (15 ML)		
	Calories	18
g	total fat	1
g	saturated fat	**trace**
g	fibre	**trace**
g	protein	1
g	carbohydrate	1
mg	cholesterol	2
mg	sodium	42
mg	potassium	38

CUCUMBER-BASIL BUTTERMILK DRESSING

This light, creamy dressing is perfect for green salads. The flavor develops upon standing, so try to make it a day in advance.

1	clove garlic	1
2/3 cup	low-fat buttermilk	150 mL
1/3 cup	reduced-fat mayonnaise	75 mL
Half	English cucumber, cut in chunks	Half
2 tbsp	chopped fresh basil OR 1/2 tsp (2 mL) dried	25 mL
1 tsp	Dijon mustard	5 mL
1/4 tsp	hot pepper sauce	1 mL
1/3 cup	low-fat yogurt	75 mL
	Salt and pepper	

In blender or food processor, while motor is running, drop in garlic. Add buttermilk, mayonnaise, cucumber, basil, mustard and hot pepper sauce; process until mixed. Stir in yogurt. Season with salt and pepper to taste. Cover and refrigerate for up to 1 week.

Makes about 2 1/2 cups (625 mL).

PER TBSP (15 ML)

Calories		10
g	total fat	1
g	saturated fat	trace
g	fibre	0
g	protein	trace
g	carbohydrate	1
mg	cholesterol	1
mg	sodium	25
mg	potassium	19

Salad Dressing Ingredients

Compare

1 tbsp (15 mL)	g fat	g saturated fat	calories
Oil—canola, olive, sunflower, corn, safflower	14	1-2	120
Mayonnaise	11	1	100
Reduced-fat mayonnaise	5	0.4	50
Miracle Whip	7	0.4	69
Miracle Whip Light	3	0	40
Sour cream (14% b.f.)	3	2	28
Low-fat sour cream	2	1.3	23
Cottage cheese (2% b.f.)	0.3	0.2	13
Yogurt (1.5% b.f.)	0.2	0.2	10
Buttermilk (1% b.f.)	0.1	trace	6

ARUGULA AND BOSTON LETTUCE SALAD WITH WALNUT OIL VINAIGRETTE

A simple salad is often the best, especially if the dressing has a flavorful walnut (or hazelnut) oil. Use any combination of fresh greens in season.

1	head Boston OR leaf lettuce	1
Half	bunch arugula, escarole OR watercress	Half
1	small head radicchio	1

Walnut Oil Vinaigrette:

2 tbsp	walnut oil	25 mL
2 tbsp	lemon juice OR rice vinegar	25 mL
1 tbsp	water	15 mL
	Salt and pepper	

Separate leaves of lettuce, arugula and radicchio; wash and dry well. Tear bite-sized pieces into salad bow.

 Walnut Oil Vinaigrette: In small dish, combine oil, lemon juice, water and salt and pepper to taste; mix well. Pour over salad and toss to mix.

Makes 8 servings.

Menu suggestions
Serve with any buffet meal or a special lunch or dinner. Because it is simple, this salad complements a variety of other dishes. When planning a buffet I choose one centerpiece dish, then other simpler dishes to go with it.

PER SERVING	
Calories	41
g total fat	3
g saturated fat	trace
g fibre	1
g protein	1
g carbohydrate	2
mg cholesterol	0
mg sodium	9
mg potassium	185

For another salad recipe, see:
Oriental Salad Rolls (page 24)

POULTRY

MENU
*Grilled Garlic-Ginger
Chicken Breasts
Grilled Sweet Peppers
Pasta tossed with Fresh
Basil and Parmesan*

PER SERVING

Calories		163
g	total fat	5
g	saturated fat	1
g	fibre	**trace**

EXCELLENT: Niacin

g	protein	26
g	carbohydrate	1
mg	cholesterol	70
mg	sodium	62
mg	potassium	240

GRILLED GARLIC-GINGER CHICKEN BREASTS

Quick and easy to prepare, this chicken tastes delicious. While the barbecue is on, grill some sweet peppers to serve along with pasta.

1 lb	boneless skinless chicken breasts	500 g
2 tbsp	lemon juice	25 mL
2 tsp	minced garlic	10 mL
2 tsp	minced gingerroot	10 mL
2 tsp	olive oil	10 mL
1 tsp	cumin	5 mL
	Pepper	

Place chicken breasts between two sheets of waxed paper; pound to 1/2-inch (1 cm) thickness.

Combine lemon juice, garlic, ginger, oil and cumin; spread over chicken. Marinate for 10 minutes at room temperature, or cover and refrigerate for up to 4 hours.

Grill on lightly greased grill 4 inches (10 cm) from heat, or broil, for 2 to 3 minutes on each side or until no longer pink inside. Season with pepper to taste.

Makes 4 servings.

PINEAPPLE-RAISIN SALSA

Fruit salsas are delicious with ham, pork or poultry. As well, they let you forget about any last-minute fuss that is involved with serving a gravy or heated sauce. A fresh or canned chopped jalapeño pepper can be used instead of hot pepper flakes.

1 1/2 cups	pineapple (1/4-inch/5 mm) cubes	375 mL
1/2 cup	diced sweet green pepper	125 mL
1/3 cup	chopped red onion	75 mL
1/3 cup	raisins	75 mL
1 tbsp	wine vinegar OR balsamic vinegar	15 mL
2 tsp	minced gingerroot	10 mL
1/4 tsp	crushed red pepper flakes	1 mL

PER 2 TBSP (25 ML)

Calories		27
g	total fat	**trace**
g	saturated fat	0
g	fibre	1

g	protein	**trace**
g	carbohydrate	7
mg	cholesterol	0
mg	sodium	1
mg	potassium	67

Mix pineapple, green pepper, onion, raisins, vinegar, gingerroot and hot pepper flakes. Transfer to 2-cup (500 mL) glass jar; cover and refrigerate for 3 hours or up to 4 days.

Makes about 2 cups (500 mL).

Microwave Mustard Herb Chicken

Even though the skin is removed from the chicken (since nearly half the fat is in the skin), this chicken is very moist and full of flavor because of the mustard-herb coating. Microwaving instead of frying the chicken ensures than no extra fat is added.

4	chicken breasts (about 2 lb/1 kg)	4
2 tbsp	Dijon mustard	25 mL
2 tbsp	low-fat yogurt	25 mL
1 tsp	dried oregano OR 1 tbsp (15 mL) fresh	5 mL
1/2 tsp	dried thyme OR 1 tbsp (15 mL) fresh	2 mL
	Pepper	

For one serving: divide recipe by four, microwave, uncovered, at High power for 4 minutes.

Remove skin from chicken. In microwaveable dish, arrange chicken in single layer with thickest portions toward outside.

In small bowl, combine mustard, yogurt, oregano, thyme, and pepper to taste; spread over chicken.

Microwave, uncovered, at High power for 8 to 10 minutes or until chicken is no longer pink inside, rotating dish after 4 minutes.

Oven Method: Prepare as above. Bake, uncovered, in 350°F (180°C) oven for 45 to 50 minutes or until chicken is no longer pink inside.

Makes 4 servings.

PER SERVING	
Calories	215
g total fat	5
g saturated fat	1
g fibre	trace

EXCELLENT: Niacin

g protein	39
g carbohydrate	1
mg cholesterol	104
mg sodium	198
mg potassium	347

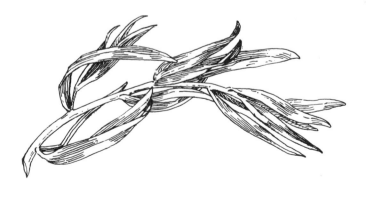

SIMMERED CHICKEN DINNER

Here's one of the fastest and easiest ways to cook a chicken, potato and vegetable dinner—in only one pot. It's also a good way to introduce children to new vegetables. This dish has sweet potatoes, which are not overpowering or as dried out as baked ones can sometimes be. My kids ate them before they realized it, and, to their surprise, quite like the new vegetable. You can use carrots, turnips, or squash cubes instead of sweet potatoes.

3 lb	chicken pieces, skinned	1.5 kg
4 cups	water	1 L
2	slices bacon, cut in pieces	2
3	leeks OR medium onions	3
2	bay leaves	2
1 tsp	dried thyme	5 mL
5	red potatoes, halved	5
1	large sweet potato (12 oz/375 g), peeled and cut into chunks	1
Half	small head cabbage	Half
1	clove garlic, minced	1
1/4 cup	chopped fresh parsley	50 mL
	Salt and pepper	

If using a whole chicken, remove skin first, then cut into pieces.

In large pot, combine chicken, water and bacon; bring to boil and skim off any foam.

Halve leeks lengthwise and clean under running water; cut into 2-inch (5 cm) lengths. If using onions, cut into quarters. Add leeks to pot along with bay leaves, thyme and red and sweet potatoes; cover and simmer for 10 minutes.

Cut cabbage into 1-inch (2.5 cm) wedges and add to pot; cover and simmer for 10 minutes or until vegetables are tender.

Using slotted spoon, transfer chicken and vegetables to six large soup bowls. Remove bay leaves. Increase heat to high; boil liquid for 3 to 5 minutes or until reduced to about 3 cups (750 mL). Stir in garlic, parsley, and salt and pepper to taste; ladle over each portion.

Makes 6 servings.

PER SERVING	
Calories	403
g total fat	8
g saturated fat	2
g fibre	6

GOOD: Riboflavin
EXCELLENT: Vitamins A and C, Thiamin, Niacin, Iron

g	protein	32
g	carbohydrate	51
mg	cholesterol	80
mg	sodium	153
mg	potassium	1188

Chicken Kabobs with Peppers and Zucchini

Sweet peppers of any color are delectable when grilled and are a good choice for kabobs. Cherry tomatoes and large mushrooms are also colorful and easy to skewer and cook fairly quickly. If using wooden skewers, soak them first in water for at least 20 minutes to prevent burning.

If fresh herbs are available, use 2 sprigs of thyme and two 2-inch (5 cm) sprigs of rosemary instead of dried herbs. Strip the leaves off the rosemary and chop the thyme, then push them between the vegetables and chicken.

1	sweet yellow pepper	1
2	small sweet red peppers	2
2	small (7-inch/18 cm) zucchini	2
1 lb	boneless skinless chicken, cubed	500 g
2 tbsp	lemon juice	25 mL
1 tsp	olive oil	5 mL
2 tsp	dried rosemary	10 mL
1/2 tsp	dried thyme	2 mL
	Pepper	

Seed peppers and cut into 1-inch (2.5 cm) pieces. Cut zucchini into 1/2-inch (1 cm) thick rounds. Alternately thread chicken, peppers and zucchini onto skewers. Combine lemon juice and oil; brush over kabobs. Sprinkle with rosemary, thyme and pepper to taste. Cover and refrigerate for up to 24 hours.

Grill over high heat, turning every 5 minutes and brushing with any remaining lemon juice mixture, for about 20 minutes or until kabobs are browned and chicken is no longer pink inside.

Makes 4 servings.

PER SERVING

Calories	169
g total fat	4
g saturated fat	1
g fibre	2

EXCELLENT: Vitamin C, Niacin

g protein	26
g carbohydrate	5
mg cholesterol	70
mg sodium	65
mg potassium	465

CHICKEN FONDUE IN GINGER BROTH

This is an easy yet elegant supper for family or guests. By using chicken stock instead of oil for cooking, and by including vegetables as well as low-fat sauces, fat and calories are kept to a minimum. Serve with rice.

Fondue Cooking Stock:

4 cups	chicken stock	1 L
2/3 cup	white wine OR 1/4 cup (50 mL) cider OR rice vinegar	150 mL
2	lemon slices	2
2	large cloves garlic, minced	2
2 tbsp	minced gingerroot	25 mL
2 tsp	granulated sugar	10 mL

Chicken and Vegetable Tray:

1 lb	boneless skinless chicken breasts	500 g
Half	bunch broccoli	Half
1	small yellow summer squash OR zucchini	1
2 cups	torn Swiss chard OR romaine lettuce	500 mL
1	sweet red pepper OR green pepper	1
1/4 lb	mushrooms	125 g
	Hot Chili Sauce (recipe follows)	
	Garlic Sauce (recipe follows)	

Fondue Cooking Stock: In fondue pot, electric skillet or electric wok, combine chicken stock, white wine, lemon slices, garlic, ginger and sugar. Just before serving, heat to simmer.

Chicken and Vegetable Tray: Cut chicken into 3/4-inch (2 cm) pieces; place on serving platter. Cut broccoli, summer squash, Swiss chard and sweet pepper into bite-sized pieces; arrange along with mushrooms on separate platter.

Using long fondue forks, spear chicken or vegetables; dip into simmering fondue broth to cook. Cook chicken pieces until no longer pink inside, and vegetables until tender-crisp. Serve with Hot Chili Sauce and Garlic Sauce for dipping.

Makes 4 servings.

PER SERVING
(Chicken without sauce)

Calories		179
g	total fat	3
g	saturated fat	1
g	fibre	3

GOOD: Vitamin A, Iron, Riboflavin
EXCELLENT: Vitamin C, Niacin

g	protein	29
g	carbohydrate	8
mg	cholesterol	70
mg	sodium	212
mg	potassium	668

Garlic Sauce

For a variation of this sauce, substitute chopped fresh basil or coriander to taste for the garlic and reduce the parsley to 1 tbsp (15 mL).

	PER TBSP (15 ML)	
	Calories	**14**
g	total fat	**1**
g	saturated fat	**trace**
g	fibre	**trace**
g	protein	**1**
g	carbohydrate	**1**
mg	cholesterol	**1**
mg	sodium	**6**
mg	potassium	**31**

1/2 cup	light sour cream OR low-fat yogurt OR a mixture of both	125 mL
2	cloves garlic, minced	2
1/4 cup	chopped fresh parsley	50 mL

In small bowl, combine sour cream, garlic and parsley.

Makes about 1/2 cup (125 mL).

Hot Chili Sauce

Young children might prefer a milder version of this medium-hot sauce; others might double the hot pepper flakes. Use for dipping.

	PER TBSP (15 ML)	
	Calories	**4**
g	total fat	**0**
g	saturated fat	**0**
g	fibre	**0**
g	protein	**trace**
g	carbohydrate	**1**
mg	cholesterol	**0**
mg	sodium	**61**
mg	potassium	**9**

1/3 cup	water	75 mL
2 tbsp	lemon OR lime juice	25 mL
1 tbsp	reduced-sodium soy sauce	15 mL
1 tsp	granulated sugar	5 mL
1/4 tsp	crushed red pepper flakes	1 mL

In small bowl, combine water, lemon or lime juice, soy sauce, sugar and hot pepper flakes.

Makes about 1/2 cup (125 mL)

GRILLED LEMON CHICKEN WITH ROSEMARY

As my days get busier and busier, my cooking seems to get simpler and simpler. Now that I have a flourishing rosemary plant growing in the garden, this is how I often cook chicken. (Pictured opposite.)

4	boneless skinless chicken breasts (about 1 lb/500 g)	4
1/4 cup	lemon juice	50 mL
2	large sprigs fresh rosemary OR 1 tbsp/ 15 mL dried	2
	Pepper	

In shallow dish, arrange chicken in single layer. Pour lemon juice over chicken and turn to coat both sides. Separate rosemary needles from stem; sprinkle over chicken. Season with pepper to taste.

Let stand at room temperature for 20 minutes or cover and refrigerate for up to 6 hours. Spray grill with nonstick vegetable coating. Grill chicken over hot coals or on medium-high setting for 4 to 5 minutes on each side or until meat is no longer pink inside.

Makes 4 servings.

PER SERVING		
Calories		149
g	total fat	3
g	saturated fat	1
g	fibre	0
g	protein	27
g	carbohydrate	2
mg	cholesterol	73
mg	sodium	64
mg	potassium	247

Herb-Baked Polenta with Parmesan (p. 184), Grilled Lemon Chicken with Rosemary (above), Sesame Broccoli (p. 145)

LEMON THYME ROAST CHICKEN

To truss a chicken
Use a cotton string to tie the legs and wings close to the body. This prevents the legs and wings from becoming overcooked and dried out before the rest of the chicken is cooked.

I don't usually follow a recipe when making stuffing for chicken. First I make bread crumbs in the food processor using whole wheat bread, then I chop an onion and add herbs and whatever else I have on hand—apples, celery or mushrooms. Here's one I often make.

2	chickens (5 lb/2.4 kg each) OR 1 capon (9 lb/4.5 kg)	2

Stuffing:

3 cups	soft breadcrumbs	750 mL
3	apples, cored and chopped	3
2	onions, chopped	2
3	stalks celery including leaves, chopped	3
3 tbsp	fresh thyme leaves OR 2 tsp/10 mL dried	45 mL
	Grated rind from 1 lemon	
	Salt and pepper	

Lemon Thyme Stuffing
This recipe makes 9 cups (1.75 L) stuffing, enough for two 5-lb (2.4 kg) roasting chickens. Wrap extra stuffing in foil and bake for 20 minutes. For 1 chicken, halve recipe.

Wipe cavity of chicken; pat dry inside and out with paper towel.

In large bowl mix the bread crumbs, apples, onions, celery, thyme and lemon until well blended. Add salt and pepper to taste.

Fill the cavity of the chicken; truss the chicken with string and place on rack, breast side up in a roasting pan. Roast in a 325°F (160°C) oven for about 35 minutes per lb (500g), or until juices run clear when chicken is pierced with fork.

Makes 16 (4 oz/125 g) servings.

PER SERVING
(of chicken)

Calories		235
g	total fat	8
g	saturated fat	2
g	fibre	1

EXCELLENT: Niacin

g	protein	30
g	carbohydrate	9
mg	cholesterol	88
mg	sodium	132
mg	potassium	344

Baked Salmon Trout with Papaya Cucumber Salsa (p. 104)

BAKED CHICKEN BREASTS WITH FRESH BASIL

This is a great choice for dinner parties because it can be prepared in advance. It's important to use fresh basil in this easy yet tasty dish that goes well with all vegetables. Make your own fresh bread crumbs in a food processor because store-bought ones are too fine and dry for this recipe.

10	boneless skinless chicken breasts (about 2 1/2 lb/1.25 kg)	10
3/4 cup	low-fat yogurt	175 mL
1/2 cup	chopped fresh basil	125 mL
2 tsp	cornstarch	10 mL
1 cup	fresh whole wheat bread crumbs*	250 mL
	Salt and pepper	
2 tbsp	freshly grated Parmesan cheese (optional)	25 mL

Arrange chicken in single layer in baking dish. Combine yogurt, basil and cornstarch; mix well and spread over chicken.

Season bread crumbs with salt and pepper to taste; add Parmesan (if using) and sprinkle over chicken. (If making in advance, cover and refrigerate for up to 6 hours.)

Bake chicken in 375°F (190°C) oven for 30 minutes or until chicken is no longer pink inside.

Makes 10 servings.

*About 2 slices of bread. If only fine dried crumbs are available, use about 3 tbsp (45 mL).

PER SERVING

Calories		165
g	total fat	3
g	saturated fat	1
g	fibre	**trace**

EXCELLENT: Niacin

g	protein	28
g	carbohydrate	4
mg	cholesterol	74
mg	sodium	99
mg	potassium	286

Easy Everyday Chicken Stir-Fry

Serve this fast, basic stir-fry over or with rice or noodles for an easy meal. The stir-fry uses vegetables available to everyone all year round. Add or substitute any other vegetables you have on hand — mushrooms, green onions, sweet peppers, snow peas or cherry tomatoes. Bottled hoisin sauce is available in the Chinese section of grocery stores; it keeps in your refrigerator for months and is a quick and easy way to add flavor. If it is unavailable, use sherry and soy sauce to taste.

1 lb	boneless skinless chicken breasts	500 g
1 tbsp	vegetable oil	15 mL
2 tbsp	chopped gingerroot	25 mL
2	small cloves garlic, minced	2
2	onions, coarsely chopped	2
2	carrots, thinly sliced on diagonal	2
2	stalks celery, diagonally sliced	2
2 cups	thinly sliced cabbage OR broccoli pieces	500 mL
2 tbsp	hoisin sauce	25 mL

Cut chicken into 1-inch (2.5 cm) cubes. In large nonstick skillet or wok, heat oil over high heat; stir-fry ginger, garlic and chicken for 3 minutes or until lightly browned. Add onions; stir-fry for 1 minute.

Add carrots, celery and cabbage or broccoli; stir-fry for 4 minutes or until vegetables are tender-crisp, adding a spoonful of water, if necessary, to prevent scorching. Stir in hoisin sauce until mixed.

Makes 4 servings.

PER SERVING

Calories		236
g	total fat	7
g	saturated fat	1
g	fibre	4

GOOD: Riboflavin, Iron
EXCELLENT: Viamins A and C, Niacin

g	protein	30
g	carbohydrate	14
mg	cholesterol	70
mg	sodium	195
mg	potassium	584

JANE FREIMAN'S CRISPY POTATO CHICKEN

Jane Freiman, New York restaurant critic and author, created this great recipe for project LEAN (Low-fat Eating for Americans Now). For a crisp, golden potato topping, be sure to pat the potato shreds as dry as possible.

1 1/3 cups	shredded peeled potato (8 oz/250 g)	325 mL
3 tbsp	Dijon mustard	45 mL
1	large clove garlic, minced	1
4	skinless chicken breasts (2 lb/1 kg)	4
1 1/2 tsp	olive oil	7 mL
	Pepper	
	Minced fresh parsley, coriander OR chives	

Place potatoes in bowl of ice water; let stand 5 minutes.

In small bowl, combine mustard and garlic. Rinse chicken and pat dry. Spread mustard mixture evenly over meaty side of chicken breasts; place bone-side down in foil-lined baking pan.

Drain potato; pat dry with paper towel. In bowl, toss potato with olive oil, mixing well. Evenly spread about 1/3 cup (75 mL) potato shreds over each breast to form ''skin''. Sprinkle lightly with pepper.

Bake in 425°F (220°C) oven for 35 to 40 minutes or until chicken is no longer pink inside and potato is golden. (If potatoes are not browning, broil for about 5 minutes or until golden, watching closely.) Sprinkle with chopped herbs to taste. Serve immediately.

Makes 4 servings.

PER SERVING

Calories		272
g	total fat	7
g	saturated fat	2
g	fibre	1

EXCELLENT: Niacin

g	protein	39
g	carbohydrate	12
mg	cholesterol	101
mg	sodium	244
mg	potassium	510

MOROCCAN CHICKEN STEW WITH COUSCOUS

I like to serve this when entertaining—for a buffet—because it tastes terrific, can be prepared in advance, and is easily eaten with a fork, so you don't need knives. Serve with couscous (page 176) or, if it isn't available, brown or white rice. Turnip can be used as well or instead of sweet potato. (Pictured after page 122.)

BUFFET DINNER MENU
(Pictured after p. 122)
Moroccan Chicken
  Stew with Couscous
Green Beans
or Asparagus
or Grilled Sweet Peppers
  and Leeks (p. 135)
Orange and Fennel
  Salad (p. 77).

1 1/4 lb	boneless skinless chicken, cubed	375 g
3	onions, thinly sliced	3
2 cups	water	500 mL
1 tbsp	minced gingerroot	15 mL
1 tsp	each turmeric, cinnamon, and granulated sugar	5 mL
1/2 tsp	saffron (optional)	2 mL
1	sweet potato, peeled and cubed	1
4	carrots, cut in chunks	4
1 cup	canned OR cooked garbanzo beans	250 mL
1/4 cup	dried currants	50 mL
1 tbsp	lemon juice	15 mL
1	small zucchini (6 oz/170 g), cut in chunks	1
2 tbsp	chopped fresh parsley OR cilantro	25 mL
	Salt and pepper	
1 1/2 cups	Couscous	375 mL

In nonstick skillet or saucepan, brown chicken over high heat; remove chicken to plate and set aside. Reduce heat to medium and add onions; cook, stirring occasionally, for about 5 minutes or until softened.

Add water, gingerroot, turmeric, cinnamon, sugar and saffron (if using); bring to a simmer. Add sweet potato and carrots; cover and simmer for 20 minutes.

Add chick-peas, currants and lemon juice. (Recipe can be prepared to this point, cooled, covered, and refrigerated for up to 2 days. Bring to a simmer before continuing.)

Add zucchini and chicken; cover and simmer for 10 minutes, or until chicken is no longer pink inside and vegetables are tender. Add parsley; season with salt and pepper to taste.

Cook couscous according to package directions or see page 176. Serve with stew.

Makes 6 servings.

PER SERVING
(Chicken Stew without Couscous)

Calories		**239**
g	total fat	**3**
g	saturated fat	**1**
g	fibre	**5**

GOOD: Iron
EXCELLENT: Vitamin A, Niacin

g	protein	**25**
g	carbohydrate	**27**
mg	cholesterol	**56**
mg	sodium	**88**
mg	potassium	**573**

MAKE-AHEAD TURKEY DIVAN

If you don't have any leftover turkey, you can poach a turkey breast to use in this recipe.

In large pot, bring 6 cups (1.5 L) water to boil. Add 1 1/2 lb (750 g) bone-in turkey breast, skin side down. Reduce heat to medium; cover and simmer for 20 to 25 minutes or until no longer pink inside. Remove from water; let cool, then slice and measure amount needed.

This recipe is from Shannon Graham, my friend and co-worker who has helped with recipe testing for all my cookbooks. It's a great way to use up leftover turkey or chicken. The sauce is very fast and easy to prepare in the microwave. I prefer to cook the broccoli in boiling water, rather than in the microwave. It's just as fast and the broccoli is more tender and brighter in color.

1	bunch broccoli	1
2 tbsp	soft margarine	25 mL
1/4 cup	all-purpose flour	50 mL
2 cups	low-fat milk	500 mL
3/4 cup	shredded fat-reduced mozzarella cheese (about 3 oz/75 g)	175 mL
2 tbsp	freshly grated Parmesan cheese	25 mL
	Pepper	
12 oz	sliced cooked turkey OR chicken (about 3 cups/750 mL)	375 g
	Paprika	

Cut broccoli into large pieces; peel stems and quarter lengthwise. Cut into 3-inch (8 cm) pieces. In large pot of boiling water, cook broccoli for 2 to 3 minutes or until tender-crisp; drain well. Place in ungreased 12- × 8-inch (3 L) baking dish.

In saucepan, melt margarine over medium-low heat; stir in flour until smooth. Whisk in milk; cook, stirring frequently, until thickened. Add mozzarella cheese and 1 tbsp (15 mL) of the Parmesan cheese; stir until melted. Add pepper to taste.

Arrange turkey on top of broccoli; pour cheese sauce over and spread evenly. Sprinkle with remaining Parmesan cheese, and paprika to taste. Bake, covered, in 350°F (180°C) oven for 25 minutes. Uncover and bake for 5 minutes longer or until hot and bubbling.

Microwave Method: In 12- × 8-inch (3 L) microwaveable dish, cover broccoli plus 2 tbsp (25 mL) water with vented plastic wrap; microwave at High power for 4 to 6 minutes or until tender-crisp. Drain and set aside.

In 4 cup (1 L) microwaveable bowl, microwave margarine at High for 10 seconds or until melted. Stir in flour until smooth; whisk in milk until smooth. Microwave at High for 5 to 7 minutes or until thickened, whisking after 2 minutes and then every minute.

PER SERVING	
Calories	**309**
g total fat	**14**
g saturated fat	**6**
g fibre	**2**

GOOD: Vitamin A, Thiamin, Iron
EXCELLENT: Vitamin C, Riboflavin, Niacin, Calcium

g	protein	**32**
g	carbohydrate	**15**
mg	cholesterol	**71**
mg	sodium	**266**
mg	potassium	**526**

Stir in mozzarella cheese and 1 tbsp (15 mL) of the Parmesan cheese until melted. Add pepper to taste.

Arrange turkey on top of broccoli; pour cheese sauce over and spread evenly. Sprinkle with remaining Parmesan cheese, and paprika to taste. Cover with waxed paper; microwave at Medium-high (70%) power for 5 to 8 minutes or until heated through. Let stand for 2 to 3 minutes.

Makes 5 servings.

MENU

*Tarragon-Orange
   Grilled Turkey
Asparagus
Citrus Quinoa Salad
   (p. 75)
Raisin Cupcakes with
   Lemon Yogurt Icing
   (p. 202)*

TARRAGON-ORANGE GRILLED TURKEY

Turkey scallopini is lean, low in calories and quick to cook. If you can't find it in the store, buy boneless, skinless chicken breasts and flatten them between waxed paper. Or buy a turkey breast, then cut the meat into thin slices and freeze the extra.

1 lb	turkey OR chicken scallopini	500 g
1/4 cup	orange juice	50 mL
1 tsp	grated orange rind	5 mL
1	medium clove garlic, minced	1
1 tsp	dried tarragon	5 mL
	Thin slices of orange	

Place turkey in shallow dish. Combine orange juice and rind, garlic and tarragon; pour over turkey and turn to coat both sides. Let stand for 5 minutes at room temperature or cover and refrigerate for up to 4 hours.

Spray grill with nonstick coating. Grill turkey over high heat or broil for about 2 minutes on each side or until no longer pink. Garnish with orange slices.

Makes 4 servings.

PER SERVING	
Calories	**130**
g total fat	**1**
g saturated fat	**trace**
g fibre	**trace**

EXCELLENT: Niacin

g	protein	**27**
g	carbohydrate	**2**
mg	cholesterol	**74**
mg	sodium	**47**
mg	potassium	**307**

TURKEY AND POTATO HASH

This tasty recipe is very handy when you want to use up the remains of a turkey, chicken, ham or roast. Since the hash isn't fried, it's important to have a large nonstick skillet.

2	large potatoes, thinly sliced (about 3 cups/750 mL)	2
1 1/2 cups	water	375 mL
1	large onion, chopped	1
1 1/2 cups	diced cooked turkey (6 oz/175 g)	375 mL
1 1/2 tsp	Worcestershire sauce	7 mL
1 tsp	minced garlic	5 mL
2	scallions, chopped	2
1 tsp	olive oil	5 mL
Dash	hot pepper sauce	Dash
	Salt and pepper	

In large nonstick skillet, bring potatoes, water and onion to boil; cover and cook over medium heat for 10 minutes or until vegetables are tender.

Add turkey, Worcestershire, garlic, scallions, oil and hot pepper sauce; mix well. Cook, uncovered, over medium heat for about 5 minutes or until mixture begins to sizzle and water has evaporated.

With spatula, scrape up crusty bits and stir them into uncooked mixture. Cook for 10 minutes longer or until mixture is lightly browned, stirring often and scraping up brown bits from bottom of pan. Season with salt and pepper to taste.

Makes 3 servings.

PER SERVING

Calories		**281**
g	total fat	**5**
g	saturated fat	**1**
g	fibre	**3**

GOOD: Thiamin, Iron
EXCELLENT: Vitamin C, Niacin

g	protein	**24**
g	carbohydrate	**34**
mg	cholesterol	**53**
mg	sodium	**86**
mg	potassium	**890**

For other poultry recipes, see:

Spicy Chicken Skewers (page 36) and
Curried Chicken and Shrimp (page 110)
Oriental Chicken Salad (page 68)

FISH AND SEAFOOD

Microwave Sole with
Mushrooms and Ginger

Cod Fillets with Red Peppers
and Onions

Pacific Snapper Fillets with
Herbs

Broiled Halibut Steaks with
Rosemary and Tomato-Basil
Sauce

Baked Salmon Trout with
Papaya-Cucumber Salsa

Papaya-Cucumber Salsa

Teriyaki Orange Fish Fillets

Salmon and Spinach Gratin

Light Salmon Loaf with Dill

Easy Fish and Tomato Stew

Curried Chicken and Shrimp

Steamed Mussels with Tomatoes
and Fennel

Yogurt Remoulade

Teriyaki Marinade

Microwave Sole with Mushrooms and Ginger

*The tantalizing flavors of Oriental seasonings, mushrooms and green
onions combine to complement the tender fillets of sole. But best of all, this
dish takes less than 10 minutes to make from start to finish. Substitute
any fish fillets, depending on what is freshest.*

6	medium mushrooms, sliced	6
1	scallion, chopped	1
2	fillets of sole (about 4 oz/125 g each)	2
1 tsp	grated gingerroot	5 mL
1 tsp	sesame oil	5 mL
1 tsp	dry sherry	5 mL
1 tsp	reduced-sodium soy sauce	5 mL

*Haddock, snapper, sole,
cod and halibut are all
very low in fat.
However, this doesn't
mean it is fine to fry fish
in added fat or to serve it
with a butter-laden
sauce. Remember, 4 oz
(125 g) sole, snapper,
cod or haddock has
1 g fat or less, but 1 tbsp
(15 mL) of butter has
11 g fat and 1 tbsp
(15 mL) of oil has 14 g
fat.*

Spread mushrooms and green onion in microwaveable dish large
enough to hold fillets in a single layer. Cover and microwave at High
power for 2 minutes; pour off any liquid.

Push mushrooms and onions to edge of dish; arrange fillets in
single layer in centre.

Combine ginger, oil, sherry and soy sauce; spread evenly
over fillets. Spoon mushrooms and onions on top. Cover and
microwave at High power for 3 minutes. Let stand, covered, for 1
to 2 minutes or until fish is opaque throughout.

Makes 2 servings.

PER SERVING		
Calories		**111**
g	total fat	**3**
g	saturated fat	**trace**
g	fibre	**1**

EXCELLENT: Niacin		

g	protein	**17**
g	carbohydrate	**3**
mg	cholesterol	**54**
mg	sodium	**237**
mg	potassium	**425**

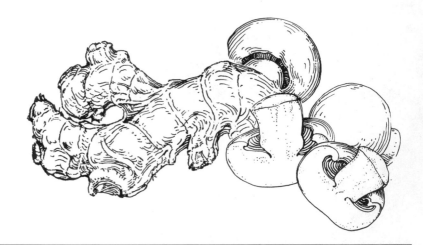

Cod Fillets with Red Peppers and Onions

Sautéed sweet red pepper strips and onion rings spooned over lightly cooked cod fillets is a colorful, easy fish dish both family and friends will enjoy.

MENU
*Cod Fillets with Red
  Peppers and Onion
Steamed Squash or
  Green Beans
Wild Rice and Bulgur
  Salad (p. 74)
or Bulgur with Ginger
  and Spring Onions
  (p. 186)*

1 tbsp	olive oil	15 mL
1	sweet red pepper, cut in thin strips	1
4	thin slices red onion	4
1 tsp	minced garlic	5 mL
1/2 tsp	dried oregano OR 1 tbsp (15 mL) fresh	2 mL
1 lb	cod fillets, cut in 4 pieces	500 g
2 tbsp	chopped fresh parsley	25 mL
	Pepper	

In nonstick skillet, heat oil over medium heat; add red pepper and sauté for 3 minutes.

Separate onion into rings and add to pan along with garlic and oregano; cook for 1 minute. Push vegetables to edge of pan.

Add cod fillets; cover and cook for 3 minutes. Turn fish; cover and cook for 2 to 3 minutes longer or until fish is opaque. Sprinkle fish with parsley; season with pepper to taste. Spoon red pepper mixture over fish and serve.

Makes 4 servings.

PER SERVING

Calories		133
g	total fat	4
g	saturated fat	trace
g	fibre	1

EXCELLENT: Vitamin C, Niacin

g	protein	20
g	carbohydrate	3
mg	cholesterol	57
mg	sodium	83
mg	potassium	522

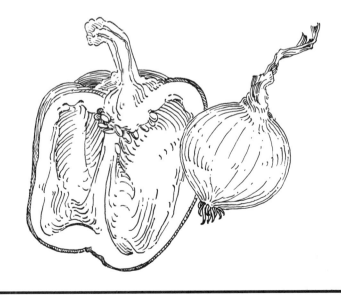

Pacific Snapper Fillets with Herbs

Topped with a creamy lemon-herb sauce, this easy-to-make fish also works well using halibut or sole fillets.

20-MINUTE DINNER
*Pacific Snapper Fillets
   with Herbs
Sesame Broccoli
   (p. 145)
Microwave Garlic
   Potatoes (p. 139)*

1 tbsp	soft margarine	15 mL
1 lb	Pacific snapper fillets	500 g
1 tbsp	chopped shallots OR onion	15 mL
1 tsp	grated lemon rind	5 mL
1/2 cup	low-fat yogurt	125 mL
2 tsp	all-purpose flour	10 mL
2 tbsp	chopped fresh parsley OR chives	25 mL
1 tbsp	chopped fresh dill, thyme OR tarragon OR 1/2 tsp (2 mL) dried	15 mL
	Salt and pepper	

In nonstick skillet, melt margarine over medium heat; cook fish for 3 minutes on each side or until nearly opaque. Transfer to hot serving plate. (The fish will continue cooking as it stands.)

Add shallots and lemon rind to skillet; cook for 1 minute or until shallots are tender. Mix yogurt with flour; stir into pan. Add parsley or chives then dill, thyme or tarragon; bring to a simmer. Season with salt and pepper to taste.

Return fish to pan to briefly reheat and coat with sauce.

Makes 4 servings.

PER SERVING

Calories		158
g	total fat	4
g	saturated fat	1
g	fibre	trace

GOOD: Thiamin
EXCELLENT: Niacin

g	protein	24
g	carbohydrate	4
mg	cholesterol	64
mg	sodium	124
mg	potassium	463

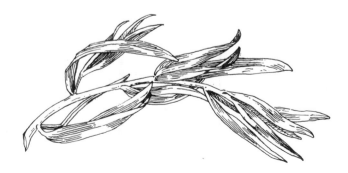

Barbecued Salmon Fillets

Barbecued salmon fillet or steak is one of my favorite summer meals —it's fast, easy and tastes terrific. Sometimes I don't do anything to the salmon: its delicate flavor and smokey taste from the barbecue is all it needs. I often grill it with lemon juice and rosemary (substitute salmon for halibut in Broiled Halibut Steaks) and omit the Tomato-Basil Sauce. Sometimes I marinate it in Teriyaki Marinade (page 112) or add a little lemon juice.

PER 2 TBSP (25 ML) SAUCE		
Calories		24
g	total fat	2
g	saturated fat	trace
g	fibre	trace
g	protein	trace
g	carbohydrate	1
mg	cholesterol	0
mg	sodium	3
mg	potassium	52

PER SERVING		
(without sauce)		
Calories		186
g	total fat	4
g	saturated fat	trace
g	fibre	trace

GOOD: Vitamin A
EXCELLENT: Niacin

g	protein	36
g	carbohydrate	trace
mg	cholesterol	85
mg	sodium	92
mg	potassium	770

BROILED HALIBUT STEAKS WITH ROSEMARY AND TOMATO-BASIL SAUCE

The sauce adds great color and flavor to the fish, but when you're in a hurry, the halibut is tasty on its own.

4	halibut steaks (about 6 oz/170 g each)	4
2 tbsp	lemon juice	25 mL
1 tbsp	olive oil	15 mL
1 tsp	dried crushed rosemary	5 mL
	Salt and pepper	

Tomato-Basil Sauce:

1/2 cup	diced ripe tomatoes	125 mL
1/4 cup	coarsely chopped fresh basil	50 mL
2 tbsp	finely chopped scallions	25 mL
1 tbsp	red wine vinegar	15 mL
1 tbsp	olive oil	15 mL
1/2 tsp	grated orange rind	2 mL
	Salt and pepper	

Place halibut steaks in large shallow dish. Combine lemon juice, oil and rosemary; season with salt and pepper to taste.

Pour marinade over halibut and turn to coat both sides. Cover and refrigerate for at least 30 minutes or up to 4 hours.

Place fish on greased broiler pan or greased grill 4 inches (10 cm) from heat; cook for about 10 minutes per inch (2.5 cm) of thickness, turning once, or until opaque throughout. Spoon Tomato-Basil Sauce (2 tbsp/25 mL) over each steak.

Tomato-Basil Sauce: In small bowl and using whisk, blend together tomatoes, basil, onions, vinegar, oil and orange rind. Season with salt and pepper to taste. Makes 3/4 cup (175 mL) sauce.

Microwave Method: Place marinated steaks in single layer in microwave dish; cover with plastic wrap and microwave on High power 4 to 5 minutes (for 3/4 inch/1.5 cm thick steaks) or until opaque.

Makes 4 servings.

BAKED SALMON TROUT WITH PAPAYA-CUCUMBER SALSA

Whole baked fish is a wonderful dish for entertaining. It's a treat to have, looks spectacular and is easy to prepare. Stuffed with a light, flavorful combination of shallots, mushrooms, dill and spinach, it's wonderful with this fresh-tasting salsa instead of the usual rich butter sauce. Salmon trout vary in size. A 3-pound (1.5 kg) trout will weigh about 1 1/2 pounds (750 g) after it has been cleaned and boned. (Do serve it with head on as it looks more attractive.) For easier serving, ask the fishmonger to remove the bones, yet leave the fish whole. (Pictured opposite page 91.)

2	salmon trout (about 3 lb/1.5 kg each) OR salmon, cleaned and boned	2
2 cups	sliced mushrooms	500 mL
1/3 cup	minced shallots	75 mL
1 tsp	olive oil	5 mL
2 cups	packed chopped fresh spinach	500 mL
1/4 cup	chopped fresh dill	50 mL
	Salt and pepper	
1	lemon, thinly sliced	1
8	sprigs fresh dill	8
	Papaya-Cucumber Salsa (recipe follows)	

Wash fish and pat dry; arrange in greased baking dish.

In microwaveable dish, combine mushrooms and shallots; sprinkle with oil. Microwave, uncovered, at High power for 2 minutes or until softened. (Or, cook in nonstick skillet over medium heat until softened.)

Combine mushroom mixture, spinach and dill; season with salt and pepper to taste. Stuff fish cavities so that stuffing stays in place without sewing. Arrange lemon slices in row on top of fish. Top with dill sprigs.

Bake fish in 400°F (200°C) oven for 25 minutes or until fish is opaque. (Test by making small cut at thickest part of fish.) Using spatulas, transfer fish to large serving platter. Garnish platter with Papaya-Cucumber Salsa around fish. To serve, discard skin.

Makes 8 servings.

SPECIAL DINNER MENU

*Oriental Salad Rolls
(p. 24)
Baked Salmon Trout
with Papaya-
Cucumber Salsa
Sprout and Snow Pea
Stir-Fry (p. 143) or
Asparagus or Sesame
Broccoli (p. 145)
Couscous with Lemon
and Fresh Basil
(p. 177)
Chris Klugman's
Orange Yogurt
Bavarian (p. 223)
Easy Date and Walnut
Squares (p. 205) or
Gingersnaps (p. 208)*

Salmon trout is higher in fat than salmon. If using salmon, fat would be about 9 g per serving.

PER SERVING
(with Papaya-Cucumber Salsa)

Calories		255
g	total fat	13
g	saturated fat	1
g	fibre	trace

GOOD: Vitamin A, Thiamin, Riboflavin
EXCELLENT: Niacin, Iron

g	protein	31
g	carbohydrate	2
mg	cholesterol	28
mg	sodium	80
mg	potassium	401

Papaya-Cucumber Salsa

If papaya isn't available, use diced, unpeeled red apple or mango or melon.

2 cups	finely diced English cucumber (unpeeled)	500 mL
2 cups	diced peeled papaya	500 mL
2 tbsp	white wine vinegar OR lime juice	25 mL
2 tbsp	chopped fresh dill	25 mL
	Pepper	

In bowl, combine cucumber, papaya, vinegar or lime juice and dill; season with pepper to taste. (Salsa can be prepared up to 1 day ahead; drain off liquid before serving.)

Makes 8 servings.

PER SERVING	
Calories	**18**
g total fat	**trace**
g saturated fat	**0**
g fibre	**1**

GOOD: Vitamin C

g	protein	**trace**
g	carbohydrate	**4**
mg	cholesterol	**0**
mg	sodium	**2**
mg	potassium	**134**

TERIYAKI ORANGE FISH FILLETS

Try this flavorful low-calorie, low-fat, easy-to-make fish dish. (Pictured opposite page 122.)

1 lb	fish fillets (perch, sole, haddock)	500 g
1 tsp	grated orange rind	5 mL
1/2 cup	orange juice	125 mL
1 tbsp	minced onion	15 mL
1 tbsp	reduced-sodium soy sauce	15 mL
1 tsp	grated gingerroot	5 mL
1/2 tsp	granulated sugar	2 mL
1 tbsp	water	15 mL
1 tsp	cornstarch	5 mL

In large skillet, arrange fish in single layer. In small bowl, mix together orange rind and juice, onion, soy sauce, ginger and sugar; pour over fish. Bring to boil; reduce heat to simmer and cook, covered, for 3 to 5 minutes or until fish is opaque and flakes easily when tested with fork.

Remove fish to serving platter, reserving orange mixture in skillet. Mix water with cornstarch until smooth; pour into skillet and bring to boil, stirring. Pour orange sauce over fish.

Makes about 4 servings.

PER SERVING	
Calories	112
g total fat	trace
g saturated fat	0
g fibre	trace
EXCELLENT: Niacin	
g protein	21
g carbohydrate	5
mg cholesterol	68
mg sodium	191
mg potassium	417

SALMON AND SPINACH GRATIN

Use canned or leftover cooked salmon in this super gratin to serve for brunch, lunch or supper along with noodles or rice and a green salad. The gratin can be prepared a few hours in advance, then covered and refrigerated, but increase the cooking time by a few minutes.

1	pkg (10 oz/284 g) fresh spinach	1
2 tbsp	soft margarine	25 mL
1 cup	sliced mushrooms	250 mL
2 tbsp	all-purpose flour	25 mL
1 cup	hot low-fat milk	250 mL
2 tbsp	chopped scallion	25 mL
	Pepper	
1	can (7.5 oz/213 g) salmon, drained	1

Topping:

2 tbsp	fresh brown bread crumbs	25 mL
2 tbsp	freshly grated Parmesan cheese	25 mL
1 tbsp	chopped fresh parsley	15 mL

Remove stems from spinach. In saucepan of boiling water, cook spinach for 3 to 5 minutes or just until wilted; drain thoroughly. Chop coarsely and spread in 8-inch (20 cm) gratin pan or microwaveable shallow baking dish. Set aside.

In small, nonstick skillet, melt 1 tsp (5 mL) of the margarine over medium-high heat; cook mushrooms, stirring often, until lightly browned. Spread mushrooms over spinach.

In small saucepan, melt remaining margarine over medium heat; stir in flour and cook, stirring, for 1 minute. Whisk in hot milk and cook, whisking for 2 minutes or until mixture simmers and is smooth and thickened. Stir in green onion; season with pepper to taste. Flake salmon and mash bones; gently stir into sauce. Spoon over mushrooms.

Topping: Combine bread crumbs, cheese and parsley; sprinkle over salmon mixture. Bake in 400°F (200°C) oven for 5 minutes, or microwave uncovered at High power for 3 minutes, or until heated through. Brown top under broiler for 2 minutes if desired.

Makes 3 servings.

Salmon is a good source of omega-3 fatty acid, which some studies show helps to reduce blood pressure and the risk of blood clots.

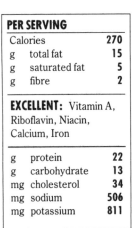

PER SERVING

Calories		**270**
g	total fat	**15**
g	saturated fat	**5**
g	fibre	**2**

EXCELLENT: Vitamin A, Riboflavin, Niacin, Calcium, Iron

g	protein	**22**
g	carbohydrate	**13**
mg	cholesterol	**34**
mg	sodium	**506**
mg	potassium	**811**

LIGHT SALMON LOAF WITH DILL

Fresh dill adds a wonderful flavor to this moist loaf. If it is unavailable, substitute fresh parsley and 1 tsp (5 mL) dried dillweed. Serve with Yogurt Remoulade, on page 112.

1 tbsp	soft margarine	15 mL
1	medium onion, chopped	1
1 cup	sliced mushrooms	250 mL
1 cup	diced celery	250 mL
2	eggs*	2
1	can (7.5 oz/213 g) salmon	1
1	cup fresh bread crumbs	250 mL
2/3 cup	milk	150 mL
1/4 cup	chopped fresh dill	50 mL
	Pepper	

In skillet, melt margarine over medium heat; cook onion, mushrooms and celery, stirring, for about 5 minutes or until tender-crisp.

In bowl, lightly beat eggs; add mushroom mixture. Drain salmon liquid into egg mixture. Flake salmon and mash bones; add to bowl along with bread crumbs, milk, dill, and pepper to taste. Stir lightly to mix.

Transfer to lightly greased 8-1/2- × 4-1/2-inch (1.5 L) loaf pan. Place in larger pan and pour in enough hot water to come 1 inch (2.5 cm) up sides of loaf pan. Bake, uncovered, in 350°F (180°C) oven for 45 to 55 minutes or until firm to the touch. Pour off any liquid.

Microwave Method: Cover and microwave loaf at High power for 7 minutes; let stand for 5 minutes.

Makes 4 servings.

Variation: Prepare above recipe but substitute 1 1/2 cups (375 mL) diced, unpeeled zucchini for the mushrooms and celery. Instead of dill, use 1/2 cup (125 mL) coarsely chopped fresh parsley.

*If you are on a cholesterol-lowering diet, use 1 whole egg and 1 egg white.

PER SERVING

Calories		201
g	total fat	10
g	saturated fat	3
g	fibre	1

GOOD: Riboflavin, Calcium
EXCELLENT: Niacin

g	protein	17
g	carbohydrate	11
mg	cholesterol	130
mg	sodium	354
mg	potassium	487

EASY FISH AND TOMATO STEW

Serve in shallow bowls with bread or over pasta, couscous, rice or boiled potatoes. Fennel adds a wonderful complementary flavor to fish. Use the seeds or 1/4 cup (50 mL) chopped fresh leaves, or a pinch of anise, or a tablespoon or two (15 to 25 mL) of Pernod liqueur. The wine is optional but the stew tastes much better when it's included.

If you keep the ingredients for this recipe on hand in your freezer and pantry, you can make a meal in minutes — even when your refrigerator is bare. If using frozen fish, use individually frozen fillets rather than the kind that was frozen in a block and, if possible, thaw before using. (However, if using a frozen block, increase cooking time to 20 minutes or until fish is opaque.) To dress up this stew for a special occasion, or when unexpected guests arrive, add clams, shrimp, crab or mussels.

2 tsp	olive oil	10 mL
1	medium onion OR leek, chopped	1
1 1/2 tsp	minced garlic	7 mL
1	large stalk celery, chopped	1
1/4 tsp	fennel seeds	1 mL
1/8 tsp	crushed red pepper flakes	0.5 mL
1	can (28 oz) tomatoes (undrained), chopped	1
1/4 cup	white wine (optional)	50 mL
1 lb	fresh or frozen fish fillets (sole, halibut, cod)	500 g
1/4 cup	chopped fresh parsley OR coriander	50 mL
	Salt and pepper	

In nonstick saucepan, heat oil over medium heat; cook onion and garlic until softened, about 5 minutes.

Add celery, fennel seeds, hot pepper flakes, tomatoes, and wine (if using); bring to boil. Reduce heat and simmer for 5 minutes.

Add fish and cook until fish is opaque, about 5 minutes for fresh, 10 minutes for frozen. Add parsley and season to taste with salt and pepper. Most fish will break up into pieces as you stir in salt and pepper; if not, cut into pieces before serving.

Makes 4 servings.

Easy Fish Stew with Scallops, Shrimp and Mussels:
Prepare Easy Fish and Tomato Stew and make the following additions. When adding fresh or thawed fish, add 1 lb (500 g) mussels (in shells, washed and debearded); cover and simmer 3 minutes, then add 1/4 lb (125 g) each scallops and medium to small shrimp (shelled, fresh or cooked). Cover and simmer another 3 minutes or until mussels open. Add parsley and continue as in above recipe. Discard any mussels that don't open.

PER SERVING	
Calories	**160**
g total fat	**3**
g saturated fat	**trace**
g fibre	**3**

GOOD: Vitamin A
EXCELLENT: Vitamin C, Niacin

g	protein	**22**
g	carbohydrate	**11**
mg	cholesterol	**57**
mg	sodium	**417**
mg	potassium	**974**

SATURDAY NIGHT INDIAN DINNER

Chapati or Indian Breads
Curried Chicken and Shrimp
Chutney, yogurt, raisins
Rice
Cucumber Raita Salad
Fresh Fruit Platter

Here is an easy Indian dinner. You can usually buy hors d'oeuvres and breads from an Indian restaurant that has them available for take-out. Try to buy some Indian breads, perhaps naan (flat bread). To serve warm, cover the flatbreads with foil and heat in a 300°F (150°C) oven for 20 minutes.

Serve hot rice and a refreshing raita salad with the curry. Raita is easy to make. Just combine chopped cucumber or tomatoes with yogurt and season with salt, pepper, cumin, garlic and parsley.

For dessert, arrange an array of fresh fruit on a large platter—grapes, melon wedges, berries, pineapple, oranges.

PER SERVING		
Calories		**355**
g	total fat	**6**
g	saturated fat	**1**
g	fibre	**2**

GOOD: Iron
EXCELLENT: Niacin

g	protein	**30**
g	carbohydrate	**44**
mg	cholesterol	**106**
mg	sodium	**122**
mg	potassium	**340**

CURRIED CHICKEN AND SHRIMP

Easy-to-make and delicious, this dish makes for no-stress entertaining. To save time, buy peeled shrimp and boneless chicken. Place small bowls of toasted slivered almonds, chopped green onions, chopped fresh coriander, raisins and chutney on the table for guests to sprinkle over their servings.

1 tbsp	vegetable oil	15 mL
1 lb	boneless skinless chicken, cubed	500 g
3	cloves garlic, minced	3
2 cups	chopped Spanish onion	500 mL
2 tbsp	minced gingerroot	25 mL
2 tbsp	curry powder*	25 mL
2	tomatoes, chopped (about 2 cups/ 500 mL)	2
1 lb	peeled large shrimp (raw OR cooked)	500 g
7 cups	hot cooked rice	1.75 L

In large nonstick saucepan, heat oil over medium heat; cook chicken, stirring often, for 5 minutes or until chicken is no longer pink inside. Remove chicken and set aside.

Add garlic, onion and gingerroot to saucepan; cook, stirring occasionally, for 4 minutes or until softened. Stir in curry powder; cook for 30 seconds.

Add tomatoes; increase heat to high and cook for about 3 minutes or until mixture has thickened. (Recipe can be prepared to this point, add chicken to tomato mixture, cover and refrigerate for up to 1 day. Reheat before continuing.)

Reduce heat to medium-low. Add shrimp and chicken; cover and simmer for 5 minutes or until shrimp are pink and chicken is heated through.

To serve, spread rice on platter; spoon curry mixture on top.

Makes 8 servings.

*Curry powder is used here as a convenience food. If you have the time to make your own, substitute 2 tsp (10 mL) each ground cardamom and coriander, 1 tsp (5 mL) each cinnamon and cumin, and 1/2 tsp (2 mL) each cayenne and turmeric.

STEAMED MUSSELS WITH TOMATOES AND FENNEL

FRIDAY NIGHT DINNER FOR FOUR

Steamed Mussels with Tomatoes and Fennel
French Bread
Salad of Greens and Herb Vinaigrette (p. 79)
Apple Streusel Pie (p. 225)

Most of the sodium in this dish is from the salty liquid released by the mussels when they open during cooking. If you are on a sodium-restricted diet, limit your amount of broth.

PER SERVING

Calories		**254**
g	total fat	**7**
g	saturated fat	**trace**
g	fibre	**3**

GOOD: Vitamin A
EXCELLENT: Vitamin C, Thiamin, Riboflavin, Niacin, Calcium, Iron

g	protein	**25**
g	carbohydrate	**20**
mg	cholesterol	**116**
mg	sodium	**1005**
mg	potassium	**1304**

Cultured mussels, which require almost no preparation time, are now available in many supermarkets — making this a fast and easy dish that's perfect for a small casual dinner party or Sunday night supper. The tomato sauce can be prepared ahead, but cook the mussels at the last minute.

4 lb	mussels	2 kg
1 tbsp	olive oil	15 mL
1	onion, chopped	1
4	cloves garlic, finely chopped	4
1	can (28 oz) plum tomatoes, drained and chopped	1
1 tsp	fennel seeds	5 mL
3 tbsp	chopped fresh parsley	50 mL
	Salt and pepper	
1 cup	dry white wine	250 mL
1	shallot, minced (optional)	1
2 tbsp	chopped scallions	25 mL

Rinse mussels; cut off any hairy beards. Discard any that do not close when lightly tapped or are cracked. Place in large pot and set aside.

In large skillet, heat oil over medium heat; cook onion and half of the garlic, stirring occasionally, until tender. Add tomatoes and fennel seeds; cook for 5 minutes. Add parsley, and salt and pepper to taste; mix well.

Meanwhile, in small bowl, combine wine, shallot (if using) and remaining garlic; pour over mussels. Cover and bring to boil; reduce heat and simmer for 5 minutes or until mussels open. Discard any that do not open. Pour tomato mixture over mussels; toss. Garnish with scallions. Serve in large soup bowls.

Makes 4 servings.

Here are some other fish and seafood recipes to try:

Creamy Oyster Chowder (page 52)
Curried Rice and Salmon Salad (page 64)
Tomato Clam Sauce for Pasta (page 148)
Easy Linguine with Scallops and Spinach (page 151)
Pasta with Tuna Cream Sauce (page 152)
Pasta with Shrimp, Zucchini and Mushrooms (page 153)

YOGURT REMOULADE

This low-calorie, quick-to-prepare sauce is delicious with the salmon loaf on page 108 or with grilled, poached or baked fish.

1/2 cup	low-fat yogurt	125 mL
2 tbsp	light sour cream	25 mL
2 tbsp	minced dill pickle	25 mL
1 tbsp	minced fresh parsley	15 mL
1 tsp	Dijon mustard	5 mL
1/4 tsp	dried tarragon	1 mL

In small bowl, combine yogurt, sour cream, dill pickle, parsley, mustard and tarragon; mix thoroughly. Pass sauce separately.

Makes about 2/3 cup (150 mL) sauce.

PER TBSP (15 ML)	
Calories	11
g total fat	trace
g saturated fat	trace
g fibre	0
g protein	1
g carbohydrate	1
mg cholesterol	1
mg sodium	39
mg potassium	33

TERIYAKI MARINADE

Use this on any kind of fish steaks or fillets, chicken wings, flank steak, lamb leg or pork tenderloin.

2 tbsp	low-sodium soy sauce	25 mL
2 tbsp	sherry	25 mL
2 tbsp	water	25 mL
1 tbsp	vegetable oil	15 mL
1 tbsp	grated gingerroot	15 mL
1 tsp	granulated sugar (optional)	5 mL

In small bowl, combine soy sauce, sherry, water, oil, gingerroot, and sugar (if using); mix well.

Makes about 1/2 cup (125 mL) enough for 1 lb (500 g) of boneless meat, fish or poultry.

PER SERVING	
(add nutrient values to one serving of marinated meat, poultry or fish)	
Calories	22
g total fat	2
g saturated fat	trace
g fibre	0
g protein	trace
g carbohydrate	1
mg cholesterol	0
mg sodium	121
mg potassium	13

Meat

Beef and Vegetable Chili

Burgers with Coriander-
Yogurt Sauce

Hamburger and Noodle
Skillet Supper

Beef and Pepper Stir-Fry

Spicy Beef Chow Mein

Beef and Vegetable Stew

No-Fuss Pot Roast
with Onions

Flank Steak with Citrus and
Pepper Marinade

Lemon Ginger Pork Loin
with Mango Salsa

Mango Salsa

Pork with Broccoli Stir-Fry

Pork Tenderloin with Orange
Ginger Sauce

Baked Ham with Marmalade
Mustard Glaze

Lamb Chops Dijon

Pilaf Supper for One

Lamb Shank and Vegetable Stew

Easy Veal Cutlets with
Tarragon Sauce

Lemon Rosemary Marinade

Everyday Marinade

Beef and Vegetable Chili

If you are cooking for a family, this is an easy quick meal — especially if you have different meal times: it's easily reheated and is nice for a packed lunch. I often add a can of pork and beans or another type of cooked beans, such as pinto, black, romano or chick-peas.

1 lb	lean ground beef	500 g
2	medium onions, chopped	2
1	large clove garlic, minced	1
1 cup	each chopped celery and carrots	250 mL
1 cup	chopped sweet green pepper (optional)	250 mL
1	can (28 oz) tomatoes, whole OR crushed (not with added purée)	1
2	cans (15 oz) red kidney beans, drained	2
2 tbsp	chili powder	25 mL
1 tbsp	lemon juice	15 mL
1 tsp	cumin	5 mL
1/4 tsp	(approx.) crushed red pepper flakes	1 mL
1 cup	water (optional)	250 mL

In large nonstick skillet or saucepan, cook beef over medium-high heat, breaking up with fork, until browned, about 5 minutes. Pour off any fat. Add onions, garlic, celery, carrots, and green pepper (if using); cook for 3 to 5 minutes or until onions are tender.

Add tomatoes, kidney beans, chili powder, lemon juice, cumin and hot pepper flakes. Cover and simmer for 10 minutes or until vegetables are tender. Add water if too thick. Taste and adjust seasoning, adding hot pepper flakes if desired.

Microwave Method: In 12-cup (3 L) microwaveable bowl, combine beef, onions, garlic, celery, carrots, and green pepper (if using); mix well, breaking up beef.

Microwave at High power for 7 to 9 minutes or until meat is no longer pink, stirring once. Stir in tomatoes, kidney beans, chili powder, lemon juice, cumin and hot pepper flakes.

Cover with waxed paper (not plastic wrap); microwave at High power for 5 minutes; stir well. Microwave at Medium-high (70%) power for about 20 minutes or until desired thickness. Taste and adjust seasoning with more hot pepper flakes if desired.

Makes 6 servings.

Variation: Adding bulgur, cracked wheat or cooked rice instead of meat to chili adds texture without adding any fat. Kidney beans plus cracked wheat or rice form a complete source of protein and are excellent sources of fibre.

Omit beef. Pour about 2 cups (500 mL) boiling water over 3/4 cup (175 mL) cracked wheat or bulgur; let stand for 15 minutes, then drain. Heat 2 tbsp (25 mL) vegetable oil in large saucepan; add onions, garlic, celery, carrots and green pepper (be sure to include). Prepare as in above recipe, adding 1 1/2 cups (375 mL) cooked prepared cracked wheat or bulgur along with kidney beans.

PER SERVING

Calories		314
g	total fat	9
g	saturated fat	3
g	fibre	11

GOOD: Vitamin C, Thiamin, Riboflavin
EXCELLENT: Vitamin A, Niacin, Iron

g	protein	24
g	carbohydrate	35
mg	cholesterol	37
mg	sodium	645
mg	potassium	1059

Burgers with Coriander-Yogurt Sauce

Use lean ground beef, lamb, pork, chicken or turkey for the patties and serve in whole wheat buns or on thick slices of toasted French bread or in a pita pocket with shredded lettuce and tomato. Fresh coriander (also called cilantro or Chinese parsley) is available in many supermarkets and in most Oriental fruit and vegetable stores. If you can't find it, use fresh dill, basil or parsley.

The best-flavored burgers are ones hot off the grill — especially chicken or turkey burgers which are juicier grilled than when they are cooked in a nonstick skillet or baked in the oven.

1 lb	lean or medium ground poultry OR meat	500 g
1	small onion, finely chopped	1
1	egg white	1
2 tbsp	fresh soft bread crumbs	25 mL
1 tbsp	chopped fresh coriander OR 1/4 cup (50 mL) chopped fresh parsley	15 mL
1/2 tsp	Worcestershire sauce	2 mL
Dash	hot pepper sauce	Dash

Coriander-Yogurt Sauce:

1/2 cup	low-fat plain yogurt	125 mL
2 tbsp	diced tomato	25 mL
1 tbsp	chopped scallion	15 mL
1 tbsp	chopped fresh coriander	15 mL
1/2 tsp	prepared horseradish	2 mL
1/2 tsp	Dijon mustard	2 mL

In bowl, combine ground meat, onion, egg white, bread crumbs, coriander, Worcestershire and hot pepper sauce; mix well. Form into 5 patties.

Coriander-Yogurt Sauce: In small bowl, combine yogurt, tomato, onion, coriander, horseradish and mustard; mix well.

Grill, broil or cook patties in nonstick skillet over medium heat for 4 minutes per side or until meat is no longer pink inside. Top with spoonful of sauce.

Makes 5 servings.

PER SERVING	
(made with turkey)	
Calories	**144**
g total fat	**4**
g saturated fat	**1**
g fibre	**trace**

EXCELLENT: Niacin

g	protein	**22**
g	carbohydrate	**4**
mg	cholesterol	**53**
mg	sodium	**99**
mg	potassium	**292**

HAMBURGER AND NOODLE SKILLET SUPPER

This made-from-scratch dish is as quick to prepare as a hamburger package dinner—and much better tasting, lower in salt and higher in fibre. When fresh tomatoes aren't in season, use a whole 14 oz (398 mL) can of tomato sauce or tomatoes. Instead of zucchini or sweet peppers, you can use chopped celery, frozen peas or corn.

3 cups	egg noodles OR 1 cup (250 mL) small pasta (about 1/4 lb/125 g)	750 mL
1 lb	ground beef	500 g
1	onion, chopped	1
1	small zucchini, cut in thin 2-inch (5 cm) long strips	1
1	sweet green OR red pepper, cubed	1
1 1/4 cups	sliced mushrooms (about 1/4 lb/125 g) (optional)	300 mL
4	tomatoes, cubed	4
1/2 cup	tomato sauce	125 mL
1/4 cup	chopped fresh parsley	50 mL
1 tsp	dried basil	5 mL
1/2 tsp	dried oregano	2 mL
	Salt and pepper	

In large pot of boiling water, cook pasta until tender but firm; drain.

Meanwhile, in large skillet or Dutch oven, cook beef over medium heat, stirring to break up, for about 5 minutes or until browned; pour off all fat. Add onion; cook for about 4 minutes or until tender. Add zucchini, sweet pepper, and mushrooms (if using); cook, stirring, over medium-high heat for about 5 minutes or until tender-crisp.

Add tomatoes, tomato sauce, parsley, basil and oregano; simmer for 5 minutes. Stir in noodles. Season with salt and pepper to taste.

Makes 5 servings.

PER SERVING	
Calories	274
g total fat	11
g saturated fat	4
g fibre	3

GOOD: Vitamin A, Riboflavin, Iron
EXCELLENT: Vitamin C, Niacin

g	protein	21
g	carbohydrate	23
mg	cholesterol	63
mg	sodium	207
mg	potassium	660

Beef and Pepper Stir-Fry

Choose red, yellow and green sweet peppers when they are in season. At other times, use broccoli, cauliflower, onions or carrots. Serve with hot cooked pasta or rice tossed with a few drops of hot pepper sauce.

1 lb	boneless lean beef,* cut in thin 2-inch (5 cm) long strips	500 g
1 tbsp	vegetable oil	15 mL
2	cloves garlic, minced	2
2 tbsp	minced gingerroot	25 mL
2	sweet peppers (1 yellow, 1 green OR red), cut in strips	2
2 cups	bean sprouts	500 mL
2 tbsp	water (optional)	25 mL
2 tbsp	reduced-sodium soy OR oyster sauce	25 mL

Marinade:

1 tbsp	cornstarch	15 mL
1 tbsp	sherry	15 mL
2 tsp	reduced-sodium soy sauce	10 mL

Marinade: In bowl, stir together cornstarch, sherry and soy sauce until smooth; add beef and stir to coat. Marinate at room temperature for 10 minutes.

In nonstick skillet or wok, heat oil over high heat; stir-fry beef, garlic and ginger for 3 minutes or until beef is browned. Transfer to plate and set aside.

Add sweet peppers to skillet; stir-fry for 3 minutes. Add bean sprouts; cook for 1 minute or until vegetables are tender-crisp, adding water if necessary to prevent scorching. Stir in soy sauce. Return beef to pan and toss to mix and reheat.

Makes 4 servings.

*Lean cuts of beef: Flank, round, rump, sirloin, sirloin tip (all visible fat removed).

PER SERVING	
Calories	**258**
g total fat	**12**
g saturated fat	**4**
g fibre	**1**

GOOD: Riboflavin, Niacin, Iron
EXCELLENT: Vitamin C

g	protein	**28**
g	carbohydrate	**8**
mg	cholesterol	**48**
mg	sodium	**612**
mg	potassium	**510**

SPICY BEEF CHOW MEIN

This tasty, budget-wise recipe is only mildly spicy, so if you like hot foods, at least double the red pepper flakes. Use fresh chow mein noodles if they are available or 4 cups (1 L) of any thin cooked noodles.

2	packages (3 oz/85 g each) namen noodles	2
1/4 cup	water	50 mL
1 tbsp	reduced-sodium soy sauce	15 mL
1 tbsp	ketchup	15 mL
1 tbsp	Worcestershire sauce	15 mL
1 tsp	granulated sugar	5 mL
2 tsp	sesame oil	10 mL
2 tsp	minced garlic	10 mL
1/8 tsp	crushed red pepper flakes	0.5 mL
1/2 lb	lean beef, cut in thin 1/4-inch (0.5 cm) wide strips	250 g
3	scallions, cut lengthwise, then diagonally in 2-inch (5 cm) pieces	3
1 cup	coarsely grated carrot	250 g
4 cups	thinly sliced cabbage	1 L

In large pot of boiling water, cook noodles for 3 minutes or until just tender (omit flavor packet, if present); drain and rinse.

Meanwhile, in bowl, combine water, soy sauce, ketchup, Worcestershire sauce, sugar and sesame oil; set aside.

In large skillet or wok sprayed with nonstick coating, cook garlic and red pepper flakes over medium-high heat for 10 seconds. Add beef; stir-fry for 1 minute. Add scallions, carrots and cabbage; stir-fry for 3 minutes. Add noodles and sauce; heat through, about 1 minute, stirring gently to coat.

Makes 4 servings.

Variation: Substitute pork or boneless chicken for beef.

PER SERVING	
Calories	206
g total fat	4
g saturated fat	1
g fibre	3

GOOD: Iron
EXCELLENT: Vitamins A and C, Niacin

g	protein	16
g	carbohydrate	26
mg	cholesterol	24
mg	sodium	372
mg	potassium	482

Beef and Vegetable Stew

Plenty of flavorful vegetables and a small amount of lean beef for a low-fat content update this stew for today's tables. Because the stew is also delicious the next day, it's a perfect make-ahead meal, too. For a special fresh flavor, add a few tablespoons of chopped fresh rosemary, thyme or oregano just before serving.

1 lb	lean stewing beef	500 g
2 cups	water	500 mL
3	medium onions, halved	3
1	bay leaf	1
1 tsp	crushed dried thyme	5 mL
1/2 tsp	crushed dried oregano	2 mL
1/2 tsp	grated orange rind	2 mL
1/8 tsp	pepper	0.5 mL
2	parsnips, peeled	2
Half	small turnip, peeled (1/2 lb/250 g)	Half
4	medium carrots, peeled	4
4	medium potatoes, peeled	4
2	stalks celery, cut in 1-in (2.5 cm) pieces	2
2 tbsp	all-purpose flour	25 mL
1/2 cup	cold water	125 mL
1 cup	frozen peas	250 mL
1/2 cup	coarsely chopped fresh parsley	125 mL

Trim all visible fat from beef and discard. Cut beef into 1- inch (2.5 cm) cubes.

Spray Dutch oven or large, heavy saucepan with nonstick coating. Heat pan over medium-high heat; cook beef, stirring, until browned on all sides. Pour in water and bring to boil, scraping up any brown bits on bottom of pan.

Add onions, bay leaf, thyme, oregano, orange rind and pepper; cover and simmer for 1 hour.

Cut parsnips, turnip and carrots into 3/4-inch (2 cm) cubes; add to pan and simmer for 10 minutes. Cut potatoes into 1-inch (2.5 cm) cubes; add to pan along with celery and simmer covered, for 20 minutes or until vegetables are tender.

Mix flour with cold water until smooth; stir into stew. Add peas and parsley; cook, stirring, until thickened and bubbly. Discard bay leaf.

Makes about 5 servings.

PER SERVING

Calories		341
g	total fat	6
g	saturated fat	2
g	fibre	8

GOOD: Riboflavin
EXCELLENT: Vitamins A and C, Thiamin, Niacin, Iron

g	protein	24
g	carbohydrate	50
mg	cholesterol	44
mg	sodium	131
mg	potassium	1112

No-Fuss Pot Roast with Onions

A popular way to cook pot roast is to sprinkle it with a package of onion soup mix, then cook it in foil. For better flavor and much less salt, make your own from scratch using sliced onions instead.

3 cups	thinly sliced onions	750 mL
3	cloves garlic, minced	3
1	lean boneless short rib roast (about 3 lb/ 1.5 kg)	1
	Pepper	
1/4 cup	water	50 mL
1 tbsp	cornstarch	15 mL
1 tbsp	cold water	15 mL

In casserole or Dutch oven, spread half of the onions and garlic. Place roast on top. Cover with remaining onions and garlic. Sprinkle with pepper to taste.

Pour in 1/4 cup (50 mL) water. Cover and cook in 325°F (160°C) oven for 2 1/2 to 3 hours or until meat is tender. Transfer meat and onions to serving platter; cover loosely with foil. Let stand for 15 minutes to make carving easier.

Meanwhile, add enough water to pan liquids, if necessary, to make 1 cup (250 mL); spoon off fat from top of liquid. Dissolve cornstarch in 1 tbsp (15 mL) water; stir into pan juices. Cook over medium-high heat, stirring, for 2 to 3 minutes or until gravy boils and thickens. Strain if desired. Cut roast into thin slices and serve with gravy.

Makes 8 servings.

PER SERVING	
Calories	202
g total fat	11
g saturated fat	5
g fibre	1

EXCELLENT: Niacin

g	protein	21
g	carbohydrate	4
mg	cholesterol	51
mg	sodium	43
mg	potassium	266

FLANK STEAK WITH CITRUS AND PEPPER MARINADE

We hardly ever have any kind of steak except flank — it's lean, full of flavor and economical. When marinated and not overcooked, it's very tender. As well as being a succulent main course, it's also good cold in sandwiches or as part of a salad plate.

1/4 cup	orange juice	50 mL
2	cloves garlic, minced	2
2 tbsp	lemon juice	25 mL
	Grated rind of 1 lemon OR orange	
1 tsp	vegetable oil	5 mL
1/4 tsp	coarse pepper	1 mL
1 lb	flank steak	500 g

In measuring cup, combine orange juice, garlic, lemon juice and rind, oil and pepper; mix well. Place steak in plastic bag or shallow dish; pour marinade over. Cover and refrigerate for 1 hour or up to 1 day, turning steak once or twice.

Remove steak from marinade; broil or barbecue for 4 to 5 minutes on each side or until desired doneness. Cut diagonally across the grain into thin slices. Serve hot or cold.

Makes 4 servings.

PER SERVING		
Calories		**211**
g	total fat	**10**
g	saturated fat	**4**
g	fibre	**trace**

EXCELLENT: Niacin

g	protein	**26**
g	carbohydrate	**3**
mg	cholesterol	**47**
mg	sodium	**56**
mg	potassium	**405**

LEMON GINGER PORK LOIN WITH MANGO SALSA

This strong-flavored marinade gives pork a wonderful flavor. Fresh and light tasting, the mango salsa is a perfect accompaniment. (Pictured opposite.)

4 lb	boneless pork loin roast (center cut OR tenderloin end), trimmed of fat	2 kg

Marinade:

1/4 cup	lemon marmalade	50 mL
2 tbsp	sherry	25 mL
2 tbsp	chopped gingerroot	25 mL
2 tsp	minced garlic	10 mL
2 tsp	Dijon mustard	10 mL
2 tsp	low-sodium soy sauce	10 mL
2 tsp	sesame oil	10 mL
1 tsp	grated lemon rind	5 mL
	Mango Salsa (page 124)	

Marinade: In small bowl, combine marmalade, sherry, ginger, garlic, mustard, soy sauce, sesame oil and lemon rind.

Place roast in large plastic bag and pour marinade over; tie shut and refrigerate for at least 4 hours or up to 24 hours, rotating bag occasionally.

Remove roast from bag, leaving as much marinade as possible clinging to roast. Set roast on rack in roasting pan.

Roast, uncovered, in 350°F (180°C) oven for 2 to 2-1/2 hours or until meat thermometer registers 160°F (70°C) and juices run clear when roast is pierced. Let stand for 15 minutes before carving into thin slices. Serve with Mango Salsa.

Makes 12 servings.

PER SERVING
without Mango Salsa

Calories		**278**
g	total fat	**14**
g	saturated fat	**5**
g	fibre	**trace**

EXCELLENT: Thiamin, Riboflavin, Niacin

g	protein	**30**
g	carbohydrate	**5**
mg	cholesterol	**67**
mg	sodium	**132**
mg	potassium	**464**

Overleaf: Orange and Fennel Salad (p. 77), Grilled Sweet Peppers and Leeks (p. 135), Moroccan Chicken Stew (p. 95)

Lemon Ginger Pork Loin with Mango Salsa (above), Sprout and Snow Pea Stir-Fry (p. 143)

Mango Salsa

I love the taste of this fresh mango relish. I like to serve it with roast chicken, turkey or pork because it's much easier than making a gravy at the last minute — not to mention that it's better for you. Papaya can be used instead of mango. Peel cucumber if skin is tough or waxed.

1	mango, peeled and finely diced	1
1/2 cup	finely diced red onion	125 mL
1/2 cup	finely diced cucumber	125 mL
2 tbsp	lime juice	25 mL
1/2 tsp	grated lime rind	2 mL
1/4 tsp	cumin	1 mL

In small bowl, combine mango, onion, cucumber, lime juice, lime rind and cumin. Cover and let stand for at least 1 hour or up to 4 hours.

Makes about 1 1/2 cups (375 mL).

PER 2 TBSP (25 ML)		
Calories		15
g	total fat	trace
g	saturated fat	0
g	fibre	trace
g	protein	trace
g	carbohydrate	4
mg	cholesterol	0
mg	sodium	1
mg	potassium	47

PORK WITH BROCCOLI STIR-FRY

Pork tenderloin is quick and easy to slice, but any lean cut of pork is fine. I keep a bottle of hoisin sauce in the refrigerator and like to add a splash to stir-frys for extra flavor. Omit it if you are on a low-sodium diet. Serve over hot rice or pasta.

3/4 lb	lean boneless pork*	375 g
1 tbsp	cornstarch	15 mL
1 tbsp	reduced-sodium soy sauce	15 mL
1 tbsp	sherry	15 mL
1	bunch broccoli	1
2 tbsp	vegetable oil	25 mL
2	cloves garlic, minced	2
2 tbsp	minced gingerroot	25 mL
1/4 cup	water	50 mL
2 tbsp	hoisin sauce (optional)	25 mL

Slice pork thinly across the grain. In bowl, stir together cornstarch, soy sauce and sherry; add pork and stir to coat well.

Separate broccoli into florets; peel stalks, then cut into 1 1/2-inch (4 cm) pieces.

In wok or large nonstick skillet, heat oil over high heat. Add pork mixture; stir-fry for 2 minutes or until meat is lightly browned. Stir in garlic, ginger and broccoli; stir-fry for 2 minutes.

Add water; cover and steam for 2 minutes or until broccoli is tender-crisp. Stir in hoisin sauce if using.

Makes 4 servings.

Variation: Substitute 3/4 lb (375 g) sliced boneless chicken or turkey for pork.

*Lean cuts of pork: Pork tenderloin is the leanest cut of pork. Other lean cuts come from the leg, picnic shoulder, and loin (tenderloin or center).

PER SERVING

Calories		220
g	total fat	10
g	saturated fat	2
g	fibre	3

GOOD: Vitamin A, Iron
EXCELLENT: Vitamin C, Thiamin, Riboflavin, Niacin

g	protein	23
g	carbohydrate	9
mg	cholesterol	46
mg	sodium	180
mg	potassium	575

Pork Tenderloin with Orange Ginger Sauce

Pork tenderloin is one of the leanest and most tender cuts of pork. It's also very easy to cook; just be careful not to overcook it because it will be too dry.

1 lb	pork tenderloin	500 g
1	medium carrot, peeled	1
4	scallions OR 1 leek	4
1/4 cup	water	50 mL
1 tsp	grated gingerroot	5 mL
1/2 tsp	minced garlic	2 mL
1 cup	orange juice	250 mL
1/2 tsp	grated orange rind	2 mL
1 tbsp	cornstarch	15 mL
Pinch	crushed red pepper flakes	Pinch
	Salt and pepper	

In roasting pan, roast pork in 350°F (180°C) oven for 50 minutes or until meat thermometer registers 160-170°F (71-75°C) and meat is no longer pink inside.

Meanwhile cut carrot and scallions or leek into thin 2-inch (5 cm) long strips.

About 15 minutes before serving, prepare sauce: In heavy saucepan, bring carrot and water to simmer; cover and cook for 5 minutes longer. Add green onions or leeks, ginger and garlic; cover and simmer for 1 minute.

Combine orange juice and rind, cornstarch and red pepper flakes; mix well. Pour over carrot mixture and bring to boil, stirring constantly. Cook, stirring, for 2 minutes longer. Season with salt and pepper to taste.

Cut pork into thin, round slices and arrange on dinner plates; spoon sauce over.

Makes 4 servings.

PER SERVING

Calories		**196**
g	total fat	**4**
g	saturated fat	**1**
g	fibre	**1**

GOOD: Riboflavin
EXCELLENT: Vitamins A and C, Thiamin, Niacin

g	protein	**27**
g	carbohydrate	**11**
mg	cholesterol	**62**
mg	sodium	**73**
mg	potassium	**680**

BAKED HAM WITH MARMALADE MUSTARD GLAZE

I like to cook ham in a liquid (either wine, port, Madeira, meat stock, orange or apple juice or a combination of these liquids) because it makes a flavorful and moist ham. For a whole ham, use the same amount of liquid but double the glaze recipe. Serve with Pineapple-Raisin Salsa (recipe on page 84).

8 lb	semi-boneless ham (shank OR butt)	4 kg
1 cup	Madeira OR port wine	250 mL
2 cups	orange juice	500 mL
Glaze:		
1/4 cup	packed brown sugar	50 mL
1/4 cup	orange marmalade	50 mL
2 tbsp	Dijon OR grainy mustard	25 mL
1 tsp	reduced-sodium soy sauce	5 mL

Glaze: In small bowl, combine sugar, marmalade, mustard and soy sauce; set aside.

Remove skin and all but 1/4-inch (5 mm) thick layer of fat on ham. Diagonally score fat side of ham to form diamond shapes; place fat side up in roasting pan. In saucepan, bring Madeira and orange juice to simmer; pour over ham.

Bake in 325°F (160°C) oven, basting occasionally, for 1 hour and 45 minutes for fully cooked ham, or 2 hours and 15 minutes for cook-before-eating ham.

Brush one-third of the glaze over ham. Cook for 45 minutes longer, brushing with remaining thirds of glaze every 15 minutes or until meat thermometer reaches 130°F (55°C) for ready-to-eat ham or 160°F (70°C) for cook-before-eating ham.

Remove from oven and let stand for 10 minutes before slicing. Serve hot or cold.

Makes 16 servings.

FAMILY HOLIDAY BUFFET DINNER MENU

*Baked Ham with
  Marmalade Mustard
  Glaze
Indonesian Fried Rice
  (p. 181)
or My Mother's
  Scalloped Potatoes
  (p. 138)
Julienne Carrots and
  Celery with Basil
  (p. 136)
or Celery and
  Mushroom Sauté
  (p. 146)
Apple Streusel Pie
  (p. 225)
or Rhubarb Strawberry
  Cobbler (p. 229)*

As long as you trim away all fat, ham is a lean cut of meat. However, it is high in sodium. Anyone on a sodium-restricted diet should eat very small portions. On a day when you do eat ham, be particularly careful to limit salt in the other foods you eat that day.

PER SERVING

Calories		**200**
g	total fat	**6**
g	saturated fat	**2**
g	fibre	**trace**

GOOD: Riboflavin
EXCELLENT: Thiamin, Niacin

g	protein	**28**
g	carbohydrate	**6**
mg	cholesterol	**61**
mg	sodium	**1512**
mg	potassium	**366**

LAMB CHOPS DIJON

Here's a fast, tasty way to cook lamb chops.

12	loin lamb chops (2 1/2 lb/1.25 kg)	12
2 tbsp	Dijon mustard	25 mL
1 tsp	dried rosemary	5 mL
1/4 tsp	whole black peppercorns, crushed	1 mL

Remove excess fat from chops; arrange in single layer on broiler pan. In small bowl, combine mustard, rosemary and peppercorns. Spread over chops.

Broil or grill 4 inches (10 cm) from heat for 5 minutes; turn and cook for 4 to 6 minutes longer for medium-rare or until desired degree of doneness.

Makes 6 servings.

**15-MINUTE SPRING OR
SUMMER DINNER**
*Lamb Chops Dijon
Asparagus
Tiny New Potatoes with
 Fresh Dill
Cherry Tomatoes
Fresh Raspberries*

PER SERVING		
Calories		**138**
g	total fat	**6**
g	saturated fat	**2**
g	fibre	**0**

GOOD: Riboflavin

g	protein	**20**
g	carbohydrate	**trace**
mg	cholesterol	**76**
mg	sodium	**105**
mg	potassium	**135**

Pilaf Supper for One

I like to use lamb in this dish because of the flavor it gives to the rice, but you can also use pork, beef or chicken—cooked or raw. Buy any small piece of lamb and freeze the extra. Double the recipe to serve two.

Half	medium onion, finely chopped	Half
2 oz	tender boneless lamb, pork OR beef, cut in 1/2-inch (1 cm) cubes OR 1/4 cup (50 mL) cooked cubed meat	50 g
1/4 cup	long-grain rice	50 mL
1/4 cup	finely diced celery OR carrot	50 mL
1 tbsp	currants OR raisins	15 mL
1/8 tsp	allspice	0.5 mL
Quarter	bay leaf	Quarter
1/2 cup	boiling water	125 mL
1/2 cup	frozen peas, thawed	125 mL
1	small tomato, coarsely chopped	1
	Salt and pepper	

Spray nonstick saucepan or small skillet with nonstick coating. Add onion and lamb; cook over medium heat, stirring often, until meat is browned and onion is tender, about 5 minutes.

Add rice, celery, currants, allspice and bay leaf; stir. Pour in boiling water; cover and simmer for 15 minutes. Stir in peas, tomato, and salt and pepper to taste; cook for 1 minute or until peas are hot and rice is tender. Discard bay leaf.

Makes 1 serving.

PER SERVING

Calories		357
g	total fat	4
g	saturated fat	2
g	fibre	7

GOOD: Vitamins A and C, Riboflavin, Niacin, Iron
EXCELLENT: Thiamin

g	protein	20
g	carbohydrate	60
mg	cholesterol	47
mg	sodium	121
mg	potassium	661

*Although the amount of
lamb may appear small,
one serving of this stew
is filling and very
flavorful. Lamb shanks
are high in fat, so it is
best to use a small
amount.*

PER SERVING	
Calories	**187**
g total fat	**2**
g saturated fat	**1**
g fibre	**5**

GOOD: Thiamin, Iron
EXCELLENT: Vitamins A
and C, Niacin

g protein	**11**
g carbohydrate	**31**
mg cholesterol	**28**
mg sodium	**282**
mg potassium	**814**

LAMB SHANK AND VEGETABLE STEW

Lamb shanks are very inexpensive and add fabulous flavor to this easy-to-make stew. If possible, make it a day in advance, then cover and refrigerate it. The next day, remove any fat that has solidified on top. As well as removing extra fat, the flavor will develop and the stew won't need thickening.

1 1/4 lb	lamb shanks	625 g
6	small onions	6
6	small potatoes, cut in chunks (1 lb/500 g)	6
Half	small turnip, peeled and cubed	Half
3	large carrots, cut in chunks	3
3	cloves garlic, minced	3
4 cups	water	1 L
1	can (8 oz) tomato sauce	1
1 tsp	each dried thyme and rosemary	5 mL
1/4 tsp	pepper	1 mL
1	bay leaf	1
1 tsp	grated orange rind	5 mL
2 tbsp	all-purpose flour (optional)	25 mL

Cut all visible fat from lamb and discard. In large casserole or Dutch oven, combine lamb shanks, onions, potatoes, turnip, carrots, garlic, water, tomato sauce, thyme, rosemary, pepper, bay leaf and orange rind; stir to mix.

Bake, covered, in 325°F (160°C) oven for 3 hours, stirring occasionally. Discard bay leaf. Remove lamb from stew; cut meat from bones and return meat to stew.

To thicken stew if desired, mix flour with 1/3 cup (75 mL) cold water until smooth; whisk into stew and stir until thickened, about 1 minute.

Makes 6 servings.

EASY VEAL CUTLETS WITH TARRAGON SAUCE

This quick and easy recipe is fine for either family or guests. Because such a tiny amount of fat is used, it's important to have a nonstick skillet. Use either veal scallopini or thin cutlets.

1 tsp	vegetable oil	5 mL
1 lb	veal cutlets	500 g
1/2 cup	dry white wine OR chicken OR veal stock	125 mL
1/2 tsp	dried tarragon OR 1 tbsp (15 mL) chopped fresh	2 mL
1 tsp	all-purpose flour	5 mL
1/4 cup	low-fat yogurt	50 mL
	Salt and pepper	

In large nonstick skillet, heat oil over high heat; add veal and brown on both sides, about 2 minutes per side. Watch carefully: if veal is overcooked, it toughens. Remove and set aside.

Add wine or stock and tarragon, stirring to scrape up brown bits from bottom of pan. Cook until liquid is reduced by half, about 2 minutes. Remove from heat.

Mix flour with yogurt; stir into pan liquid and mix well. Return veal to pan and turn to coat with sauce. Season with salt and pepper to taste.

Makes 4 servings.

Chicken Breasts with Tarragon Sauce

This veal dish can also be made with boneless chicken breasts. Pound chicken breasts between waxed paper until about 1/4-inch (5 mm) thick so they will cook faster and appear larger.

In large nonstick skillet, heat oil over high heat; cook chicken for about 5 minutes or until browned on both sides.

Leave the chicken in the pan and add the wine or stock and tarragon; reduce heat to medium and cook, uncovered for about 5 minutes or until chicken is no longer pink inside and liquid is reduced by half.

Remove chicken to a side plate; mix flour into yogurt; stir into pan liquid until mixed well. Return chicken to pan and coat with sauce; season with salt and pepper to taste.

PER SERVING	
Calories	**167**
g total fat	**6**
g saturated fat	**trace**
g fibre	**0**
g protein	**22**
g carbohydrate	**2**
mg cholesterol	**87**
mg sodium	**56**
mg potassium	**265**

Here are some other meat recipes to try:

Smoky Sausage Lentil Soup (page 46)
Beef 'n' Bean Minestrone (page 53)
Penne with Italian Sausage, Tomato and Herbs (page 155)
Family Favorite Lasagna (page 159)
Tomato Ham Pasta Dinner for One (page 163)
Favorite Spaghetti (page 164)
Chinese Noodles with Mushrooms and Pork (page 166)

LEMON ROSEMARY MARINADE

Use this marinade for pork, chicken, lamb or fish. It's enough for 1 to 2 pounds (500 g to 1 kg) of chops, kabobs or fillets.

4	sprigs fresh rosemary OR 2 tsp (10 mL) dried	4
1	small onion, sliced	1
1 tsp	minced garlic	5 mL
2 tbsp	lemon juice	25 mL
1 tbsp	olive oil	15 mL
1 tbsp	water	15 mL

Remove leaves from rosemary sprigs. In small bowl, combine rosemary leaves, onion, garlic, lemon juice, oil and water.

Pour over meat or combine with meat in plastic bag; cover and refrigerate for 1 hour or overnight.

Makes about 1/4 cup (50 mL).

PER SERVING
(add nutrient values to one serving of marinated meat, poultry or fish)

Calories		**20**
g	total fat	**2**
g	saturated fat	**trace**
g	fibre	**trace**
g	protein	**trace**
g	carbohydrate	**1**
mg	cholesterol	**0**
mg	sodium	**0**
mg	potassium	**23**

EVERYDAY MARINADE

Pour this over beef, pork OR lamb kabobs, steak, roast or chops, then cover and refrigerate for 1 hour or up to 24 hours, turning meat occasionally.

2	cloves garlic, minced	2
1	medium onion, chopped	1
1/4 cup	wine vinegar	50 mL
1 tbsp	vegetable oil	15 mL
1 tbsp	reduced-sodium soy sauce	15 mL
1/2 tsp	dry mustard OR curry powder	2 mL

In small bowl combine garlic, onion, vinegar, oil, soy sauce and mustard; mix well.

Makes about 1/2 cup (125 mL), enough for up to 2 pounds (1 kg) meat.

Ginger Marinade
Add 2 tbsp (25 mL) minced fresh gingerroot to Everyday Marinade.

PER SERVING
(add nutrient values to one serving of marinated meat, poultry or fish)

Calories		**23**
g	total fat	**2**
g	saturated fat	**trace**
g	fibre	**trace**
g	protein	**trace**
g	carbohydrate	**2**
mg	cholesterol	**0**
mg	sodium	**61**
mg	potassium	**36**

VEGETABLES

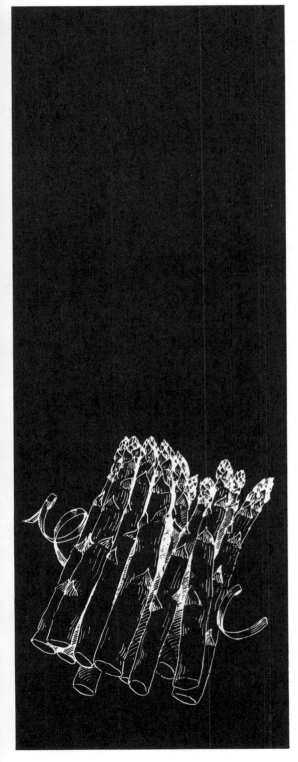

Easy Baked Leeks

You can prepare this recipe for leeks (one of my favorite vegetables) in advance, then reheat in the oven or microwave. Bake it along with whatever else you have in the oven by increasing the baking time 10 minutes if the oven isn't as hot as required or decreasing it if the oven is hotter. Use about one large leek or two small leeks per person.

10	medium to large leeks	10
1 tbsp	soft margarine	15 mL
	Pepper	
2 tbsp	freshly grated Parmesan cheese	25 mL

Trim base and tough green leaves from leeks, leaving tender green and white parts. Beginning at top green part, cut leeks lengthwise about three-quarters down; spread leaves apart and wash under cold running water.

In large pot of simmering water, cook leeks, covered, for 10 minutes or until tender when pierced with a knife; drain and arrange in single layer in baking dish. Brush with margarine and season with pepper to taste; sprinkle with Parmesan. Cover with foil. (Leeks can stand at room temperature for a few hours or be refrigerated up to 24 hours.) Bake, covered, in 350°F (180°C) oven for 25 minutes.

Makes 10 servings.

PER SERVING	
Calories	53
g total fat	2
g saturated fat	**trace**
g fibre	2
g protein	1
g carbohydrate	9
mg cholesterol	1
mg sodium	41
mg potassium	109

Grilled Sweet Peppers and Leeks

A combination of sweet peppers, leeks, yellow zucchini and green zucchini makes a colorful and fabulous-tasting vegetable dish. This is a great dish for entertaining because you can grill all the vegetables in advance, then reheat them in a 375°F (190°C) oven for 15 minutes just before serving. (Pictured after page 122.)

12	small leeks	12
2	small green zucchini	2
2	small yellow zucchini (summer squash)	2
6	sweet peppers (red, yellow, green)	6
4	sprigs fresh rosemary OR 1 tbsp (15 mL) dried	4
2 tbsp	olive oil	25 mL
	Salt and pepper	

Trim all but 1-inch (2.5 cm) of green from leeks; wash under cold water. In saucepan of boiling water, cook leeks for 5 to 10 minutes or until tender; drain.

Cut zucchini and squash into 1/2-inch (1 cm) thick diagonal slices. Seed peppers and cut into quarters or strips. Remove leaves from rosemary. Brush oil over zucchini, squash and peppers; sprinkle with rosemary and toss to mix.

Grill peppers, zucchini and squash over medium-hot coals or on medium setting, turning occasionally, for 15 to 20 minutes or until tender. Grill leeks for 5 minutes or until heated through. Season with salt and pepper to taste. Arrange on large serving platter.

Makes 12 servings.

PER SERVING	
Calories	**79**
g total fat	**3**
g saturated fat	**trace**
g fibre	**3**

GOOD: Iron
EXCELLENT: Vitamin C

g	protein	**2**
g	carbohydrate	**14**
mg	cholesterol	**0**
mg	sodium	**15**
mg	potassium	**301**

JULIENNE CARROTS AND CELERY WITH BASIL

I think of celery as an old-fashioned vegetable that I really enjoy but all too often forget about. If fresh basil isn't available, use any fresh herb such as parsley, dill, coriander or thyme; if using fresh tarragon, use only 2 tbsp (25 mL). Chop the basil just before using because it darkens if done in advance. (Pictured opposite page 122.)

1 lb	carrots, peeled (6 medium)	500 g
1	head celery	1
1 cup	chicken stock OR water	250 mL
1/4 cup	chopped fresh basil	50 mL
1 tbsp	soft margarine	15 mL
	Salt and pepper	

Cut carrots and celery into julienne strips about 2 inches (5 cm) long.

In saucepan, bring stock to boil; add carrots, cover and boil for 5 minutes. Add celery; cover and simmer for 5 minutes longer or until vegetables are tender-crisp. Drain and add basil and margarine; season with salt and pepper to taste and mix lightly. Serve hot.

Makes 6 servings.

Carrot and celery salad
If I have any extra of this, I turn it into a salad by letting it cool, then mixing with a little light mayonnaise and yogurt.

PER SERVING	
Calories	**57**
g total fat	**2**
g saturated fat	**1**
g fibre	**2**

EXCELLENT: Vitamin A

g protein	**2**
g carbohydrate	**8**
mg cholesterol	**0**
mg sodium	**218**
mg potassium	**360**

BRAISED CARROTS WITH FENNEL

Tender new carrots teamed with mild licorice-tasting fennel is a lovely vegetable combination.

1	medium bulb fennel (about 3/4 lb/375 g)	1
1 cup	chicken stock	250 mL
2 cups	thinly sliced small carrots	500 mL
2 tbsp	chopped shallots OR onion	25 mL
1/4 cup	chopped fresh parsley	50 mL
	Pepper	

Trim stalk from fennel bulb; chop and save a few wispy fronds.

Remove outer layer of fennel bulb if discolored or bruised; trim root end. Cut into 1/4-inch (5 mm) thick pieces about 1-inch (2.5 cm) long.

In saucepan, bring chicken stock to boil; add carrots, shallots or onion and fennel. Cover and simmer for 15 minutes or until vegetables are tender; uncover and boil to reduce liquid until nearly gone. Stir in parsley and reserved fennel fronds. Season with pepper to taste. Serve hot.

Makes 4 servings.

PER SERVING		
Calories		**74**
g	total fat	**1**
g	saturated fat	**trace**
g	fibre	**2**

GOOD: Iron
EXCELLENT: Vitamins A and C

g	protein	**5**
g	carbohydrate	**14**
mg	cholesterol	**0**
mg	sodium	**255**
mg	potassium	**604**

MY MOTHER'S SCALLOPED POTATOES

When my friend Elizabeth Baird was helping me name some of these recipes we both commented that this was the way our mothers made scalloped potatoes — hence the name. This comforting dish has always been one of my favorites; I'm quite happy to have it as my main course along with a green salad and a vegetable or tiny amount of meat. To save time, I slice the potatoes and chop the onions in a food processor and warm the milk in the microwave.

8	medium potatoes, thinly sliced	8
1	large onion, chopped	1
2 tbsp	all-purpose flour	25 mL
	Salt and pepper	
2 cups	hot low-fat milk	500 mL
1 cup	shredded fat-reduced Cheddar cheese	250 mL

Spray 13- × 9-inch (3 L) baking dish with nonstick coating.

Arrange one-third of the potatoes over bottom; sprinkle with half of the onion, then half of the flour. Season with salt and pepper to taste. Repeat layers; arrange remaining potatoes over top. Pour hot milk over. Sprinkle with cheese.

Bake, uncovered, in 350°F (180°C) oven for 1 hour or until potatoes are tender.

Makes 8 servings.

PER SERVING	
Calories	**192**
g total fat	**4**
g saturated fat	**2**
g fibre	**3**

GOOD: Niacin, Calcium

g protein	**8**
g carbohydrate	**32**
mg cholesterol	**13**
mg sodium	**106**
mg potassium	**608**

MICROWAVE GARLIC POTATOES

This is my favorite fast potato dish in the summer and fall when tiny red potatoes are readily available. They can be served hot or at room temperature, so you don't have to worry about split-second timing when serving with barbecued meats. The potatoes can also be baked in a conventional oven or boiled, and you can substitute medium potatoes, cut in half.

2 lb	small red potatoes (unpeeled)	1 kg
2 tbsp	olive oil	25 mL
1 tsp	minced fresh garlic	5 mL
1/3 cup	chopped fresh dill, basil OR parsley	75 mL
	Salt and pepper	

Wash potatoes, then prick with fork. Arrange in single layer in microwaveable dish. Microwave, uncovered, at High power for 10 to 13 minutes or until tender when pierced with fork, rearranging once.

Meanwhile, combine oil and garlic; let stand for at least 15 minutes or up to 30 minutes. Pour over hot cooked potatoes. Sprinkle with fresh dill and toss to mix; season with salt and pepper to taste.

Makes 6 servings.

PER SERVING

Calories		172
g	total fat	5
g	saturated fat	1
g	fibre	2

GOOD: Vitamin C

g	protein	3
g	carbohydrate	30
mg	cholesterol	0
mg	sodium	9
mg	potassium	597

MUSHROOM-STUFFED POTATOES

This recipe is adapted from a Prince Edward Island Potato Marketing Commission Board brochure.

4	baking potatoes (about 8 oz/250 g each)	4

Stuffing:

1 tbsp	soft margarine	15 mL
1/2 cup	finely chopped onion	125 mL
1/4 cup	finely chopped celery	50 mL
2 tbsp	finely chopped sweet red OR green pepper	25 mL
2 cups	chopped fresh mushrooms	500 mL
1/4 cup	finely chopped fresh parsley	50 mL
1/4 cup	low-fat milk	50 mL
	Pepper	
1/2 cup	shredded reduced-fat Cheddar cheese	125 mL

Scrub potatoes; prick with fork. Bake in 400°F (200°C) oven for 50 to 60 minutes or until tender.

Stuffing: In saucepan, melt margarine over medium heat; cook onion, celery, red or green pepper and mushrooms, stirring, until vegetables are tender.

Cut slice from top of each potato; scoop out pulp to bowl, reserving shells. Mash pulp until free of lumps. Stir in vegetables, parsley, milk, and pepper to taste. Add more milk to taste if necessary. Spoon mixture into shells, smoothing top. (Potatoes can be prepared to this point, cooled and packaged for freezing.*) Sprinkle with cheese. Bake in 400°F (200°C) oven for 10 minutes or until filling is hot and cheese is melted.

Microwave Method: Scrub potatoes; prick with fork. Microwave at High power for 12 to 16 minutes or until almost tender. Let stand, covered, until tender.

Stuffing: In microwaveable dish, microwave margarine at High power for 20 seconds or until melted. Add onion, celery, red or green pepper and mushrooms; microwave at High for 2 minutes. Stir; microwave at High for 1 minute longer. Assemble stuffed potatoes as above.

Arrange potatoes in circle in microwave; cover with waxed paper. Microwave at High 1 minute per potato. (If potatoes have been refrigerated before microwaving, add 1 minute of cooking time for each potato.) Sprinkle with cheese; microwave for 1 to 2 minutes longer or until cheese melts.

Microwave frozen stuffed potatoes at High power:

1 potato: 3 to 5 minutes
2 potatoes: 5 to 7 minutes
3 potatoes: 7 to 9 minutes
4 potatoes: 9 to 11 minutes

Then sprinkle with cheese and microwave for 1 to 2 minutes longer or until cheese melts.

Makes 4 servings.

*Stuffed potatoes can be frozen for up to 1 month. When ready to use, bake frozen in 400°F (200°C) oven for 50 to 60 minutes or until heated through. Top with cheese and bake until cheese melts, about 2 minutes.

PER SERVING	
Calories	285
g total fat	6
g saturated fat	2
g fibre	5

GOOD: Thiamin, Iron
EXCELLENT: Vitamin C, Niacin

g protein	9
g carbohydrate	50
mg cholesterol	10
mg sodium	123
mg potassium	965

ROSE MURRAY'S BAKED ASPARAGUS

My friend and cookbook author Rose Murray showed me how to cook asparagus this way. It has a slightly different texture and flavor from boiled asparagus and tastes absolutely delicious. Very thin asparagus might take less baking time, fat stalks might take a little longer. For extra flavor, sprinkle asparagus with Parmesan cheese and bread crumbs before baking.

1 lb	asparagus	500 g
2 tsp	melted soft margarine OR olive oil	10 mL
1/4 tsp	salt	1 mL

Spray baking sheet with nonstick coating. Break off tough ends of asparagus. Arrange asparagus in single layer on prepared baking sheet. Brush with melted margarine or oil; sprinkle with salt. Bake in 500°F (260°C) oven for about 8 minutes or until tender.

Makes 4 servings.

PER SERVING	
Calories	31
g total fat	2
g saturated fat	trace
g fibre	1

g protein	1
g carbohydrate	2
mg cholesterol	0
mg sodium	151
mg potassium	174

Eggplant-Tomato Gratin

Serve this delicious dish as a main course or side vegetable. For years, I only had eggplant recipes where it was fried in huge amounts of oil. In Italy, I learned they also boil, bake and steam it before using it in a variety of ways.

2	eggplants (1 lb/500 g each)	2
1 cup	shredded reduced-fat mozzarella cheese	250 mL
2 tbsp	freshly grated Parmesan cheese	25 mL

Tomato Sauce:

1	can (28 oz) plum tomatoes (undrained)	1
1/4 cup	tomato paste	50 mL
1	onion, finely chopped	1
2	cloves garlic, minced	2
1	large bay leaf	1
1 tbsp	dried basil	15 mL
1 tsp	dried oregano	5 mL
	Pepper	

This is a handy all-purpose tomato sauce recipe to use with pasta, on top of polenta, with lasagna or as a pizza base. If I have any fresh herbs on hand such as basil, thyme, dill, or parsley, I add them for extra flavor.

Cut eggplants in half lengthwise; prick skin with fork. Place cut side down on lightly greased baking sheet; bake in 450°F (230°C) oven for 20 minutes or until tender. Let cool, then cut crosswise into 1/2-inch (1 cm) thick slices.

Tomato Sauce: Meanwhile, in food processor, purée tomatoes; pour into large heavy saucepan. Add tomato paste, onion, garlic, bay leaf, basil and oregano. Simmer, uncovered, for 20 to 30 minutes or until sauce has thickened and onions are tender (you should have about 3 cups/750 mL). Season with pepper to taste. Remove bay leaf.

In 8-inch (2 L) square baking dish, spread thin layer of sauce; cover with layer of eggplant. Repeat with sauce, then eggplant, then sauce. Sprinkle with mozzarella and Parmesan. Bake in 400°F (200°C) oven for 25 to 30 minutes or until bubbly.

Makes 6 main-course servings.

PER SERVING	
Calories	**141**
g total fat	**4**
g saturated fat	**2**
g fibre	**6**

GOOD: Vitamins A and C, Thiamin, Niacin, Calcium, Iron

g	protein	**9**
g	carbohydrate	**20**
mg	cholesterol	**13**
mg	sodium	**353**
mg	potassium	**826**

Sprout and Snow Pea Stir-Fry

My friend Stevie Cameron is a fabulous cook. I came up with this recipe after tasting it at a dinner party at her house. (Pictured opposite page 123.)

4 cups	snow peas (8 oz/250 g)	1 L
2 tsp	vegetable oil	10 mL
2 tsp	minced garlic	10 mL
2 tbsp	minced gingerroot	25 mL
2 cups	bean sprouts (4 oz/125 g)	500 mL
3 tbsp	water (optional)	45 mL
2 tsp	reduced-sodium soy sauce	10 mL

Remove stem end and string from snow peas. In large nonstick skillet or wok, heat oil over high heat. Add garlic, gingerroot and snow peas; stir-fry for 1 minute.

Add bean sprouts; stir-fry for 1 minute or until vegetables are tender-crisp, adding water if necessary to prevent burning. Stir in soy sauce.

Makes 4 servings.

PER SERVING	
Calories	54
g total fat	2
g saturated fat	**trace**
g fibre	3

GOOD: Vitamin C

g protein	2
g carbohydrate	6
mg cholesterol	0
mg sodium	85
mg potassium	178

GRILLED EGGPLANT WITH GARLIC AND ROSEMARY

Eggplant cooked on the barbecue has a rich smoky flavor. Be sure to slice it 1/2 inch (1 cm) thick because thicker slices tend to burn before they become tender inside. Serve with other grilled vegetables (see page 135) or broiled tomatoes.

1	eggplant (about 1 lb/500 g)	1
2 tbsp	olive OR vegetable oil	25 mL
1 tbsp	water	15 mL
1	small clove garlic, minced	1
2 tsp	crushed dried rosemary OR 1 tbsp (15 mL) fresh	10 mL

Cut eggplant into 1/2-inch (1 cm) thick slices. Combine oil, water and garlic; brush over both sides of eggplant.

Grill on greased rack about 6 inches (15 cm) from medium-hot coals or on medium setting for 8 to 10 minutes (with lid down); turn and sprinkle with rosemary. Grill for 8 to 10 minutes longer or until lightly browned outside and soft and creamy inside. (Alternatively, broil on baking sheet for 4 to 6 minutes per side.) Serve hot or warm.

Makes 6 servings.

Eggplant, tomato and mozzarella salad
Arrange overlapping slices of Grilled Eggplant with Garlic and Rosemary, thick slices of tomato and thin slices of mozzarella cheese. Drizzle with Everyday Vinaigrette (p. 79).

Eggplant, tomato and cheese
In shallow baking dish, arrange overlapping slices of Grilled Eggplant, sliced tomato and thin slices of reduced-fat mozzarella. Bake in 350°F (180°C) oven for 25 minutes or until vegetables are heated through and cheese melts. Serve hot.

PER SERVING	
Calories	61
g total fat	5
g saturated fat	1
g fibre	2
g protein	1
g carbohydrate	5
mg cholesterol	0
mg sodium	2
mg potassium	182

SESAME BROCCOLI

Oriental seasonings add wonderful flavors to broccoli. (Pictured opposite page 90.)

1 tbsp	sesame seeds	15 mL
1	bunch broccoli (1 lb/500 g)	1
2 tbsp	orange juice	25 mL
2 tsp	sesame oil	10 mL
2 tsp	reduced-sodium soy sauce	10 mL
1 tsp	grated gingerroot	5 mL

In small pan, cook sesame seeds over medium heat for 3 minutes, shaking pan occasionally; set aside.

Cut broccoli into florets; peel stalks and diagonally slice. Boil broccoli for 5 to 6 minutes or steam until tender-crisp; drain and place in serving dish.

Combine orange juice, sesame oil, soy sauce and gingerroot; toss with broccoli. Sprinkle with sesame seeds.

Makes 5 servings.

Brassica Vegetables
Some studies have suggested that consumption of these vegetables may reduce the risk of cancer, particularly of the bowel and colon.

Brassica vegetables include cabbage, broccoli, cauliflower, turnips and rutabaga, collard greens, kale, kohlrabi, bok choy and brussels sprouts.

To prepare in advance, cook broccoli, then quickly cool in ice water; toast sesame seeds and mix seasonings. Just before serving, blanch broccoli in boiling water; drain and combine as in recipe.

PER SERVING	
Calories	**56**
g total fat	**3**
g saturated fat	**trace**
g fibre	**2**

EXCELLENT: Vitamin C

g	protein	3
g	carbohydrate	6
mg	cholesterol	0
mg	sodium	74
mg	potassium	171

CELERY AND MUSHROOM SAUTÉ

A dash of sesame oil adds fabulous flavor to this vegetable dish. Serve with meats or poultry.

1 tsp	soft margarine	5 mL
1	small onion, thinly sliced	1
4 cups	diagonally sliced celery	1 L
3 cups	thickly sliced mushrooms (8 oz/250 g)	750 mL
1 tsp	reduced-sodium soy sauce	5 mL
1 tsp	sesame oil	5 mL
1 tsp	water	5 mL
	Pepper OR hot pepper sauce	

In nonstick skillet, melt margarine over medium-high heat; stir-fry onion for 1 minute. Add celery and mushrooms; stir-fry for 6 to 8 minutes or until tender-crisp.

In small dish, combine soy sauce, sesame oil and water; pour over vegetables. Season with pepper or hot pepper sauce to taste. Mix well. Serve hot.

Makes 6 servings.

Sesame oil

Sesame oil adds wonderful flavor to stir-frys and salad dressings. Some brands of sesame oil have more flavor than others. I like one with lots of flavor, so I can keep the fat as low as possible by using a small amount.

Look for toasted sesame oil and avoid virgin sesame oil. Generally, a darker-colored sesame oil will have more flavor than a light-colored one. Store it in the refrigerator to prevent it from becoming rancid.

PER SERVING	
Calories	33
g total fat	2
g saturated fat	**trace**
g fibre	2
g protein	1
g carbohydrate	4
mg cholesterol	0
mg sodium	81
mg potassium	361

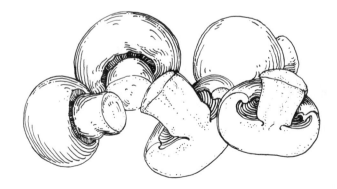

PASTA

Tomato Clam Sauce for
Pasta

Pasta e Fagioli

Linguine with Asparagus
and Red Pepper

Easy Linguine with Scallops
and Spinach

Pasta with Tuna Cream Sauce

Pasta with Shrimp, Zucchini
and Mushrooms

Penne with Tomato, Black
Olive and Feta

Penne with Italian Sausage,
Tomato and Herbs

Spicy Thai Noodles with
Vegetables (Pad Thai)

Mushroom and Sweet Pepper
Lasagna

Family Favorite Lasagna

Pasta with Sweet Peppers,
Cheese and Basil

Kids' Easy Macaroni and
Cheese with Vegetables

Tomato Ham Pasta
Dinner for One

Favorite Spaghetti

Lighthearted Fettuccine
Alfredo

Chinese Noodles with
Mushrooms and Pork

TOMATO CLAM SAUCE FOR PASTA

Serve this tasty, quick sauce over any kind of hot cooked pasta. Using crushed tomatoes saves time and gives a thicker sauce. Otherwise use two 19 oz/540 mL cans of plum tomatoes and purée in food processor, then cook a little longer to thicken sauce.

1 tbsp	olive oil	15 mL
1	medium onion, chopped	1
1	clove garlic, minced	1
1	can (28 oz) crushed tomatoes	1
1	bay leaf	1
1 tbsp	dried basil	15 mL
1 tsp	dried oregano	5 mL
1	can (6 1/2 oz) clams (undrained)	1
1/2 tsp	granulated sugar (optional)	2 mL
1/2 cup	chopped fresh parsley	125 mL

In saucepan, heat oil over medium heat; cook onion, stirring often, until tender.

Add garlic, tomatoes, bay leaf, basil, oregano and clams; simmer, uncovered, for 5 minutes or until flavors are blended. Taste and add sugar (if using). Stir in parsley.

Makes about 4 cups (1 L), enough for 1 1/2 lb (750 g) pasta, 6 main-course servings.

PER SERVING
(sauce only)

Calories		**79**
g	total fat	**3**
g	saturated fat	**trace**
g	fibre	**2**

GOOD: Vitamin C, Iron

g	protein	**4**
g	carbohydrate	**12**
mg	cholesterol	**8**
mg	sodium	**501**
mg	potassium	**456**

Pasta e Fagioli

This hearty pasta and bean dish proves that healthy eating is not expensive. If you have the time, to save money, reduce sodium and improve texture and flavor, instead of using canned beans, cook dried beans and peas; use 2 cups (500 mL), cooked, of each.

2 cups	small pasta CR broken noodles (6 oz/175 g)	500 mL
1 tbsp	olive oil	15 mL
1	large onion, chopped	1
2	medium carrots, chopped	2
2 tsp	minced garlic	10 mL
1/4 tsp	crushed red pepper flakes	1 mL
1 tsp	each dried basil, rosemary and oregano	5 mL
1	can (28 oz) plum tomatoes (undrained), chopped	1
1	can (19 oz) kidney beans, drained and rinsed	1
1	can (19 oz) garbanzo beans, drained and rinsed	1
	Salt and pepper	
2 tbsp	freshly grated Parmesan cheese	25 mL
1/2 cup	chopped fresh parsley	125 mL

In large pot of boiling water, cook pasta until tender but firm; drain. Meanwhile, in large saucepan, heat oil over medium heat; cook onion, carrots, garlic and hot pepper flakes until tender.

Add basil, rosemary, oregano and tomatoes; bring to a boil. Add beans, chick-peas and cooked pasta; mix gently and simmer for 2 minutes.

Season with salt and pepper to taste. Serve in soup bowls and sprinkle with Parmesan, then parsley.

Makes 6 servings, about 1 1/4 cup (300 mL) each.

PER SERVING	
Calories	367
g total fat	5
g saturated fat	1
g fibre	13

GOOD: Niacin, Thiamin
EXCELLENT: Vitamins A and C, Iron

g	protein	16
g	carbohydrate	67
mg	cholesterol	1
mg	sodium	673
mg	potassium	889

LINGUINE WITH ASPARAGUS AND RED PEPPER

We have pasta for dinner at least once a week, mainly using whatever we have in the refrigerator. The large pot I use for cooking pasta has a steamer tray on top in which I steam vegetables such as asparagus, broccoli or sweet peppers while cooking the pasta. Then I toss everything, together with a touch of olive oil and some Parmesan or feta cheese.

1 lb	linguine OR other pasta	500 g
1 lb	asparagus, cut in 2-inch (5 cm) lengths	500 g
1	large sweet red pepper, cut in thin strips	1
2 tbsp	olive oil	25 mL
2 tbsp	chicken stock OR water	25 mL
3	cloves garlic, minced	3
1/2 cup	freshly grated Parmesan cheese	125 mL
1/2 cup	chopped fresh parsley	125 mL
1 tsp	dried basil OR 1/4 cup (50 mL) chopped fresh	5 mL

In large pot of boiling water, cook pasta until tender but firm. In top of pasta cooking pot or steamer, steam asparagus and red pepper for 3 minutes or until tender-crisp; drain.

Meanwhile, in small saucepan or microwaveable dish, combine oil, stock and garlic; cook over medium heat for 1 minute or microwave at High power for 20 seconds or until garlic is tender.

Drain pasta and return to cooking pot; toss with cooked asparagus and pepper, oil mixture, cheese, parsley and basil. Serve immediately.

Makes 5 servings.

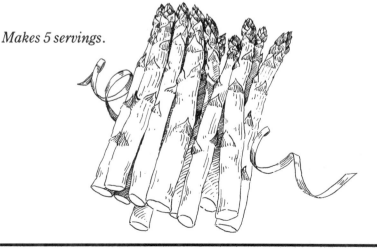

Linguine with Broccoli and Carrots

Follow directions for Linguine with Asparagus and Red Pepper, but substitute 1 lb (500 g) broccoli for asparagus and 3 medium carrots for sweet red pepper. Cook until tender-crisp.

PER SERVING	
Calories	**447**
g total fat	**9**
g saturated fat	**2**
g fibre	**5**

GOOD: Niacin, Calcium, Iron
EXCELLENT: Vitamin C

g	protein	**17**
g	carbohydrate	**74**
mg	cholesterol	**6**
mg	sodium	**176**
mg	potassium	**490**

EASY LINGUINE WITH SCALLOPS AND SPINACH

Tasty and colorful, this quick pasta dish is also relatively low in fat, high in complex carbohydrates and a good source of iron and vitamin A.

FRIDAY NIGHT SUPPER
*Lighthearted Caesar
Salad (page 62)
Easy Linguine with
Scallops and Spinach
Braised Carrots with
Fennel (page 137)
Rhubarb Apple Crisp
(page 230)*

If you are on a low-calorie or lower-fat diet, you can substitute 1% or 2% cottage cheese for the reduced-fat cream cheese. Purée cottage cheese in a blender or food processor or pass through a sieve, then stir into cooking liquid with lemon rind and dill.

1/2 lb	linguine	250 g
1/2 cup	chicken stock OR white wine	125 mL
1	onion, minced	1
1/2 lb	scallops (halved if large)	250 g
1/3 cup	light cream cheese	75 mL
2 tbsp	chopped fresh dill OR 1 tsp (5 mL) dried basil	25 mL
1 tsp	grated lemon rind	5 mL
2 cups	shredded spinach	500 mL
	Salt and pepper	
2 tbsp	freshly grated Parmesan cheese	25 mL

In large pot of boiling water, cook linguine until tender but firm; drain and return to pot.

Meanwhile, in small saucepan, bring stock to simmer; add onion and scallops. Cover and simmer for 4 minutes or until scallops are opaque throughout. (Time will vary depending on size of scallops: bay scallops will cook in 2 minutes.) Using slotted spoon, remove scallops to bowl and keep warm.

Stir cream cheese, dill and lemon rind into hot cooking liquid; stir over medium heat until smooth. Pour over pasta and toss. Add spinach and scallops; toss. Season with salt and pepper to taste. Sprinkle each serving with Parmesan cheese.

Makes 3 servings.

PER SERVING	
Calories	**420**
g total fat	**9**
g saturated fat	**4**
g fibre	**4**

GOOD: Vitamin A, Iron
EXCELLENT: Niacin

g	protein	**23**
g	carbohydrate	**62**
mg	cholesterol	**42**
mg	sodium	**424**
mg	potassium	**552**

PASTA WITH TUNA CREAM SAUCE

I like to use penne or bowtie-shaped pasta for this quick and easy dinner. Just run the frozen peas under hot water to thaw slightly.

8 oz	penne, ziti OR other tubular pasta	250 g
2 tbsp	soft margarine	25 mL
2 tbsp	minced onion	25 mL
2 tbsp	all-purpose flour	25 mL
1 2/3 cup	low-fat milk	400 mL
1 cup	thawed frozen peas	250 mL
1	can (6 1/2 oz/184 g) tuna, (packed in water) drained	1
1/3 cup	chopped fresh parsley OR dill OR basil	75 mL
1/3 cup	chopped scallions	75 mL
1/4 cup	freshly grated Parmesan cheese	50 mL
	Hot pepper sauce	

In large pot of boiling water, cook pasta until tender but firm. Drain and return to pot.

Meanwhile, in saucepan, melt margarine over medium heat; add onion and cook until tender. Stir in flour and cook for a few seconds. Gradually whisk in milk and bring to simmer, stirring constantly until simmering and thickened.

Add peas, tuna (broken into chunks), parsley, scallions, cheese, and hot pepper sauce. Pour over pasta and stir gently to mix. Serve immediately.

Microwave Method: Cook pasta as above. In microwaveable bowl or 4-cup (1 L) measure, microwave margarine and onion at Medium-high (70%) power for 1 minute or until onion is tender. Stir in flour; gradually whisk in milk. Microwave at High power for 3 to 5 minutes or until boiling and thickened, whisking after each minute. Add remaining ingredients and mix with pasta.

Makes 4 servings (1 1/2 cups/375 mL each).

Pasta with Salmon Cream Sauce
Follow recipe for Pasta with Tuna Cream Sauce, but substitute 1 cup (250 mL) cooked salmon or 1 can (7 1/2 oz/213 g) for tuna. If using canned salmon, reduce milk to 1 1/3 cups (325 mL) and include juices from can.

PER SERVING

Calories		439
g	total fat	10
g	saturated fat	4
g	fibre	4

GOOD: Vitamin A, Thiamin, Riboflavin, Calcium, Iron
EXCELLENT: Niacin

g	protein	28
g	carbohydrate	56
mg	cholesterol	41
mg	sodium	257
mg	potassium	509

PASTA WITH SHRIMP, ZUCCHINI AND MUSHROOMS

Pasta picks up the delicate shrimp flavor in this wonderful, light dish. I make it with any kind of pasta and like to add some fresh herbs such as basil or dill. (Pictured opposite page 154.)

When entertaining, you can cook pasta a few hours in advance; drain, rinse under cold water, then let stand covered in cold water. Just before serving, reheat in boiling water for 1 or 2 minutes, then add sauce.

1 lb	pasta (penne OR rigatoni)	500 g
3 tbsp	olive oil OR soft margarine	45 mL
4	small (7-inch/18 cm) zucchini, julienned	4
1/2 lb	mushrooms, sliced	250 g
2 lb	large raw shrimp, peeled and deveined	1 kg
3	cloves garlic, minced	3
1	large tomato, diced	1
1/2 cup	chopped fresh parsley	125 mL
1/4 cup	freshly grated Parmesan cheese	50 mL
2 tbsp	lemon juice	25 mL
	Salt and pepper	

For the most flavorful shrimp, buy medium to large raw shrimp in the shell. Cook in simmering water until pink; cool, then remove the shell. Leaving the shell on while cooking adds flavor to the shrimp.

In large pot of boiling water, cook pasta until tender but firm; drain and return to pot.

Meanwhile in large nonstick skillet, heat 1 tbsp (15 mL) of the oil over high heat; stir-fry zucchini and mushrooms until tender-crisp, about 3 minutes. Transfer to bowl.

In skillet, heat remaining oil over high heat; cook shrimp and garlic, stirring, for 3 minutes or until shrimp is opaque. Add tomato and cook for 1 minute.

Add shrimp and zucchini mixtures (including all liquids) to pot with hot pasta. Add parsley, cheese, lemon juice; toss to mix. Season with salt and pepper to taste.

Makes 8 servings.

PER SERVING		
Calories		376
g	total fat	9
g	saturated fat	2
g	fibre	4

GOOD: Niacin, Iron

g	protein	25
g	carbohydrate	50
mg	cholesterol	90
mg	sodium	195
mg	potassium	445

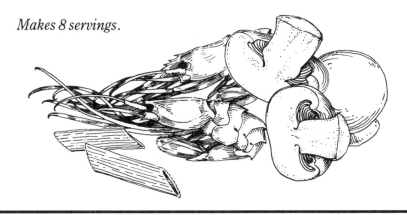

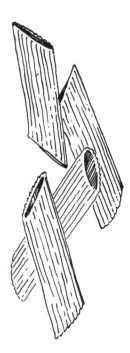

PENNE WITH TOMATO, BLACK OLIVE AND FETA

This is one of my favorite pasta dishes to make in the fall when tomatoes are at their best. (Pictured opposite.)

1 lb	penne OR fusilli OR other short pasta	500 g
1 tbsp	olive oil	15 mL
1 tsp	minced garlic	5 mL
4	large tomatoes, cut in wedges	4
1/3 cup	black olives, halved	75 mL
1/2 cup	crumbled feta cheese	125 mL
1/2 cup	chopped fresh parsley	125 mL
2 tbsp	chopped fresh basil OR 2 tsp (10 mL) dried	25 mL
1/4 cup	freshly grated Parmesan cheese	50 mL

In large pot of boiling water, cook pasta until tender but firm; drain and return to pot to keep warm.

Meanwhile, in large nonstick skillet, heat oil over medium heat; stir in garlic. Add tomatoes and cook, stirring, for 3 minutes or until heated through.

Transfer to pot with drained pasta; add olives, feta cheese, parsley, and basil; toss gently to mix.

Sprinkle each serving with Parmesan.

Makes 4 main-course servings.

PER SERVING

Calories		609
g	total fat	15
g	saturated fat	6
g	fibre	7

GOOD: Thiamin
EXCELLENT: Vitamins A and C, Riboflavin, Niacin, Calcium, Iron

g	protein	23
g	carbohydrate	96
mg	cholesterol	32
mg	sodium	561
mg	potassium	698

Penne with Italian Sausage, Tomato and Herbs

This is a dish that often comes to mind when I stop at the store at 6:00 p.m. wondering what to cook for dinner. I like hot Italian sausage or a Macedonia type; for a less spicy version, use sweet Italian sausage or some of each. I usually chop the onions and garlic in the food processor, then while they are cooking, whirl the tomatoes in the processor. (Pictured opposite page 154.)

1 lb	hot Italian sausage	500 g
1 lb	penne OR corkscrew-shaped pasta	500 g
1 tsp	vegetable oil	5 mL
1	large onion, chopped	1
3	cloves garlic, minced	3
1	can (28 oz) tomatoes (undrained), coarsely chopped	1
2 tsp	dried basil	10 mL
1 tsp	dried oregano	5 mL
1/2 cup	chopped fresh parsley	125 mL
	Pepper	
2 tbsp	freshly grated Parmesan cheese (optional)	25 mL

In skillet, cook sausage over medium heat until no longer pink in centre, about 15 to 20 minutes. Drain well; cut into thin round slices.

Meanwhile, in large pot of boiling water, cook pasta until tender but firm; drain and return to pot.

In nonstick pan, heat oil over medium heat; cook onion until tender, about 5 minutes. Add garlic, tomatoes, basil and oregano; simmer uncovered for 10 minutes. Add cooked sausage. Pour over pasta; toss to mix. Sprinkle with parsley, pepper to taste, and Parmesan (if using); toss again.

Makes 6 servings.

Pasta with Shrimp and Tomatoes

Follow instructions for Penne with Italian Sausage, Tomato and Herbs, but substitute 1 lb (500 g) large cooked shrimp for the sausage, or use 1/2 lb (250 g) each cooked shrimp and sausage. Add shrimp to tomato mixture when adding cooked sausage.

PER SERVING

Calories		480
g	total fat	15
g	saturated fat	4
g	fibre	5

GOOD: Vitamin C, Iron
EXCELLENT: Thiamin, Niacin

g	protein	21
g	carbohydrate	66
mg	cholesterol	38
mg	sodium	671
mg	potassium	679

Harvest Vegetable Curry (p. 171)

30-MINUTE DINNER
Spicy Thai Noodles with
  Vegetables
Sliced Tomatoes and/or
  Cucumbers
Peaches or Plums

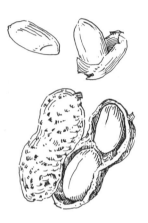

Spicy Thai Noodles with Vegetables (Pad Thai)

A common everyday dish in Thailand, this wonderful noodle recipe is from Karen Barnaby, Toronto caterer and Thai cooking teacher. Pad Thai has many versions, often with shrimp or stir-fried meat or chicken. Rice noodles are available at many supermarkets; choose the flat rice noodles jantaboon. *If these aren't available, use Chinese rice noodles or vermicelli, or even Italian capellini.*

8 oz	flat rice noodles	250 g
1 tbsp	vegetable oil	15 mL
2 tsp	minced fresh garlic	10 mL
2 cups	thinly sliced cabbage	500 mL
1	medium carrot, cut in julienne strips	1
2	eggs, lightly beaten	2
3 cups	bean sprouts	750 mL
1 cup	julienned green onions	250 mL
1/4 cup	chopped fresh coriander (optional)	50 mL
1/4 cup	chopped peanuts	50 mL

Seasoning Sauce:

3 tbsp	fish sauce (*nam pla* OR Thai fish sauce)* OR 2 tbsp (25 mL) rice vinegar	50 mL
1/4 cup	ketchup	50 mL
2 tbsp	water	25 mL
2 tbsp	molasses	25 mL
2 tbsp	reduced-sodium soy sauce	25 mL
1 tsp	granulated sugar	5 mL
1/4 tsp	crushed red pepper flakes	1 mL

Cover rice noodles in hot water; soak for 20 minutes. Drain well.

   Seasoning Sauce: In small bowl, combine fish sauce, ketchup, water, molasses, soy sauce, sugar and hot pepper flakes; set aside.

   In large nonstick skillet, heat oil over medium-high heat; stir in garlic, then cabbage and carrot. Stir-fry for 5 minutes or until vegetables are tender-crisp. Push vegetables to side of pan; pour in eggs and stir to scramble.

   Add drained noodles and sauce; reduce heat to medium and

stir-fry until noodles soften about 4 minutes. Add 2 cups (500 mL) of the bean sprouts and green onions; stir until mixed and heated through. Transfer to serving platter or individual plates. Sprinkle with coriander (if using), peanuts and remaining bean sprouts.

Makes 5 main-course servings, 8 side-dish servings.

Variations: Before adding eggs, add 1 cup (250 mL) chopped raw chicken or pork and/or 1 cup (250 mL) cooked or raw shrimp to pan; stir-fry until cooked. Then add eggs and continue as in above recipe.

*Fish sauce is a staple ingredient in Thai cooking. It is available in some supermarkets and most Oriental grocery stores. It keeps on the shelf for at least a year.

PER SERVING	
Calories	**208**
g total fat	**5**
g saturated fat	**1**
g fibre	**2**

EXCELLENT: Vitamin A

g protein	**4**
g carbohydrate	**37**
mg cholesterol	**54**
mg sodium	**242**
mg potassium	**256**

Types of Oriental Noodles

I substitute one for the other in many recipes, (cook according to package directions) and suggest you use whatever is available. Often found at supermarkets and at most Oriental grocery stores.

Rice Noodles or Rice Sticks or Rice Vermicelli:
Dried rice noodles are opaque white in color. Usually in a very thin, angel hair noodle but also available in a variety of shapes and thicknesses. A broad fettuccine type of rice noodle is pictured opposite page 59 in Thai Noodle Salad. To use, soak in cold water for 20 minutes, then add to soups or stir frys. To use in salads, cover in boiling water and let stand for 5 minutes.

Bean Thread or Cellophane Noodles:
These dried translucent noodles are made from mung beans. To use, soak in warm water until softened, then add to soups or stir frys.

Wheat Noodles:
In some areas, these are available fresh as well as dried and come in a variety of shapes from thin noodles to won ton wrappers. The thin noodles are used in Cantonese chow mein; cook in boiling water, about 3 minutes for fresh or 5 minutes for dried.

Mushroom and Sweet Pepper Lasagna

Sweet green peppers and mushrooms make this a delicious variation on an old favorite.

**Italian sausage
lasagna**
*Prepare Mushroom and
Sweet Pepper Lasagna
but add 1 lb (500 g)
Italian sausage (I use
half sweet and half hot
sausage). Omit oil and
cook sausage in
nonstick skillet over
medium-high heat until
firm and nearly cooked
through, about
15 minutes; remove
and cut into thin slices.
Discard fat from pan
and continue cooking
vegetables as in
Mushroom and Sweet
Pepper Lasagna.
Return sausage to pan
and add tomato sauce.*

9	lasagna noodles (1/2 lb/250 g)	9

Tomato Sauce:

2 tsp	vegetable oil	10 mL
1	large onion, chopped	1
1/2 lb	fresh mushrooms, sliced	250 g
3	cloves garlic, minced	3
1/4 cup	chopped fresh parsley	50 mL
1 tsp	each dried basil and oregano	5 mL
1/4 cup	tomato paste	50 mL
1	can (16 oz) tomatoes (undrained)	1
2	sweet red, yellow OR green peppers, coarsely chopped	2
	Salt and pepper	

Filling:

2 cups	low-fat cottage cheese	500 mL
1/3 cup	freshly grated Parmesan cheese	75 mL
1 tsp	dried oregano	5 mL
3 cups	shredded reduced-fat mozzarella cheese (3/4 lb/375 g)	750 mL

Tomato Sauce: In large nonstick skillet, heat oil over medium heat; cook onion and mushrooms for 5 minutes or until tender, stirring often. Add garlic, parsley, basil, oregano, tomato paste and tomatoes, mashing with potato masher to break up tomatoes; simmer, uncovered, for 10 minutes. Add sweet peppers; simmer for 10 minutes or until sauce is thickened. Season with salt and pepper to taste.

Meanwhile, in large pot of boiling water, cook noodles for 8 to 10 minutes or until tender but firm. Drain under cold running water and set aside in single layer on dampened tea towel.

Filling: Combine cottage cheese, half of the Parmesan, and the oregano; mix well.

Assembly: In 13- × 9-inch (3.5 L) baking dish, spread 1 cup (250 mL) tomato sauce over bottom. Top with layer of noodles. Cover with half of the cottage cheese mixture, then one-third of the mozzarella cheese and one-third of the remaining sauce. Add another layer of noodles; spread with remaining cottage cheese mixture. Layer with half of the remaining mozzarella, then half of the sauce and final layer of noodles. Top with remaining sauce and mozzarella, then Parmesan. (Lasagna can be prepared to this point, covered and refrigerated for up to 1 day. Add 15 minutes to baking time.)

Bake, covered, in 350°F (180°C) oven for 30 minutes. Uncover and bake for 10 to 15 minutes longer or until hot and bubbly. Remove from oven and let cool for 5 minutes before serving.

Makes 8 servings.

PER SERVING

Calories		322
g	total fat	11
g	saturated fat	6
g	fibre	3

GOOD: Vitamin A, Riboflavin, Iron
EXCELLENT: Vitamin C, Niacin, Calcium

g	protein	25
g	carbohydrate	33
mg	cholesterol	31
mg	sodium	623
mg	potassium	528

Vegetarian Lasagna
Follow recipe for Family Favorite Lasagna, but omit beef (and egg if desired). Instead, in a nonstick pan, heat 1 tbsp (15 mL) vegetable oil over medium heat; add 8 cups (2 L) shredded unpeeled zucchini and 3/4 lb (375 g) coarsely chopped mushrooms along with onions and garlic. Cook until tender. Continue with recipe.

PER SERVING	
Calories	**389**
g total fat	**13**
g saturated fat	**7**
g fibre	**3**

GOOD: Vitamins A and C, Thiamin, Iron
EXCELLENT: Calcium, Riboflavin, Niacin

g protein	**31**
g carbohydrate	**36**
mg cholesterol	**73**
mg sodium	**617**
mg potassium	**656**

PER SERVING	
vegetarian (with egg)	
Calories	**352**
g total fat	**11**
g saturated fat	**5**
g fibre	**5**

GOOD: Vitamin A, Vitamin C, Iron
EXCELLENT: Niacin, Calcium, Riboflavin

g protein	**25**
g carbohydrate	**41**
mg cholesterol	**52**
mg sodium	**599**
mg potassium	**913**

FAMILY FAVORITE LASAGNA

This is your classic lasagna made as healthy as possible by using lean beef, tomato paste (not tomato sauce, because it is higher in sodium), 2% cottage cheese (not ricotta or cream cheese), low-fat or part-skim mozzarella (not regular mozzarella or Cheddar) to keep sodium fat at a minimum.

3/4 lb	lean ground beef	375 g
2	onions, chopped	2
2	cloves garlic, minced	2
1	can (16 oz) tomatoes (undrained)	1
1 cup	water	250 mL
1	can (6 oz) tomato paste	1
2 tsp	dried oregano	10 mL
1 tsp	dried basil	5 mL
	Pepper	
9	lasagna noodles	9
2 cups	low-fat cottage cheese	500 mL
2 cups	shredded reduced-fat mozzarella cheese	500 mL
1	egg, lightly beaten	1
1/2 cup	freshly grated Parmesan cheese	125 mL

In large nonstick skillet or Dutch oven, cook beef over medium heat for about 5 minutes or until browned, breaking up with fork; pour off fat. Add onions and garlic; cook for 3 to 5 minutes or until softened. Add tomatoes, breaking up with fork. Add water, tomato paste, oregano and basil; bring to boil. Reduce heat to medium-low and simmer uncovered and stirring occasionally, for 20 minutes or until mixture has spaghetti sauce consistency. Season with pepper to taste. If too acidic, add 1 tsp (5 mL) granulated sugar to taste.

In large pot of boiling water, cook lasagna noodles for 10 to 12 minutes or until tender but firm. Drain and rinse under cold water; drain well.

Combine cottage cheese, mozzarella, egg and half of the Parmesan.

Cover bottom of 13- × 9-inch (3.5 L) baking dish sparingly with some of the tomato sauce; top with layer of lasagna noodles. Cover with half of the cheese mixture. Repeat with remaining sauce, noodles and cheeses to make 3 layers of each; then a final layer of tomato sauce. Sprinkle with remaining Parmesan cheese.

Bake, uncovered, in 350°F (180°C) oven for 45 minutes or until hot and bubbly. Remove from oven and let stand for 5 to 10 minutes before serving.   *Makes 8 servings.*

PASTA WITH SWEET PEPPERS, CHEESE AND BASIL

This colorful pasta dish makes a great supper: it will make four servings (unless you have teenage boys!) if you serve it with a vegetable such as broccoli or green beans, a salad and French bread.

1/2 lb	pasta (rigatoni OR fusilli)	250 g
1 tsp	olive oil	5 mL
1	small onion, minced	1
1	clove garlic, minced	1
1	each medium sweet red and yellow pepper, cut in strips	1
1	large tomato, chopped	1
1/2 cup	finely shredded fresh basil OR 2 tsp (10 mL) dried leaves	125 mL
1 cup	crumbled feta cheese (4 oz/120 g)	250 mL
6	black olives (preferably Kalamata OR Greek type), sliced	6

In large pot of boiling water, cook pasta until tender but firm; drain and return to pot.

Meanwhile, in large nonstick skillet, heat oil over medium heat; cook onion and garlic for 3 minutes. Add red and yellow peppers; cook for 3 minutes, stirring often. Add tomato; cook until peppers are tender, about 2 minutes. Add to hot pasta along with basil, cheese and olives; toss well.

Makes 3 servings.

When using dried herbs, I never use the ground or powdered form. The dried leaf form has much better flavor and appearance than the ground. For the most flavor, crush the leaves by rubbing them between your palms before adding to the recipe.

PER SERVING

Calories		**435**
g	total fat	**12**
g	saturated fat	**6**
g	fibre	**5**

GOOD: Niacin, Calcium, Iron
EXCELLENT: Vitamin C, Riboflavin

g	protein	**16**
g	carbohydrate	**65**
mg	cholesterol	**35**
mg	sodium	**520**
mg	potassium	**421**

KIDS' EASY MACARONI AND CHEESE WITH VEGETABLES

This is a quick and easy version of pasta that most children will enjoy.

1 cup	macaroni OR other small pasta (1/2 lb/ 250 g)	250 mL
2	medium carrots, thinly sliced	2
1 cup	frozen peas	250 mL
1/3 cup	low-fat milk	75 mL
2 tbsp	cream cheese	25 mL
1/2 tsp	dried basil OR 2 tbsp (25 mL) chopped fresh	2 mL
1/2 cup	shredded reduced-fat mozzarella OR Cheddar cheese	125 mL
1 tbsp	freshly grated Parmesan cheese	15 mL
1	scallion, chopped	1
	Salt and pepper	

In large pot of boiling water, cook pasta until tender but firm.

Meanwhile, steam or boil carrots for 4 minutes. Add peas and cook until carrots are tender-crisp, about 3 minutes. Drain and return to pot.

In small saucepan over medium heat or in microwave, heat milk until steaming. Whisk in cream cheese until smooth; stir in basil. Add to pasta along with vegetables, mozzarella and Parmesan cheeses and scallions; toss to mix. Season with salt and pepper to taste.

Makes 3 servings, 1 1/2 cups (375 mL) each.

Variation: Prepare above recipe except instead of cream cheese whisk 1 egg into 1/3 cup (75 mL) cold milk; pour over hot cooked macaroni and stir over low heat for 1 minute. Add mozzarella and vegetables; stir and cook for another minute or until cheese has melted and sauce thickened slightly.

PER SERVING
with Cream Cheese

Calories	303
g total fat	8
g saturated fat	5
g fibre	5

GOOD Niacin, Calcium
EXCELLENT: Vitamin A

g protein	14
g carbohydrate	43
mg cholesterol	25
mg sodium	243
mg potassium	407

PER SERVING
with Eggs

Calories	298
g total fat	7
g saturated fat	3
g fibre	5

GOOD: Thiamin, Riboflavin, Niacin, Calcium
EXCELLENT: Vitamin A

g protein	16
g carbohydrate	42
mg cholesterol	88
mg sodium	232
mg potassium	371

Tomato Ham Pasta Dinner for One

Any shaped pasta can be used, but for a more interesting looking dish, try some of the unique shapes such as farfalle or radiatori. Use the remaining bunch of broccoli in a stir-fry, a soup or an omelette.

1 cup	farfalle (bow-tie shape pasta) (2 oz/50 g)	250 mL
1 cup	broccoli florets	250 mL
1 tsp	vegetable oil	5 mL
1	small tomato, coarsely chopped	1
Half	clove garlic minced	Half
1 tbsp	chopped fresh basil OR 1/4 tsp (1 mL) dried	15 mL
1	thin slice ham OR smoked turkey (1 oz/ 30 g), cut in strips	1
1 tbsp	freshly grated Parmesan cheese	15 mL
	Salt and pepper	

In pot of boiling water, cook pasta until tender but firm, about 10 minutes. About 2 minutes before pasta is cooked, add broccoli; cook until tender-crisp; drain.

Meanwhile, in nonstick skillet, heat oil over medium-high heat: cook tomato, garlic, basil and ham, stirring often, until tomato is heated through, about 2 minutes. Pour over drained pasta and broccoli; toss to mix. Sprinkle with Parmesan. Season with salt and pepper to taste.

Makes 1 serving.

PER SERVING

Calories		386
g	total fat	10
g	saturated fat	2
g	fibre	7

EXCELLENT: Vitamins A and C, Thiamin, Riboflavin, Niacin, Calcium, Iron

mg	protein	21
g	carbohydrate	56
mg	cholesterol	20
mg	sodium	515
mg	potassium	690

Favorite Spaghetti

A quick dinner that over the years has been my kids' favorite is this spaghetti with meat sauce. Sometimes I use only tomato paste, other times, crushed tomatoes with added purée, sometimes both tomato paste and tomatoes.

1 lb	extra lean ground beef*	500 g
2	onions, chopped	2
1	large clove garlic, minced	1
1	can (6 oz) tomato paste	1
1	can (28 oz) tomatoes	1
1 cup	water	250 mL
2 tsp	dried oregano	10 mL
1 tsp	dried basil	5 mL
1/2 tsp	dried thyme	2 mL
1/4 tsp	pepper	1 mL
1 lb	spaghetti	500 g
2 tbsp	freshly grated Parmesan cheese	25 mL

In large heavy skillet, brown beef over medium heat; pour off all fat. Stir in onions and garlic; cook, stirring occasionally until softened.

Stir in tomato paste, tomatoes (breaking up with back of spoon), water, oregano, basil, thyme and pepper; bring to boil. Reduce heat and simmer for 10 minutes. Add water if too thick. Taste and adjust seasoning if desired.

Meanwhile, in large pot of boiling water, cook spaghetti until tender but firm; drain and arrange on plates; spoon sauce over each serving. Sprinkle with Parmesan cheese.

Makes 6 servings.

*Nutrient figures are based on using extra lean ground beef. Buy this when it is on special. At other times, unless you are on a fat-restricted diet, buy lean or even regular ground beef and be sure to drain off all fat before adding onion.

PER SERVING	
Calories	484
g total fat	10
g saturated fat	4
g fibre	5

GOOD: Vitamin A
EXCELLENT: Vitamin C, Thiamin, Riboflavin, Niacin, Iron

g	protein	27
g	carbohydrate	71
mg	cholesterol	39
mg	sodium	314
mg	potassium	962

LIGHTHEARTED FETTUCCINE ALFREDO

This light version of a classic favorite has a surprisingly rich flavor.

1/2 lb	fettuccine OR spaghetti	250 g
1 cup	low-fat cottage cheese	250 mL
1/4 cup	freshly grated Parmesan cheese	50 mL
1/4 cup	low-fat milk	50 mL
1	egg	1
1/4 tsp	nutmeg	1 mL
1/4 tsp	pepper	1 mL
1/2 cup	chopped fresh parsley OR basil	125 mL

In large pot of boiling water, cook fettuccine until tender but firm; drain and return to saucepan.

Meanwhile, in food processor, process cottage cheese until smooth. Add Parmesan cheese, milk, egg, nutmeg and pepper; blend until smooth. Pour into saucepan with hot cooked pasta; cook over medium heat for 1 minute, stirring constantly. Sprinkle with parsley or basil. Serve immediately.

Makes 4 servings.

Variations: Add one or more of the following:
1 cup (250 mL) chopped cooked ham
1 can (7 1/2 oz/220 g) salmon, drained and flaked
1 can (6 1/2 oz/184 g) tuna, drained and flaked
1 cup (250 mL) frozen peas, thawed
1/2 cup (125 mL) kernel corn or chopped green onion
1 cup (250 mL) cooked sliced mushrooms
1 cup (250 mL) cooked julienned carrots, zucchini, sweet peppers
    or leeks
4 cups (1 L) cooked broccoli florets

Compare:
This version of Fettuccine Alfredo uses milk and cottage cheese instead of butter and cream.

Compare the grams of fat per serving:

This version: 5
With 1/4 cup/50 mL butter instead of milk: 16
With 1 cup/250 mL whipping cream instead of cottage cheese: 24

PER SERVING	
Calories	312
g total fat	5
g saturated fat	2
g fibre	2

GOOD: Thiamin
EXCELLENT: Riboflavin, Niacin

g	protein	19
g	carbohydrate	46
mg	cholesterol	64
mg	sodium	349
mg	potassium	251

Here are some other pasta and noodle recipes to try:

Skewered Tortellini (page 25)
Thai Noodle Salad (page 63)
Garden Pasta Salad with Basil Dressing (page 76)
Hamburger and Noodle Skillet Supper (page 117)
Spicy Beef Chow Mein (page 119)

CHINESE NOODLES WITH MUSHROOMS AND PORK

Chinese vermicelli, or rice noodles, are available at many supermarkets and Chinese grocery stores and cook in just three minutes. If not available, use the thinnest noodles you can find. Large regular fresh mushrooms can be used instead of dried. If you don't have carrots on hand, use any other colorful vegetable. Ground beef, lamb or turkey can be used or, for a vegetarian dish, omit all meat.

6	dried Chinese mushrooms	6
6 oz	Chinese vermicelli OR rice noodles	170 g
1/2 lb	lean ground pork OR beef	250 g
1 cup	thin carrot strips	250 mL
1 tbsp	minced gingerroot	15 mL
6	scallions, minced	6

Seasoning Sauce:

1/3 cup	chicken stock	75 mL
1/4 cup	rice vinegar	50 mL
1 tbsp	sesame oil	15 mL
1 tsp	reduced-sodium soy sauce	5 mL
1/4 tsp	crushed red pepper flakes	1 mL

Cover mushrooms with hot water; let stand for 5 minutes or until softened. Remove mushrooms and cut in strips, discarding tough stems.

Seasoning Sauce: In small bowl, combine chicken stock, vinegar, sesame oil, soy sauce and red pepper flakes; set aside.

Cook noodles according to package directions or in boiling water until tender, about 3 minutes; drain.

In nonstick skillet over high heat, stir-fry pork for 1 minute or until almost browned, breaking up with back of spoon; pour off any fat. Add carrots and ginger; stir-fry for 2 minutes or until carrots are tender-crisp. Stir in mushrooms, then noodles, then seasoning sauce, stirring until mixed well and heated through, 1 to 2 minutes. Transfer to serving platter and sprinkle with scallions.

Makes 4 servings.

Variation: Use medium ground beef or lamb or ground chicken or turkey instead of pork.

PER SERVING	
Calories	**337**
g total fat	**11**
g saturated fat	**3**
g fibre	**5**

EXCELLENT: Vitamin A, Thiamin, Riboflavin, Niacin

g	protein	**17**
g	carbohydrate	**46**
mg	cholesterol	**31**
mg	sodium	**505**
mg	potassium	**489**

GRAINS, LEGUMES AND MEATLESS MAIN DISHES

GRAINS

Canada's latest guidelines for healthy eating recommend including more complex-carbohydrate foods (such as grains) in our diet so that we will eat less fat and more fibre. The less refined the grains are, the better they are for us. In general, grains are a good source of complex carbohydrates, fibre and protein and supply us with iron, calcium, phosphorous and B vitamins.

Here is a general guide for cooking grains. When you have package directions, follow them. As with beans, the cooking time will vary depending on the length of storage. Grains stored for a longer time will take longer to cook. Some grains (such as bulgur) come in a variety of sizes. The smaller the size — the faster the cooking time.

Grain and Use	Method of Cooking
CORN Corn Meal: Tortillas, dumplings, stuffings, bread, polenta, cereal, muffins.	For cereal: Add 1 cup (250 mL) cornmeal to 4 cups (1 L) boiling water. Cover. Simmer 25-30 minutes.
WHEAT Bulgur: Soups, pilafs, stuffing, tabbouleh, salads, cereal. Served like rice.	Add 1 cup (250 mL) bulgur to 2 cups (500 mL) boiling water. Cover. Simmer 25-35 minutes. For salads, cover bulgur with hot water and soak 1 hour. Drain well.
Couscous: With meats and poultry, stews, lamb. Served like rice.	Follow package directions for amount of liquid or add 1 cup (250 mL) couscous to 1 1/2 cups (375 mL) boiling water. Cover. Remove from heat and let stand 5 minutes.
Wheat germ: Crumb coatings; replaces nuts in cakes and cookies. Add to muffins, breads, pancakes.	Follow package instructions or individual recipes.
Cracked wheat: Cereals, puddings, breads, salads. Served like rice.	For cereal: Add 1 cup (250 mL) cracked wheat to 2 cups (500 mL) boiling water. Cover. Simmer 30-40 minutes.
Wheat berries: Pilafs, salads, baking, Swiss muesli.	Add 1 cup (250 mL) wheat berries to 2 cups (500 mL) boiling water. Cover. Simmer for 60-90 minutes.
Kasha (toasted buckwheat): Pilafs, stuffings, breads.	Add 1 cup (250 mL) kasha to 2 cups (500 mL) boiling water. Cover. Simmer 10-15 minutes.
OATS Oat bran: Muffins, cereal, cookies.	For cereal: Follow package directions or add 1 cup (250 mL) oat bran to 3 cups (750 mL) boiling water. Cook 2 minutes. Remove from heat. Cover and let stand 2-4 minutes.
Rolled oats: Cereal, granola, muesli, muffins, cakes, cookies, breads.	For cereal: Add 1 1/3 cups (325 mL) rolled oats to 2 cups (500 mL) boiling water. Follow package directions for cooking time.
RICE White rice: Desserts, pilafs, risottos, stuffing, salads, soups, curries, casseroles or with meats.	Add 1 cup (250 mL) rice to 2 cups (500 mL) boiling water. Cover. Simmer 15-20 minutes.
Brown rice: Pilafs, stuffing, salads, soups, casseroles, or with meats.	Rinse rice. Add 1 cup (250 mL) brown rice to 2 cups (500 mL) boiling water. Cover. Simmer 45-60 minutes.
Basmati rice: With meats, casseroles.	Rinse rice. Add 1 cup rice (250 mL) to 1 1/2 cups (375 mL) boiling water. Simmer 15-20 minutes.

Arborio rice: Risotto	Add 1 cup (250 mL) arborio to 2 cups (500 mL) boiling water. Cover. Simmer 18-20 minutes.
Wild rice (not a rice but treated like one): Curries, pilafs, stuffings, salads, often mixed with other rices.	Rinse. Add 1 cup (250 mL) wild rice to 3 cups (750 mL) boiling water. Cover. Simmer 45-60 minutes.
Red rice: Desserts, molds, salads, curries.	Rinse. Add 1 cup (250 mL) red rice to 1 3/4 cups (425 mL) boiling water. Cover. Simmer 18-20 minutes.
Black rice: Puddings, Oriental dishes.	Rinse. Add 1 cup (250 mL) black rice to 1 3/4 cups (425 mL) boiling water. Cover. Simmer 35-40 minutes.
Wehani rice: Pilafs or with meat.	Follow package instructions or rinse and add 1 cup (250 mL) wehani rice to 2 cups (500 mL) boiling water. Cover. Simmer 30 minutes.
OTHER Pearl barley: Soups, hot cereal, stews, pilafs, stuffings.	Add 1 cup (250 mL) pearl barley to 2 cups (500 mL) boiling water. Cover. Simmer 45 minutes.
Quinoa: Cereals, pilafs, soups, desserts, stuffing, salads.	Rinse. Add 1 cup (250 mL) quinoa to 2 cups (500 mL) water. Bring to boil. Cover. Simmer 12-15 minutes.
Millet: Pilafs, soups, bread, stuffings, puddings.	Add 1 cup (250 mL) millet to 2 cups (500 mL) boiling water. Cover. Simmer 30-40 minutes.

LEGUMES

Dried Beans, Peas and Lentils

Legumes (which are the seeds of such plants as the lentil, garden pea, lima bean or kidney bean) are a source of protein almost as good as meat. If you serve them with a grain or bread, you have a complete source of protein. Legumes are also excellent sources of B vitamins, iron, other minerals and a very high source of dietary fibre. They are high in complex carbohydrates and except for soybeans, low in fat.

Preparation:
Before cooking, dried legumes (except lentils and split peas) should be soaked to return moisture to them, to reduce cooking time and save vitamins and minerals and to help reduce flatulence. Rinse and sort before soaking to remove any grit or pebbles.

Long soak:
Cover dried beans with 3 to 4 times their volume of water and let stand for 4 to 8 hours or overnight. Drain and cook as directed.

Quick soak:
Cover dried beans with 3 to 4 times their volume of water; bring to a boil and simmer for 2 minutes. Remove from heat and let stand 1 hour; drain and cook as directed.

Cooking:
In large saucepan, cover drained, soaked beans or lentils with 2 1/2 times their volume of fresh water. Don't add salt. Bring to a boil; reduce heat and simmer, covered, until tender. See chart for cooking times. Drain if necessary.

Yield:
1 cup (250 mL) dried beans or lentils yields 2 to 2 1/2 cups (500 to 625 mL) cooked.

Cooking times for Beans, Peas and Lentils
Adapted from The Food Advisory Division of Agriculture Canada

	Soaking Method	*Suggested Cooking Time*
Black (turtle) beans	quick or overnight soak	1 3/4 hours
Cranberry (roman) beans	quick or overnight soak	45 minutes
Great northern beans	quick soak	60 minutes
	overnight soak	75 minutes
Kidney beans		
red	quick or overnight	60 minutes
white	quick soak	40 minutes
	overnight soak	60 minutes
Lentils		
green	no soaking	30 minutes
red	no soaking	10 minutes
Lima Beans		
large	quick soak	20 minutes
	overnight soak	40 minutes
small	quick or overnight	35 minutes
Navy (pea) Beans	quick soak	90 minutes
	overnight soak	50 minutes
Peas		
whole yellow	quick soak	60 minutes
	overnight soak	40 minutes
split yellow	no soaking	75 minutes
split green	no soaking	75 minutes
Pinto beans	quick or overnight	45 minutes
Small red beans	quick soak	50 minutes
	overnight soak	40 minutes
Soy Beans	quick soak	3 1/2 hours
	overnight soak	4 hours
Yellow-eyed beans	quick soak	60 minutes
	overnight soak	50 minutes

Reducing Gas from Beans:
Apparently the more you eat beans, the less you'll be bothered by flatulence. However, let your body become used to beans gradually.

In the past, some recipes recommended using the soaking liquid because of its possible nutrient content. Now this isn't recommended because of the flatulence associated with using the soaking water. In fact, if you really want to reduce flatulence, it's now recommended that you change the soaking liquid a few times, drain the cooking water after 30 minutes, add fresh water and cook until beans are tender. Thoroughly cooked beans will reduce the possibility of gas. Rinse beans after cooking. Drain canned beans and rinse well before using.

Harvest Vegetable Curry

Serve this colorful and flavorful main-course vegetable dish over couscous, bulgur or brown rice. The chick-peas and grain complement each other to form complete protein. (Pictured on cover.)

FALL DINNER
Tomato Slices with Chèvre and Basil (p. 78)
Harvest Vegetable Curry
Peach Shortcake (p. 219)

If you don't have a large steamer, cook vegetables in as little water as possible. Sometimes I microwave the carrots, squash and zucchini together, covered, on High power for 6 minutes, then add garbanzo beans and microwave for another minute. I simmer the broccoli, onion and sweet pepper together in a small amount of water for 5 minutes or until tender-crisp and drain. Then I toss all the vegetables with curry sauce mixture.

2	carrots, sliced	2
2 cups	peeled cubed squash (about 1-inch/ 2.5 cm pieces)	500 mL
2 cups	broccoli florets	500 mL
1	sweet red pepper, cut in strips	1
1	small (6-inch/15 cm) yellow zucchini, cut in wedges	1
1	red onion, cut in wedges	1
1 cup	cooked garbanzo beans	250 mL
1 tbsp	olive OR vegetable oil	15 mL
1 tbsp	curry powder	15 mL
2 tbsp	minced gingerroot	25 mL
1 tsp	cumin	5 mL
3	cloves garlic, minced	3
1/4 tsp	crushed red pepper flakes (optional)	1 mL
1/2 cup	chicken OR vegetable stock OR water	125 mL
2 tbsp	lemon juice	25 mL
3 cups	hot cooked brown rice OR couscous OR bulgur	750 mL
2 tbsp	chopped fresh coriander OR parsley	25 mL

Steam carrots and squash for 5 minutes; add broccoli, red pepper, zucchini and red onion; steam for 5 minutes. Add chick-peas; steam for 3 to 5 minutes or until all vegetables are tender-crisp.

Meanwhile, in small saucepan, heat oil over medium heat; cook curry powder, gingerroot, cumin, garlic and hot pepper flakes (if using), stirring often, for 2 minutes. Add stock and lemon juice; simmer, uncovered, for 2 minutes.

Toss vegetables with sauce. Serve over hot rice or couscous. Sprinkle with coriander or parsley.

Makes 6 main-course servings.

PER SERVING		
Calories		**263**
g	total fat	**4**
g	saturated fat	**trace**
g	fibre	**8**

GOOD: Thiamin, Niacin, Iron
EXCELLENT: Vitamins A and C

g	protein	**8**
g	carbohydrate	**50**
mg	cholesterol	**0**
mg	sodium	**386**
mg	potassium	**708**

Speedy Lentil and Bean Casserole

QUICK DINNER FROM THE PANTRY

*Speedy Lentil and Bean
  Casserole
Corn or Peas
Whole Wheat Toast
Canned Apricots or
  Plums
Cookies*

This is one of the fastest family dinner dishes I know how to make, but even better than that, everyone loves it. Packed with nutrients, high in fibre yet low in fat, canned beans and lentils are quick to prepare. This dish can be seasoned in any number of ways: instead of rosemary you can add either hot pepper flakes, chili, curry or oregano to taste.

*To reduce sodium, use
low-sodium canned
tomatoes. Rinse canned
lentils before using.*

1 tbsp	vegetable oil	15 mL
1	large onion, chopped	1
2	stalks celery, sliced	2
1	can (19 oz) kidney beans, drained and rinsed	1
1	can (15 oz) lentils, drained	1
1	can (16 oz) tomatoes, drained	1
1/2 tsp	dried rosemary OR thyme	2 mL
	Pepper	
1 1/2 cups	shredded reduced-fat Cheddar OR mozzarella cheese	375 mL

In flameproof casserole, heat oil over medium heat; cook onion and celery until onion is softened.

Add beans, lentils, tomatoes, rosemary, and pepper to taste; stir and break up tomatoes with back of spoon. Bring to simmer. Sprinkle with cheese; broil until cheese melts.

Microwave Method: In microwaveable casserole, combine oil, onion and celery; cover and cook at High power for 3 to 4 minutes or until onion is softened. Add beans, lentils, tomatoes (break up with back of spoon), rosemary and pepper to taste; cover and microwave at High power for 5 minutes or until heated through. Sprinkle with cheese and microwave until cheese melts and is bubbly.

Makes 4 servings.

PER SERVING	
Calories	414
g total fat	12
g saturated fat	5
g fibre	15

GOOD: Vitamins A and C, Riboflavin
EXCELLENT: Thiamin, Niacin, Calcium, Iron

g	protein	29
g	carbohydrate	51
mg	cholesterol	25
mg	sodium	1021
mg	potassium	1177

Curried Lentils with Coriander

This is an adaptation of a recipe using a combination of dhal (lentils): black, pink, split and green. I tested the recipe using all green lentils — the flavor is wonderful.

One-half cup (125 mL) of cooked lentils has a very high amount of dietary fibre, 8 grams of protein, no fat and is a good source of iron and niacin.

2 cups	green lentils	500 mL
2 tbsp	vegetable oil	25 mL
2	medium onions, chopped	2
1 tsp	each ginger, coriander, cumin and turmeric	5 mL
1 tsp	minced garlic	5 mL
1/2 tsp	salt	2 mL
3	whole cloves	3
2	whole cardamom	2
1	3-inch (8 cm) stick cinnamon OR 1/2 tsp (2 mL) ground	1
1/4 tsp	crushed red pepper flakes	1 mL
1 cup	chopped tomatoes (fresh OR canned)	250 mL
1/3 cup	chopped scallions (include tops)	75 mL
1/4 cup	chopped fresh coriander	50 mL

Wash lentils in cold water; drain. In saucepan, bring 6 cups (1.5 L) water and lentils to boil; reduce heat, cover and simmer for 20 to 30 minutes or until tender; drain.

Meanwhile in large saucepan over medium heat, combine oil, onions, ginger, coriander, cumin, turmeric, garlic, salt, cloves, cardamom, cinnamon and red pepper flakes; cook for 10 minutes or until onions are softened, stirring frequently.

Add tomatoes and drained lentils; simmer over low heat for 3 minutes. Discard cloves, cardamom and cinnamon stick. Stir in scallions and coriander. Serve hot.

Makes 8 servings, about 1/2 cup (125 mL) each.

PER SERVING		
Calories		207
g	total fat	4
g	saturated fat	**trace**
g	fibre	6

GOOD: Thiamin, Niacin
EXCELLENT: Iron

g	protein	13
g	carbohydrate	31
mg	cholesterol	0
mg	sodium	162
mg	potassium	635

Bean and Vegetable Burritos

My kids really like these. They're easy to prepare, especially if you have some salsa or spicy tomato sauce on hand. Serve with yogurt. Flour tortillas are available in the refrigerated section of most supermarkets.

1 tsp	vegetable oil	5 mL
2	medium onions, chopped	2
3	cloves garlic, minced	3
1	sweet green pepper, chopped	1
1 cup	finely diced zucchini	250 mL
1	large carrot, grated	1
2 tsp	chili powder	10 mL
1 tsp	each dried oregano and cumin	5 mL
1 1/2 cups	Winter Salsa (page 190)	375 mL
1	can (16 oz) refried beans	1
5	10-inch (25 cm) flour tortillas	5
2/3 cup	shredded Cheddar cheese	150 mL

In nonstick skillet, heat oil over medium heat; cook onions, stirring occasionally, for 3 minutes. Add garlic, green pepper, zucchini and carrot; cook, stirring often, for 5 minutes. Stir in chili powder, oregano and cumin.

Stir 2/3 cup (150 mL) of the Winter Salsa into refried beans. Spread about 1/3 cup (75 mL) refried bean mixture in thin layer over each tortilla, leaving about 1-inch (2.5 cm) border; cover with vegetable mixture. Roll up each tortilla and place seam side down in lightly oiled 13- × 9-inch (3.5 L) baking dish.

Bake in 400°F (200°C) oven for 15 minutes. Sprinkle with cheese and bake for 5 minutes longer. Serve with remaining salsa.

Makes 5 servings.

PER SERVING

Calories		310
g	total fat	9
g	saturated fat	4
g	fibre	9

GOOD: Riboflavin, Niacin, Calcium
EXCELLENT: Vitamins A and C, Iron

g	protein	14
g	carbohydrate	45
mg	cholesterol	16
mg	sodium	596
mg	potassium	743

HERE ARE SOME OTHER
RECIPES USING LEGUMES:
Mexican Bean Dip
(page 35)
Jiffy Mexican Burritos
(page 39)
Old-Fashioned Quebec
Pea Soup (page 44)
Smoky Sausage Lentil
Soup (page 46)
Lentil Spinach Soup
with Curried Yogurt
(page 47)
Black Bean and Ham
Soup (page 49)
Beef 'n' Bean
Minestrone (page 53)
Jiffy Bean, Broccoli and
Tomato Chowder
(page 59)
Red Bean Salad with
Feta and Peppers
(page 65)
Lunchtime Lentil Salad
(page 71)
Beef and Vegetable
Chili (page 114)
Pasta e Fagioli
(page 149)

Old-Fashioned Baked Beans

I make these often to have after skiing. Homemade beans are a treat and are great for feeding a crowd. Not to mention being good for us. Sometimes I add a smoked pork hock, but that will increase the fat and sodium so shouldn't be done if you make these often.

1 lb	white pea or navy beans	500 g
2	medium onions, sliced	2
1/4 cup	molasses	50 mL
2 tbsp	tomato paste OR 1/2 cup (125 mL) ketchup	25 mL
1 tbsp	packed brown sugar	15 mL
1 tbsp	vinegar	15 mL
1 tsp	salt	5 mL
1/2 tsp	dry mustard	2 mL
1/4 tsp	black pepper OR red pepper flakes	1 mL
4 cups	hot water	1 L
2	slices bacon, chopped (2 oz/50 g)	2

Rinse beans; discard any discolored ones. In large saucepan, soak beans overnight or quick soak as below; drain. Add water to cover by at least 2 inches (5 cm), bring to boil and simmer for 30 minutes; drain.

In bean pot or 8-cup (2 L) casserole, spread onion slices. Mix molasses, tomato paste, sugar, vinegar, salt, mustard and pepper; pour into casserole. Add drained beans and hot water; sprinkle with bacon.

Cover and bake in 250°F (120°C) oven for 6 hours; uncover and bake for 1 hour longer, adding enough water if necessary to keep beans covered.

Makes 8 servings, about 3/4 cup (175 mL) each.

Instead of soaking overnight:
Quick Soaking Method 1: Place rinsed beans in large saucepan; cover with 2 inches (5 cm) water; bring to a boil. Boil 2 minutes. Remove from heat; cover and let stand 1 hour. Drain and rinse.
Quick Soaking Method 2: Place rinsed beans in large saucepan; cover with 2 inches (5 cm) water; bring to a boil. Boil 10 minutes; drain. Cover with cold water; let soak 30 minutes; drain.

PER SERVING

Calories		251
g	total fat	4
g	saturated fat	1
g	fibre	9

GOOD: Calcium
EXCELLENT: Thiamin, Iron

g	protein	12
g	carbohydrate	43
mg	cholesterol	3
mg	sodium	344
mg	potassium	991

Couscous

A staple in Morocco, couscous is made from semolina wheat and looks like a grain. A quick-cooking variety, which only needs to be soaked in boiling water, is now available in most health food stores and some supermarkets. Follow package directions for amount of liquid to add or, if bought in bulk, the following recipe.

2 cups	chicken stock OR water	500 mL
2 tsp	olive oil	10 mL
1 1/2 cups	quick-cooking couscous*	375 mL
	Salt and pepper	

In saucepan, bring stock and oil to boil; add couscous and salt and pepper to taste. Cover and remove from heat; let stand for 5 minutes. Fluff with fork and serve hot.

Makes 6 servings.

*Almost all couscous sold in supermarkets and health food stores is a quick cooking type.

15-MINUTE SPRING DINNER
*Grilled Lamb Chops
Curried Couscous with
  Currants
Asparagus
Sliced Tomatoes*

Curried Couscous with Currants

Because couscous is so fast and easy to prepare, I serve it often, especially with fish or grilled chicken.

1 1/2 cups	chicken stock OR water*	375 mL
1 1/2 cups	couscous	375 mL
1	onion, minced	1
1/3 cup	currants OR raisins	75 mL
1 tbsp	soft margarine OR olive oil	15 mL
1 tsp	curry powder	5 mL
1/2 tsp	ground cumin OR cardamom OR coriander OR combination	2 mL
	Pepper	

In saucepan, bring chicken stock to boil; add couscous and remove from heat. Cover and let stand for 5 minutes or until grains are tender and liquid is absorbed.

Meanwhile, in saucepan or microwaveable dish cook onion in 1 tbsp (15 mL) water over medium heat or microwave at High power for 1 1/2 minutes or until tender.

Fluff couscous with fork. Add onion, currants or raisins, margarine, curry powder, cumin, and pepper to taste; stir with fork.

Makes 8 servings.

*Follow couscous package directions for amount of liquid, if different from this amount.

PER SERVING	
Calories	124
g total fat	2
g saturated fat	**trace**
g fibre	2
g protein	3
g carbohydrate	24
mg cholesterol	0
mg sodium	16
mg potassium	78

Couscous with Lemon and Fresh Basil

Couscous, available in most supermarkets and health food stores, is made from semolina wheat. It's very easy to prepare. All you need to do is soak it in boiling water for 5 minutes, then add seasonings and serve. It also reheats well.

2 cups	chicken stock*	500 mL
1 tbsp	olive oil	15 mL
1 1/2 cups	couscous	375 mL
2 tbsp	lemon juice	25 mL
1/2 cup	lightly packed chopped fresh basil	125 mL
	Pepper	

In saucepan, bring chicken stock to boil; add oil and couscous. Remove from heat; cover and let stand for 5 minutes or until grains are tender and liquid is absorbed.

Fluff couscous with fork; add lemon juice, and basil. Season with pepper to taste.

Makes 8 servings.

*Follow couscous package directions for amount of liquid, if different from this amount.

PER SERVING	
Calories	120
g total fat	2
g saturated fat	**trace**
g fibre	1
g protein	5
g carbohydrate	19
mg cholesterol	0
mg sodium	262
mg potassium	94

El Paso Pilaf

Tom Ney, food editor, Prevention Magazine, *developed this tasty recipe for Project LEAN, a low-fat educational program that I am involved with.*

2 tsp	olive oil	10 mL
1/2 cup	chopped onion	125 mL
1	can (15 oz) red kidney beans, drained	1
2 1/2 cups	chicken stock OR water	625 mL
1 cup	long grain rice	250 mL
1 cup	fresh OR frozen corn	250 mL
1 cup	chunky salsa	250 mL
1/4 cup	dry green lentils	50 mL
1/4 cup	chopped sweet red OR green pepper	50 mL
1/2 tsp	chili powder	2 mL
1	clove garlic, minced	1
12	thick slices tomato (optional)	12

In large saucepan, heat oil over medium heat; cook onion for 5 minutes or until tender but not browned. Add beans, chicken stock, rice, corn, salsa, lentils, sweet pepper, chili powder and garlic; bring to a boil.

Reduce heat, cover and simmer for 20 to 25 minutes or until rice and lentils are tender and most of the liquid is absorbed. Serve over tomato slices (if using).

Makes 6 servings.

EASY FALL DINNER
*Curried Pumpkin Soup (p. 55)
El Paso Pilaf
Low-Cal Coleslaw (p. 72)
Plum and Nectarine Cobbler (p. 228)*

If you are on a sodium-restricted diet, use water instead of stock and rinse beans before using.

PER SERVING

Calories		**259**
g	total fat	**3**
g	saturated fat	**trace**
g	fibre	**6**

GOOD: Thiamin, Niacin, Iron

g	protein	**11**
g	carbohydrate	**48**
mg	cholesterol	**0**
mg	sodium	**498**
mg	potassium	**521**

MAKE-AHEAD RISOTTO WITH FRESH BASIL AND RADICCHIO

This risotto-style recipe is great for entertaining since it can be prepared a few hours in advance and reheated. Usually risotto is prepared just before serving and is made with arborio or a short-grain rice; when preparing it in advance use a converted long-grain rice. I serve this as a first course or as part of a main course with a roast or chicken. If radicchio isn't available, use wispy, thin slices of red cabbage.

1/3 cup	olive oil	75 mL
2	onions, chopped	2
4 cups	long-grain converted rice	1 L
1 1/2 cups	dry white wine	375 mL
9 cups	simmering chicken stock*	2.250 L
2 cups	thinly sliced radicchio	500 mL
1 cup	chopped fresh parsley	250 mL
1 cup	chopped fresh basil OR 1 tbsp (15 mL) dried	250 mL
1/2 cup	freshly grated Parmesan cheese	125 mL
	Salt and pepper	

In large heavy saucepan, heat oil over medium heat; cook onions, stirring occasionally until softened. Stir in rice and cook, stirring, for 3 minutes. Add wine and cook, stirring, until wine is absorbed.

Set 1 cup (250 mL) of the stock aside. Add remaining stock 1 cup (250 mL) at a time, stirring until all stock is absorbed but rice is still moist before adding another cup. (This will take 15 to 20 minutes.) Remove from heat, cover and refrigerate for up to 4 hours.

To serve, reheat rice over medium heat; stir in remaining hot stock until absorbed yet rice is still moist. Stir in radicchio, parsley and basil. Add Parmesan, and salt and pepper to taste. Serve immediately.

Makes 12 servings.

*To reduce sodium, use half water and half chicken stock or, for those on a sodium-restricted diet, use low-sodium chicken stock or water.

PER SERVING	
Calories	364
g total fat	8
g saturated fat	2
g fibre	2

GOOD: Niacin

g protein	10
g carbohydrate	59
mg cholesterol	3
mg sodium	653
mg potassium	328

ELIZABETH BAIRD'S MUSHROOM RISOTTO

My friend and Canadian Living Magazine *food editor Elizabeth Baird makes a delicious risotto. When making a risotto, you stir a little stock at a time into the rice until it is absorbed. It takes about 20 minutes in all and the result is a lovely creamy dish (without any cream). If you have guests, have them visit with you in the kitchen while you stir, or get them to stir. For best results, choose a short-grain rice, preferably Italian arborio, which is available in supermarkets.*

Oyster mushrooms, or any specialty fresh or dried mushrooms, can be used instead of some of the regular mushrooms. If the mushrooms are dried, be sure to use the mushroom soaking liquid as part of the stock.

3 cups	chicken stock	750 mL
2 tbsp	soft margarine	25 mL
1	medium onion, chopped	1
1	clove garlic, minced	1
1/2 cup	coarsely chopped sweet red pepper	125 mL
6 cups	sliced mushrooms (1 lb/500 g)	1.5 L
1 1/2 cups	arborio rice	375 mL
1 cup	dry white wine OR extra chicken stock	250 mL
	Salt and pepper	
1/2 cup	chopped scallions	125 mL
	Chopped fresh parsley	
1/4 cup	freshly grated Parmesan cheese	50 mL

In saucepan, bring stock to low simmer.

Meanwhile, in wide shallow saucepan or large skillet, melt half of the margarine over medium-high heat; cook onion, garlic, red pepper and mushrooms, stirring, for about 10 minutes or until tender and most of the liquid released by mushrooms has evaporated.

Add rice, stirring to coat. Stir in about half of the wine; cook, stirring often, until wine is absorbed, about 2 minutes. Add remaining wine and cook, stirring often, until wine is absorbed.

Add hot chicken stock 1/4 cup (50 mL) at a time, stirring after each addition, until all of the stock is absorbed and rice has swelled to double its size and is tender but still a little firm, about 20 minutes.

Stir in remaining margarine, and extra stock if necessary to make risotto creamy and moist. Season with salt and pepper to taste. Spoon into warmed pasta bowls and sprinkle with onions, parsley and cheese.

Makes 4 main-course servings, 6 appetizer servings.

PER APPETIZER SERVING

Calories		264
g	total fat	6
g	saturated fat	2
g	fibre	2

GOOD: Riboflavin
EXCELLENT: Niacin

g	protein	8
g	carbohydrate	41
mg	cholesterol	3
mg	sodium	492
mg	potassium	416

INDONESIAN FRIED RICE

Serve this curried rice dish as a vegetable, or add cooked meat or shrimp and serve as a main course.

4 cups	water	1 L
2 cups	whole grain OR long-grain rice	500 mL
1 tbsp	vegetable oil	15 mL
1	medium onion, chopped	1
1	stalk celery, chopped	1
1	medium carrot, diced	1
2	cloves garlic, chopped	2
1 tbsp	grated gingerroot	15 mL
1 tbsp	reduced-sodium soy sauce	15 mL
1 tsp	each curry powder and cumin	5 mL
1/4 tsp	hot pepper sauce	1 mL
1	sweet green pepper, diced	1
1 cup	shredded cabbage	250 mL
1/2 cup	frozen peas	125 mL
	Salt	

In saucepan, bring water to boil; add rice. Reduce heat, cover and simmer for 20 minutes or just until tender (don't overcook). Rinse under cold running water; drain well and pat dry. Set aside.

In large heavy saucepan, heat oil over medium-high heat; cook onion until softened, stirring constantly. Add celery, carrot, garlic, ginger, soy sauce, curry powder, cumin and hot pepper sauce; cook, stirring, for 2 minutes. Add green pepper, cabbage and peas, cook for 2 minutes.

Add rice and cook, stirring constantly until heated through and rice is light brown. Season with salt to taste. Serve hot.

Makes 6 servings.

Variations: Add 1/2 lb (250 g) peeled, deveined, and halved medium shrimp along with green pepper and cabbage.

Or, before adding cooked rice, add 2 cups (500 mL) diced cooked chicken, ham, pork or lamb and heat thoroughly.

PER SERVING		
Calories		**266**
g	total fat	**3**
g	saturated fat	**trace**
g	fibre	**3**

GOOD: Vitamin C
EXCELLENT: Vitamin A

g	protein	**5**
g	carbohydrate	**54**
mg	cholesterol	**0**
mg	sodium	**110**
mg	potassium	**216**

CHINESE RICE AND VEGETABLE STIR-FRY

Yellow or red sweet peppers and snow peas are an attractive color combination, though I use whatever vegetables I have on hand for this easy meal. Serve with a tossed green or spinach salad. If possible, use brown rice for its high vitamin and fibre content.

2 tbsp	vegetable oil	25 mL
1/2 cup	chopped onion	125 mL
1	carrot, chopped	1
Half	sweet pepper, coarsely chopped	Half
2 cups	chopped packed bok choy OR chopped cabbage	500 mL
1 cup	bean sprouts	250 mL
1/4 lb	snow peas (2 cups/500 mL)	125 g
2 cups	cooked rice	500 mL
2 tbsp	reduced-sodium soy sauce	25 mL
2	eggs, lightly beaten	2
2 tbsp	toasted sesame seeds* OR slivered almonds	25 mL

In large nonstick skillet or wok, heat oil over medium-high heat. Add onion and carrot; stir-fry until onion is softened.

Add sweet pepper, bok choy, bean sprouts and snow peas; stir-fry for 3 to 5 minutes or until tender-crisp, adding 1 tbsp (15 mL) water at a time if necessary to prevent scorching.

Stir in rice, soy sauce and eggs; stir-fry for 2 to 3 minutes or until eggs are set.

Sprinkle with sesame seeds or almonds.

Makes 4 main-course servings.

*To toast sesame seeds or almonds: Cook in small skillet over medium-low heat for about 5 minutes or until golden brown, shaking pan occasionally.

MEDITERRANEAN BARLEY AND BROWN RICE BAKE

Barley is an excellent source of soluble fibre (the same kind of fibre as oat bran). This dish can be prepared in advance, refrigerated and baked before serving.

1/2 cup	brown rice	125 mL
1/2 cup	pearl OR pot barley	125 mL
2 1/2 cups	water	625 mL
3 cups	sliced zucchini	750 mL
2/3 cup	chopped onion	150 mL
1	sweet green OR yellow pepper, cut in strips	1
2/3 cup	water	150 mL
1/3 cup	tomato paste	75 mL
1	clove garlic, minced	1
1 tsp	dried basil OR oregano	5 mL
1/2 tsp	granulated sugar	2 mL
1	large tomato, sliced	1
3/4 cup	shredded reduced-fat mozzarella OR Cheddar cheese	175 mL

Rinse rice and barley under cold water. In saucepan, bring water to boil; stir in rice and barley. Cover and reduce heat; simmer for 40 minutes or until water is absorbed and rice is tender.

Spray 11- × 7-inch (2 L) baking dish with nonstick vegetable coating; spread rice mixture in bottom.

In saucepan with small amount of boiling water, cook zucchini, onion and sweet pepper for 2 to 3 minutes or until tender-crisp; drain. Spread over rice mixture.

In small bowl, combine water, tomato paste, garlic, basil and sugar; pour over vegetables. Arrange tomato slices on top. Cover and bake in 325°F (160°C) oven for 25 minutes or until heated through. Sprinkle with cheese; bake, uncovered, for 5 minutes or until cheese melts.

Makes 6 servings.

PER SERVING		
Calories		196
g	total fat	3
g	saturated fat	1
g	fibre	5

GOOD: Niacin
EXCELLENT: Vitamin C

g	protein	8
g	carbohydrate	36
mg	cholesterol	8
mg	sodium	239
mg	potassium	494

HERB-BAKED POLENTA WITH PARMESAN

For a long time, I wasn't interested in making polenta. I thought it was very bland and probably difficult to make. It isn't; however, it does require stirring for 15 to 20 minutes unless you use the quick-cooking cornmeal (then follow package instructions), but you can prepare it in advance.

Mark Dowling, a Toronto chef, makes the best polenta I've tasted. He adds extra flavor by cooking it with onions and herbs, then sprinkling with cheese. It's delicious served as part of a brunch or instead of a starch at dinner. (Pictured opposite page 90.)

1	medium onion, minced	1
4 cups	water	1 L
1/2 tsp	each dried rosemary, thyme and salt	2 mL
1 cup	cornmeal	250 mL
1 tsp	olive oil	5 mL
1/4 cup	freshly grated Parmesan cheese	50 mL

In large saucepan, cover and simmer onion and 1/4 cup (50 mL) of the water for 5 minutes or until tender. Add remaining water, rosemary, thyme and salt; bring to boil.

Very gradually, add cornmeal, stirring constantly (it should take at least 3 minutes). Continuing to stir, cook cornmeal over medium-low heat for 15 to 20 minutes or until very thick. (If it cooks for less than 15 minutes, the cornmeal won't be cooked.)

Spray baking sheet with nonstick coating. Evenly spread polenta over baking sheet in 9-inch (23 cm) square or circle about 3/4 inch (2 cm) thick. Let cool or refrigerate for up to 24 hours.

Drizzle oil over polenta and brush to distribute evenly. Sprinkle with cheese. Cut into wedges or squares and separate slightly to have crisp edges. Bake in 375°F (190°C) oven for 12 to 15 minutes or until hot and golden. Serve hot.

Makes 8 servings.

PER SERVING	
Calories	83
g total fat	2
g saturated fat	1
g fibre	1
g protein	2
g carbohydrate	14
mg cholesterol	2
mg sodium	205
mg potassium	43

POLENTA WITH SAUTÉED MUSHROOMS

For a light supper, top baked polenta with flavorful mushrooms. You can use a few wild mushrooms, fresh or dried, instead of some of the regular mushrooms.

	Herb-Baked Polenta with Parmesan (facing page)	
1 tbsp	soft margarine OR olive oil	15 mL
1	medium onion, chopped	1
1	small clove garlic, minced	1
1 lb	mushrooms, halved	500 g
1/3 cup	coarsely chopped fresh parsley	75 mL
	Salt and pepper	

In large nonstick skillet, heat margarine over medium heat; cook onion and garlic until tender, about 5 minutes. Add mushrooms and stir-fry over high heat for 5 minutes or until tender and browned. Add parsley. Season with salt and pepper to taste. Spoon over hot Baked Polenta.

Makes 6 servings.

PER SERVING	
Calories	153
g total fat	5
g saturated fat	1
g fibre	3

GOOD: Niacin

g protein	5
g carbohydrate	24
mg cholesterol	3
mg sodium	275
mg potassium	291

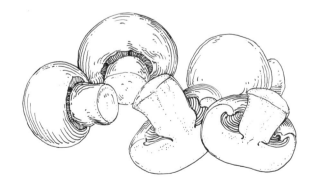

BULGUR WITH GINGER AND SPRING ONIONS

Bulgur has a light nutty flavor, slightly crunchy texture and is high in fibre. It's available at some supermarkets and most health food stores. Substitute cracked wheat if bulgur isn't available. Serve instead of rice.

2 cups	water	500 mL
1 1/2 cups	chicken stock	375 mL
1 1/4 cups	bulgur	300 mL
1 tbsp	grated gingerroot	15 mL
1/2 cup	finely chopped scallions	125 mL

In saucepan, bring water and chicken stock to boil; add bulgur and ginger. Cover and simmer for 15 minutes or until tender (cooking time will be about 10 minutes longer for cracked wheat). Stir in scallions.

Makes 6 servings.

Here are some other recipes using grains to try:

Old-Fashioned Mushroom Barley Soup (page 56)
Curried Rice and Salmon Salad (page 64)
Southwest Rice and Bean Salad (page 73)
Wild Rice and Bulgur Salad (page 74)
Citrus Quinoa Salad (page 75)
Moroccan Chicken Stew with Couscous (page 95)
Pilaf Supper for One (page 129)

PER SERVING	
Calories	138
g total fat	1
g saturated fat	**trace**
g fibre	3

GOOD: Niacin

g	protein	5
g	carbohydrate	28
mg	cholesterol	0
mg	sodium	198
mg	potassium	159

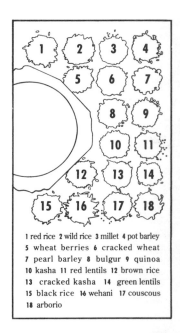

1 red rice 2 wild rice 3 millet 4 pot barley
5 wheat berries 6 cracked wheat
7 pearl barley 8 bulgur 9 quinoa
10 kasha 11 red lentils 12 brown rice
13 cracked kasha 14 green lentils
15 black rice 16 wehani 17 couscous
18 arborio

Wild Rice and Bulgur Salad (p. 74)

Swiss Muesli with Bananas

There are many variations of this healthy Swiss breakfast dish — this one is more authentic than the dried version. Though nuts and seeds can be added, I haven't done so in order to keep fat at a minimum. It's delicious topped with any fresh fruit.

1/2 cup	hot water	125 mL
1/2 cup	rolled oats	125 mL
1 cup	low-fat yogurt	250 mL
1/4 cup	raisins	50 mL
2 tbsp	wheat bran	25 mL
2 tbsp	oat bran	25 mL
2 tbsp	liquid honey	25 mL
1	apple, cored and diced	1
3	bananas, sliced	3

In bowl, pour hot water over rolled oats; let stand for 20 minutes or until water is absorbed.

Add yogurt, raisins, natural bran, oat bran, honey and apple; mix well. Cover and refrigerate overnight or for up to 2 days. Spoon into individual bowls and top with bananas.

Makes 4 servings.

Leslie's Muesli

My long-time friend Leslie King taught me how to make this, and now it's what I most often have for breakfast. Leslie lives on a farm in Vermont and buys a large variety of grains, seeds and dried fruit at the local co-op. In this simplified version, you only measure the first time you make it; after that you just add what you have on hand. Serve with milk or yogurt and top with any kind of fresh fruit — banana, strawberries or blueberries. (Pictured opposite page 219.)

3 cups	rolled oats (not instant)	750 mL
1 cup	raisins OR mixture of dried fruits	250 mL
1/2 cup	each oat bran and wheat bran	125 mL
1/2 cup	toasted wheat germ	125 mL
1/2 cup	pumpkin OR sunflower seeds	125 mL

Combine rolled oats, raisins or chopped dried fruit, oat bran, wheat bran, wheat germ and seeds; store in airtight container for up to 6 months.

Makes 10 servings, 1/2 cup (125 mL) each.

PER SERVING

Calories		257
g	total fat	2
g	saturated fat	1
g	fibre	5

GOOD: Thiamin, Riboflavin

g	protein	7
g	carbohydrate	56
mg	cholesterol	4
mg	sodium	47
mg	potassium	679

If you omit the pumpkin or sunflower seeds, you reduce the grams of fat per serving to 3. (Homemade granola has an average of 17 g fat per 1/2 cup/ 125 mL.)

PER SERVING

Calories		227
g	total fat	6
g	saturated fat	1
g	fibre	7

EXCELLENT: Thiamin, Iron

g	protein	9
g	carbohydrate	38
mg	cholesterol	0
mg	sodium	5
mg	potassium	371

Plum and Nectarine Cobbler (p. 228)

MICROWAVE LEEK AND MUSHROOM FLAN

Serve this for brunch or a quick meatless dinner along with a green vegetable, salad and whole wheat bun. Chopped onion can be used instead of leeks.

This flan is also delicious made with 1 whole egg plus 3 egg whites. The cholesterol is then 109 mg per serving.

1 cup	thinly sliced leek (white part only)	250 mL
1 tsp	vegetable oil	5 mL
1/2 lb	mushrooms, coarsely chopped (about 3 cups/750 mL)	250 g
2	eggs lightly beaten	2
2	egg whites, lightly beaten*	2
2 tbsp	milk	25 mL
Pinch	paprika	Pinch
	Salt and pepper	

In 8 1/2- × 4-inch (1.5 L) microwaveable dish, toss leeks with oil. Cover with plastic wrap and microwave at High power for 1 minute.

Add mushrooms; cover and microwave at High power for 4 minutes or until mushrooms are nearly tender. Stir in egg, egg whites, milk, paprika, and salt and peper to taste.

Microwave, uncovered, at Medium (50%) power for 6 to 8 minutes or until mixture is set. Serve hot.

Makes 2 servings.

*Using egg whites makes this dish light in texture and keeps the cholesterol count down (all the cholesterol in eggs is in the yolks).

PER SERVING

Calories		167
g	total fat	8
g	saturated fat	2
g	fibre	2

GOOD: Iron
EXCELLENT: Riboflavin, Niacin, Folate

g	protein	14
g	carbohydrate	11
mg	cholesterol	217
mg	sodium	154
mg	potassium	484

SPANISH OMELETTE

This light, colorful omelette is designed for someone on a diet who wants to avoid egg yolks. It's important to use a nonstick pan over high heat.

2	egg whites	2
1 tbsp	milk	15 mL
Pinch	turmeric OR paprika	Pinch
	Salt and pepper	
1 tsp	soft margarine	5 mL
2 tbsp	diced cooked ham (optional)	25 mL
2 tbsp	finely chopped tomato	25 mL
1 tbsp	finely chopped scallion	15 mL

In bowl, whisk egg whites until frothy; add milk, turmeric, and salt and pepper to taste. Heat large nonstick skillet over high heat until hot; add margarine and swirl to coat bottom of pan.

Pour in egg mixture and shake pan over high heat until egg sets. Sprinkle ham (if using), tomato and scallion over egg. Remove from heat and using fork, lift one-third of omelette and fold it over center, tilt pan and roll omelette over onto plate.

Makes 1 serving.

Variations: Add chopped cooked or raw vegetables, fresh herbs or a small amount of low-fat cheese or flaked fish such as salmon.

PER SERVING

Calories		79
g	total fat	4
g	saturated fat	1
g	fibre	trace

GOOD: Riboflavin

g	protein	8
g	carbohydrate	3
mg	cholesterol	1
mg	sodium	143
mg	potassium	179

Here are some other meatless recipes to try:

Pasta e Fagioli (page 149)
Linguine with Asparagus and Red Pepper (page 150)
Penne with Tomato, Black Olive and Feta (page 154)
Spicy Thai Noodles with Vegetables (page 156)
Mushroom and Sweet Pepper Lasagna (page 158)
Pasta with Sweet Peppers, Cheese and Basil (page 161)
Kids' Easy Macaroni and Cheese with Vegetables (page 162)
Lighthearted Fettuccine Alfredo (page 165)

SWEET PEPPER AND MUSHROOM PIZZA

Vegetable toppings make the best-tasting pizza—juicy and flavorful. You can also add zucchini, broccoli, cauliflower, artichokes, sliced tomato or eggplant. Forget about anchovies or olives because they're high in salt. I don't like too much cheese or any pepperoni at all because they make a salty, greasy pizza. Instead I love to add fresh basil.

2	12-inch (30 cm) uncooked pizza crusts	2
1/4 cup	tomato paste	50 mL
3/4 cup	water	175 mL
1 1/2 tsp	dried oregano	7 mL
Half	sweet red pepper, cut in strips	Half
Half	sweet yellow OR green pepper, cut in strips	Half
1 cup	sliced mushrooms	250 mL
1	small onion, thinly sliced	1
2 cups	shredded reduced-fat mozzarella cheese	500 mL

Place each pizza crust on nonstick baking sheet or pizza pan. Combine tomato paste and water with oregano; spread over each crust.

Arrange red and yellow peppers, mushrooms and onion on each crust. Sprinkle with cheese. Bake in 450°F (230°C) oven for 12 minutes or until cheese is bubbly.   *Makes 8 servings.*

PER SERVING

Calories		189
g	total fat	7
g	saturated fat	3
g	fibre	1

GOOD: Vitamin C, Niacin, Calcium

g	protein	10
g	carbohydrate	22
mg	cholesterol	19
mg	sodium	323
mg	potassium	189

WINTER SALSA

Make this version of salsa in winter when canned tomatoes are a better choice than fresh ones. Use the salsa as a dip with nachos or as a sauce for burritos.

1	can (16 oz) tomatoes	1
2 tsp	cider vinegar	10 mL
1 1/2 tsp	each cumin and chili powder	7 mL
4	scallions, chopped	4
1	clove garlic, minced	1
Half	sweet green pepper, chopped	Half
2 tbsp	chopped fresh coriander (optional)	25 mL

In food processor or by hand, chop tomatoes. Transfer to bowl and stir in vinegar, cumin, chili powder, onions, garlic, green pepper and coriander (if using). Cover and refrigerate for up to 4 days. *Makes about 3 cups (750 mL).*

PER 2 TBSP (25 ML)

Calories		7
g	total fat	trace
g	saturated fat	0
g	fibre	trace

g	protein	trace
g	carbohydrate	1
mg	cholesterol	0
mg	sodium	39
mg	potassium	68

BAKED GOODS

Lemon Tea Loaf

*Pumpkin Loaf with Orange
Glaze*

Cinnamon Carrot Bread

Banana Cake with Orange Icing

Buttermilk Herb Quick Bread

Apple Streusel Muffins

Apple Date Muffins

Blueberry Lemon Muffins

Wheat Germ Raisin Muffins

Oat Bran Raisin Muffins

*Buttermilk Oatmeal Raisin
Scones*

*Raisin Cupcakes with Lemon
Yogurt Icing*

Whole Wheat Blueberry Biscuits

Pineapple Carrot Bars

Easy Date and Walnut Squares

Applesauce Spice Cookies

Lemon Sugar Cookies

Gingersnaps

Hermits

Cornmeal Peach Pancakes

LEMON TEA LOAF

This tangy cake is an excellent choice to serve for dessert with fresh fruit or sorbet.

1 cup	granulated sugar	250 mL
1/4 cup	soft margarine	50 mL
1	egg	1
2 tbsp	low-fat yogurt	25 mL
1/2 cup	low-fat milk	125 mL
1 1/2 cups	all-purpose flour	375 mL
1 tsp	baking powder	5 mL
	Grated rind of 1 lemon	

Glaze:

	Juice of 1 lemon	
1/4 cup	granulated sugar	50 mL

Line 8- × 4-inch (1.5 L) loaf pan with foil; grease lightly.

In large bowl, cream sugar and margarine. Beat in egg and yogurt; beat in milk. Mix flour and baking powder; beat into egg mixture until blended. Stir in lemon rind.

Spoon into prepared pan; bake in 350°F (180°C) oven for 1 hour or until cake tester inserted in center comes out dry. Let cake stand in pan for 3 minutes.

Glaze: In small bowl, combine lemon juice and sugar, mixing well; pour over top of warm cake.

Remove foil and cake from pan and place on rack. Loosen foil and let cake cool completely before cutting.

Makes 16 slices.

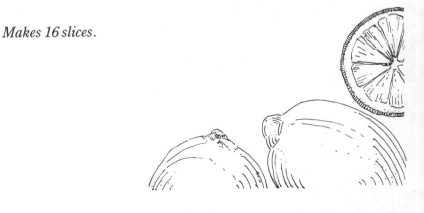

PER SLICE		
Calories		139
g	total fat	3
g	saturated fat	1
g	fibre	trace
g	protein	2
g	carbohydrate	25
mg	cholesterol	14
mg	sodium	51
mg	potassium	37

PUMPKIN LOAF WITH ORANGE GLAZE

This doesn't last long around our house because it's a favorite for packed lunches and after-school snacks. Use canned or fresh cooked pumpkin or squash for this tasty quick bread.

1 cup	whole wheat flour	250 mL
2/3 cup	all-purpose flour	150 mL
1 1/2 tsp	cinnamon	7 mL
1 tsp	baking soda	5 mL
1/2 tsp	baking powder	2 mL
1/2 tsp	nutmeg	2 mL
1/4 tsp	salt	1 mL
1/3 cup	soft margarine	75 mL
2/3 cup	granulated sugar	150 mL
1/2 tsp	vanilla	2 mL
2	eggs	2
1 cup	cooked pumpkin	250 mL
1/3 cup	water	75 mL
3/4 cup	raisins	175 mL

Glaze:

2 tbsp	confectioners' sugar	25 mL
1/4 cup	orange juice	50 mL

Lightly grease and flour 9- × 5-inch (2 L) loaf pan.

In small bowl, combine whole wheat flour, all-purpose flour, cinnamon, baking soda, baking powder, nutmeg and salt.

In large bowl, cream margarine, sugar and vanilla; add eggs one at a time, beating well after each addition. Stir in pumpkin. Alternately stir in flour mixture and water just until smooth. Stir in raisins and pour into prepared pan.

Bake in 350°F (180°C) oven for 1 hour or until cake tester inserted in center comes out clean. Let cool in pan for 10 minutes; turn out onto rack.

Glaze: Pierce hot cake with fork. Mix sugar with orange juice; pour over cake. Let cool completely.

Makes 16 slices.

PER SLICE		
Calories		155
g	total fat	5
g	saturated fat	1
g	fibre	2

EXCELLENT: Vitamin A

g	protein	3
g	carbohydrate	27
mg	cholesterol	27
mg	sodium	156
mg	potassium	140

Cinnamon Carrot Bread

This carrot bread is packed with flavor as well as nutrients. It's great as an afternoon snack or with a packed lunch.

1 cup	raisins	250 mL
3/4 cup	all-purpose flour	175 mL
3/4 cup	whole wheat flour	175 mL
2 tsp	cinnamon	10 mL
1 tsp	ground ginger	5 mL
1/2 tsp	nutmeg	2 mL
1 tsp	each baking soda and baking powder	5 mL
1/4 tsp	salt	1 mL
1	egg	1
3 tbsp	vegetable oil	45 mL
3/4 cup	low-fat yogurt	175 mL
1/2 cup	packed brown sugar	125 mL
1 tsp	vanilla	5 mL
1 cup	finely shredded carrot	250 mL

Topping:

1 tbsp	rolled oats	15 mL
1 tbsp	oat bran	15 mL

Pour boiling water over raisins and let stand for 5 minutes; drain thoroughly.

Combine all-purpose and whole wheat flours, cinnamon, ginger, nutmeg, baking soda, baking powder, salt and raisins; set aside.

In large bowl, beat egg until fluffy; beat in oil. Mix in yogurt, sugar and vanilla; stir in carrot. Add flour mixture; stir until combined. Pour into greased and foil or waxed paper-lined 8- × 4-inch (1.5 L) loaf pan.

Topping: Combine rolled oats and oat bran; sprinkle over batter. Bake in 350°F (180°C) oven for 50 to 55 minutes or until toothpick inserted in center comes out clean. Let stand in pan for 5 minutes. Remove from pan and let cool before slicing.

Makes about 13 slices.

PER SLICE		
Calories		166
g	total fat	4
g	saturated fat	trace
g	fibre	2

GOOD: Vitamin A

g	protein	4
g	carbohydrate	30
mg	cholesterol	17
mg	sodium	171
mg	potassium	216

BANANA CAKE WITH ORANGE ICING

I make this cake when I have over-ripe bananas to use up (my kids think one brown mark makes them inedible). It's delicious with or without icing. My mother often used to make this in a loaf pan.

1/4 cup	soft margarine	50 mL
3/4 cup	granulated sugar	175 mL
2	eggs	2
1 tsp	vanilla	5 mL
1 cup	mashed ripe bananas (about 3)	250 mL
1 tsp	grated orange rind (optional)	5 mL
2 cups	all-purpose flour	500 mL
2 tsp	baking powder	10 mL
1 tsp	baking soda	5 mL
1/2 cup	buttermilk OR sour milk*	125 mL

Orange Icing:

1 1/2 cups	confectioners' sugar	375 mL
2 tbsp	low-fat yogurt	25 mL
1 tsp	grated orange rind	5 mL
1 tsp	orange juice	5 mL

In bowl, cream margarine; add sugar and beat well. Add eggs one at a time, beating well after each addition. Beat in vanilla, bananas, and orange rind (if using).

Mix together flour, baking powder and baking soda; beat into egg mixture alternately with buttermilk. Spray 9-inch (2.5 L) springform or square pan with nonstick coating; spoon in batter.

Bake in 350°F (180°C) oven for 40 minutes or until cake springs back when pressed in center or until tester inserted in center comes out clean. Let cool in pan for 10 minutes; remove from pan and let cool on rack.

Orange Icing: In small bowl, combine sugar, yogurt, orange rind and juice; mix until smooth. Spread over cake. Cut into wedges.

Makes 12 servings.

*To sour milk, add 2 tsp (10 mL) lemon juice or vinegar to 1/2 cup (125 mL) milk and let stand for 10 minutes.

PER PIECE	
Calories	253
g total fat	5
g saturated fat	1
g fibre	1
g protein	4
g carbohydrate	49
mg cholesterol	37
mg sodium	195
mg potassium	130

BUTTERMILK HERB QUICK BREAD

Serve this textured flavorful bread anytime, from breakfast to snacks, with salads, soups or bean dishes. Be sure to use the crumbled leaf form of herbs, not the ground.

1 cup	whole wheat flour	250 mL
1/2 cup	all-purpose flour	125 mL
1/2 cup	cornmeal	125 mL
2 tsp	baking powder	10 mL
1/2 tsp	baking soda	2 mL
1/2 tsp	salt	2 mL
1 tsp	dried dillweed	5 mL
1/2 tsp	each crumbled dried oregano, basil and thyme	2 mL
1/2 tsp	fennel seeds (optional)	2 mL
1 1/4 cups	buttermilk	300 mL
1	egg, beaten	1
2 tbsp	liquid honey	25 mL
2 tbsp	vegetable oil	25 mL
1 tbsp	sesame seeds	15 mL

In bowl, combine whole wheat and all-purpose flours, cornmeal, baking powder, baking soda, salt, dillweed, oregano, basil, thyme, and fennel seeds (if using).

Combine buttermilk, egg, honey and oil; stir into flour mixture just until blended. Spoon into foil or waxed paper-lined 8- × 4-inch (1.5 L) loaf pan; sprinkle with sesame seeds.

Bake in 350°F (180°C) oven for 45 to 50 minutes or until tester inserted in center comes out clean. Turn out and cool on rack.

Makes about 15 slices.

PER SLICE	
Calories	101
g total fat	3
g saturated fat	trace
g fibre	1
g protein	3
g carbohydrate	16
mg cholesterol	15
mg sodium	186
mg potassium	84

APPLE STREUSEL MUFFINS

These moist cinnamon muffins are perfect for breakfast or snack time.

1 1/3 cups	whole wheat flour	325 mL
1/2 cup	oat bran	125 mL
1/3 cup	granulated sugar	75 mL
1 tbsp	baking powder	15 mL
1 tbsp	cinnamon	15 mL
1/4 tsp	salt	1 mL
1 1/4 cup	chopped peeled apple	300 mL
1	egg, lightly beaten	1
1 cup	low-fat milk	250 mL
1/4 cup	vegetable oil	50 mL

Topping:

2 tbsp	packed brown sugar	25 mL
1/4 tsp	cinnamon	1 mL
1/4 tsp	nutmeg	1 mL

In large bowl, mix together flour, oat bran, sugar, baking powder, cinnamon and salt. Stir in chopped apple.

In separate bowl, combine egg, milk and oil; stir into flour mixture just until moistened. Do not overmix. Spoon into nonstick or paper-lined muffin cups, filling three-quarters full.

Topping: Combine sugar, cinnamon and nutmeg; sprinkle over muffins. Bake in 400°F (200°C) oven 15 to 20 minutes or until golden and firm to the touch.

Makes 12 muffins.

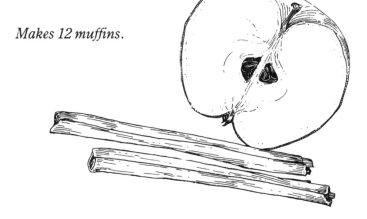

PER MUFFIN		
Calories		157
g	total fat	6
g	saturated fat	1
g	fibre	2
g	protein	4
g	carbohydrate	23
mg	cholesterol	19
mg	sodium	128
mg	potassium	136

APPLE DATE MUFFINS

These moist, good-tasting muffins are great for breakfast or packed lunches.

3/4 cup	whole wheat flour	175 mL
1/2 cup	all-purpose flour	125 mL
1/2 cup	wheat bran	125 mL
1 tsp	baking powder	5 mL
1 tsp	baking soda	5 mL
1 tsp	cinnamon	5 mL
1/3 cup	chopped dates	75 mL
1	egg, lightly beaten	1
1/4 cup	packed brown sugar	50 mL
2 tbsp	vegetable oil	25 mL
1 cup	low-fat milk	250 mL
1 cup	grated peeled apple	250 mL

In large bowl, combine whole wheat and all-purpose flours, bran, baking powder, baking soda and cinnamon; stir in dates. In another bowl, beat egg with sugar and oil; stir in milk and apple. Pour into flour mixture and stir just enough to moisten, being careful not to overmix.

Spoon into nonstick or paper-lined medium muffin tins, filling almost to top. Bake in 375°F (190°C) oven for about 20 minutes or until firm to the touch.

Makes 12 muffins.

Carrot raisin muffins

Prepare Apple Date Muffins, but substitute grated carrots for the apple. Use raisins instead of dates.

PER MUFFIN

Calories		119
g	total fat	3
g	saturated fat	1
g	fibre	2
g	protein	3
g	carbohydrate	21
mg	cholesterol	19
mg	sodium	133
mg	potassium	149

Blueberry Lemon Muffins

Warm from the oven and bursting with fresh flavor, these moist muffins need no butter.

1 tbsp	lemon juice	15 mL
1 cup	milk	250 mL
1	egg, beaten	1
1/4 cup	vegetable oil	50 mL
1/4 cup	molasses	50 mL
1 cup	wheat bran	250 mL
3/4 cup	whole wheat flour	175 mL
3/4 cup	all-purpose flour	175 mL
1/3 cup	packed brown sugar	75 mL
1 1/2 tsp	grated lemon rind	7 mL
1 1/2 tsp	baking powder	7 mL
1/2 tsp	baking soda	2 mL
1 cup	blueberries (fresh OR frozen)	250 mL

To make it easy to pour the molasses from the measuring cup, first measure the oil into the measuring cup, remove oil, then measure molasses.

In bowl, stir lemon juice into milk; let stand for 1 minute to sour. Stir in egg, oil and molasses.

In large bowl, combine bran, whole wheat and all-purpose flours, sugar, lemon rind, baking powder and baking soda. Add milk mixture and blueberries; mix just until combined.

Spoon into nonstick or paper-lined muffin tins. Bake in 375°F (190°C) oven for 20 to 25 minutes or until firm to the touch.

Makes 12 muffins.

PER MUFFIN

Calories		159
g	total fat	6
g	saturated fat	1
g	fibre	3

GOOD: Iron

g	protein	4
g	carbohydrate	25
mg	cholesterol	19
mg	sodium	112
mg	potassium	347

WHEAT GERM RAISIN MUFFINS

Chopped figs or dates instead of raisins are also good in these muffins.

1 cup	raisins	250 mL
1 3/4 cups	whole wheat flour	425 mL
3/4 cup	wheat germ	175 mL
1/3 cup	granulated sugar	75 mL
1 tbsp	baking powder	15 mL
1/2 tsp	salt	2 mL
3 tbsp	vegetable oil	45 mL
1 1/2 cups	low-fat milk	375 mL
1	egg, beaten	1

Pour boiling water over raisins and let stand for 10 minutes; drain.

In bowl, combine flour, wheat germ, sugar, baking powder and salt; stir in raisins. Combine oil, milk and egg; pour into flour mixture and stir just until combined. Spoon into nonstick or paper-lined muffin tins, filling each three-quarters full. Bake in 375°F (190°C) oven for 18 to 20 minutes or until firm to the touch.

Makes 15 muffins.

PER MUFFIN	
Calories	**159**
g total fat	**4**
g saturated fat	**1**
g fibre	**3**

GOOD: Thiamin

g	protein	**5**
g	carbohydrate	**27**
mg	cholesterol	**16**
mg	sodium	**154**
mg	potassium	**224**

OAT BRAN RAISIN MUFFINS

These easy-to-make moist muffins have the particularly nice accent of orange rind. Grated lemon rind could be used instead.

1 cup	oat bran	250 mL
1 cup	whole wheat flour	250 mL
1/4 cup	packed brown sugar	50 mL
2 tsp	baking powder	10 mL
1/2 cup	raisins	125 mL
1 1/4 cups	low-fat milk	300 mL
1	egg	1
1/4 cup	molasses OR liquid honey	50 mL
2 tbsp	vegetable oil	25 mL
1 tsp	grated orange rind	5 mL

In large bowl, combine oat bran, whole wheat flour, sugar, baking powder and raisins. Add milk, egg, molasses or honey, oil and orange rind; stir just until combined.

Spoon batter into nonstick or paper-lined muffin tins. Bake in 400°F (200°C) oven for 20 minutes or until firm to the touch.

Makes 12 muffins.

PER MUFFIN	
Calories	**160**
g total fat	**4**
g saturated fat	**1**
g fibre	**3**

g	protein	**5**
g	carbohydrate	**28**
mg	cholesterol	**20**
mg	sodium	**68**
mg	potassium	**276**

Buttermilk Oatmeal Raisin Scones

Hot from the oven, these are a wonderful treat for Sunday brunch. Serve with apple butter or homemade jam.

1/4 cup	granulated sugar	50 mL
1 1/2 cups	whole wheat flour	375 mL
1 1/2 cups	rolled oats	375 mL
1 tbsp	baking powder	15 mL
1/2 tsp	baking soda	2 mL
1/2 tsp	salt	2 mL
3 tbsp	soft margarine	45 mL
1 cup	raisins	250 mL
1 1/4 cups	buttermilk	300 mL

Set aside 1 1/2 tsp (7 mL) of sugar for topping. In bowl, combine whole wheat flour, rolled oats, remaining sugar, baking powder, soda and salt. Rub in margarine until mixture is crumbly. Stir in raisins, then buttermilk.

On lightly floured surface, knead dough about 10 times. Divide into 3 pieces. Pat each piece into a round about 3/4-inch (2 cm) thick. Transfer to baking sheet then cut with knife to divide each round into four quarters. Sprinkle with reserved sugar. Bake in 425°F (220°C) oven for 15 to 20 minutes or until lightly browned. Serve hot.

Makes 12 scones.

Buttermilk

Even though buttermilk sounds rich, it isn't. Buttermilk used to be the liquid left over when cream was made into butter. Now it is made commercially by adding special bacteria to skim or 2% milk. In buttermilk, the milk sugar lactose has been converted to lactic acid so it can be consumed by people who have trouble with regular milk.

Buttermilk's tart taste and thick consistency make it ideal for salad dressings and some cold soups. It's also good in muffins and pancakes.

PER SCONE		
Calories		184
g	total fat	4
g	saturated fat	1
g	fibre	3
GOOD: Thiamin		
g	protein	5
g	carbohydrate	34
mg	cholesterol	1
mg	sodium	276
mg	potassium	236

RAISIN CUPCAKES WITH LEMON YOGURT ICING

This recipe is from my mother-in-law, Olive Lindsay. The cupcakes are a special hit with all the grandchildren at family gatherings.

1 1/2 cups	raisins	375 mL
1 1/2 cups	all-purpose flour	375 mL
1 tsp	baking soda	5 mL
1 tsp	cinnamon	5 mL
1/4 tsp	cloves	1 mL
1/4 cup	low-fat yogurt OR buttermilk	50 mL
2 tbsp	soft margarine	25 mL
3/4 cup	granulated sugar	175 mL
1	egg, beaten	1

Lemon Yogurt Icing:

3/4 cup	sifted confectioners' sugar	175 mL
1 tbsp	low-fat yogurt	15 mL
1/2 tsp	grated lemon rind	2 mL
1/2 tsp	lemon juice	2 mL

Spray muffin tins with nonstick coating or line with paper liners.

In saucepan, cover raisins with water; bring to boil. Reduce heat and simmer for 20 minutes; drain, reserving 1/2 cup (125 mL) liquid. Let cool.

In bowl, sift together flour, baking soda, cinnamon and cloves.

In separate large bowl, beat yogurt, margarine and sugar until well mixed. Add egg and beat well. Stir in reserved cooled liquid alternately with dry ingredients, making 2 additions of each. Add cooled raisins and mix well.

Spoon into prepared muffin tins. Bake in 375°F (190°C) for 20 to 25 minutes or until toothpick inserted in center comes out clean. Let cool.

Lemon Yogurt Icing: In small bowl, combine sugar, yogurt, lemon rind and juice; mix until smooth. Spread on cooled cupcakes.

Makes 12 cupcakes.

PER CUPCAKE		
Calories		222
g	total fat	3
g	saturated fat	1
g	fibre	1
g	protein	3
g	carbohydrate	48
mg	cholesterol	18
mg	sodium	125
mg	potassium	188

WHOLE WHEAT BLUEBERRY BISCUITS

My daughter, Susie, makes these every summer at the cottage for breakfast or brunch. Instead of buttermilk, she usually sours milk by adding 1 tbsp (15 mL) of lemon juice or vinegar to 1 cup (250 mL) milk, then letting it stand for 10 minutes before stirring.(Pictured opposite page 219.)

1 cup	all-purpose flour	250 mL
1 cup	whole wheat flour	250 mL
1 tbsp	granulated sugar	15 mL
1 tbsp	baking powder	15 mL
1/2 tsp	baking soda	2 mL
1/2 tsp	salt	2 mL
1/4 cup	soft margarine	50 mL
1 cup	blueberries	250 mL
1 cup	buttermilk* OR sour milk	250 mL

In bowl, combine all-purpose and whole wheat flours, sugar, baking powder, baking soda and salt. Using fingers, rub in margarine until mixture resembles coarse crumbs.

Stir in blueberries; add buttermilk and mix lightly. Drop by spoonfuls into 10 mounds. Bake in 425°F (220°C) oven for 12 to 15 minutes or until golden.

Makes 10 biscuits.

*Buttermilk has the same fat content as the milk it is made from — skim, 1% or 2%, so it isn't high in fat.

PER BISCUIT	
Calories	150
g total fat	5
g saturated fat	1
g fibre	2
g protein	4
g carbohydrate	23
mg cholesterol	1
mg sodium	333
mg potassium	110

PINEAPPLE CARROT BARS

These squares are really delicious and will be especially appreciated by those who don't like overly sweet desserts. They lasted about 10 minutes in my house!

1/2 cup	packed brown sugar	125 mL
2 tbsp	vegetable oil	25 mL
1 tsp	vanilla	5 mL
1	egg	1
1 cup	whole wheat flour	250 mL
1 tbsp	cinnamon	15 mL
1 tsp	baking powder	5 mL
1 tsp	baking soda	5 mL
1 cup	finely grated carrots	250 mL
2/3 cup	drained crushed unsweetened pineapple	150 mL
1/2 cup	raisins	125 mL
1/4 cup	low-fat milk	50 mL

In large bowl, combine sugar, oil, vanilla and egg. Stir well and set aside.

In separate bowl, combine flour, cinnamon, baking powder and baking soda; add to sugar mixture, stirring well. Stir in carrots, pineapple, raisins and milk.

Pat mixture into 13- × 9-inch (3.5 L) baking pan lightly coated with cooking spray. Bake in 350°F (180°C) oven for 25 minutes or until top is golden. Let cool before cutting into bars. Store in refrigerator, loosely covered.

Makes 24 bars.

PER SQUARE		
Calories		63
g	total fat	1
g	saturated fat	**trace**
g	fibre	1
g	protein	1
g	carbohydrate	12
mg	cholesterol	9
mg	sodium	66
mg	potassium	84

EASY DATE AND WALNUT SQUARES

My sister-in-law Nancy Williams gave me the recipe for these yummy squares. Dates are an excellent source of fibre and iron.

1	egg	1
2	egg whites	2
1 cup	granulated sugar	250 mL
3 tbsp	melted soft margarine	45 mL
1 1/4 cups	finely chopped dates, packed	300 mL
1/4 cup	chopped walnuts	50 mL
1/3 cup	all-purpose flour	75 mL
1 tsp	baking powder	5 mL

In bowl and using electric mixer, beat egg, egg whites and sugar for about 5 minutes or until light in color. Beat in margarine, dates and walnuts. Stir in flour and baking powder until well combined.

Pour into lightly greased 8-inch (2 L) square baking dish. Bake in 350°F (180°C) oven for 35 minutes or until set. Let cool completely before cutting into squares.

Makes 20 squares.

Variation: A less sweet, more cake-like version of these squares makes a tasty choice for a packed lunch. Prepare above recipe but reduce sugar to 1/2 cup (125 mL), increase flour to 1/2 cup (125 mL). When cool, sift 1 tsp (5 mL) confectioners' sugar over squares.

PER SQUARE		
Calories		**107**
g	total fat	**3**
g	saturated fat	**1**
g	fibre	**1**
g	protein	**1**
g	carbohydrate	**20**
mg	cholesterol	**11**
mg	sodium	**37**
mg	potassium	**91**

APPLESAUCE SPICE COOKIES

These are an easy-to-make, soft cookie. For variety, add chopped dried fruit such as apricots, figs, dates or raisins.

1/3 cup	soft margarine*	75 mL
1/2 cup	granulated sugar	125 mL
1 1/2 cups	applesauce	375 mL
1 tsp	vanilla	5 mL
1	egg	1
2 cups	whole wheat flour	500 mL
1 tsp	each cinnamon and nutmeg	5 mL
1/2 tsp	cloves	2 mL
1 tsp	baking powder	5 mL
1/2 tsp	baking soda	2 mL

Sugar Topping:

1 tbsp	granulated sugar	15 mL
1/4 tsp	cinnamon	2 mL

Using electric mixer, cream margarine and sugar until smooth; add applesauce, vanilla and egg; beat well. Add flour, cinnamon, nutmeg, cloves, baking powder and baking soda; mix well.

Drop by spoonfuls onto baking sheet sprayed with nonstick vegetable coating. Bake in 350°F (180°C) oven for 15 to 20 minutes or until evenly browned.

Sugar Topping: Combine sugar with cinnamon; sprinkle over hot cookies. Let cool on racks.

Makes 36 medium cookies.

*Diet and calorie-reduced margarines are not recommended for baking.

PER COOKIE	
Calories	57
g total fat	2
g saturated fat	trace
g fibre	1
g protein	1
g carbohydrate	9
mg cholesterol	6
mg sodium	42
mg potassium	36

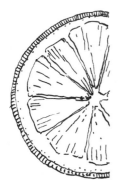

Lemon Sugar Cookies

Shannon Graham, who helps me with recipe testing, came up with these cookies, which everyone loves.

1/4 cup	soft margarine*	50 mL
2/3 cup	granulated sugar	150 mL
1	egg	1
2 tbsp	lemon juice	25 mL
1 1/4 cups	all-purpose flour	300 mL
1/3 cup	whole wheat flour	75 mL
	Grated rind of 2 lemons	
1/2 tsp	baking soda	2 mL
1 tbsp	granulated sugar	15 mL

In large bowl and using electric mixer, cream margarine and sugar. Add egg and lemon juice; beat until light and fluffy.

In separate bowl, combine all-purpose flour, whole wheat flour, lemon rind and baking soda. Stir into egg mixture; mix well. Shape tablespoonfuls (15 mL) of dough into balls; place about 2 inches (5 cm) apart on lightly greased baking sheets. Using back of fork, press to 1/4-inch (5 mm) thickness. Sprinkle with sugar. Bake in 350°F (180°C) oven for 10 minutes or until firm.

Makes 40 cookies.

*Diet or calorie-reduced margarines are not recommended for baking.

PER COOKIE	
Calories	44
g total fat	1
g saturated fat	**trace**
g fibre	**trace**
g protein	1
g carbohydrate	7
mg cholesterol	5
mg sodium	27
mg potassium	11

Average Fat and Calories for Store-Bought Packaged Cookies

For two cookies	g total fat	calories
sandwich type	6.7	148
chocolate chip	4.4	98
oatmeal cookie	4.1	117
arrowroot	2.3	70
vanilla wafers	1.9	54
gingersnap	1.3	59

GINGERSNAPS

These crisp cookies are great for packed lunches or with fresh fruit for dessert. They also freeze well.

1/4 cup	soft margarine	50 mL
1/2 cup	molasses	125 mL
1/2 tsp	baking soda	2 mL
1 1/2 tsp	boiling water	7 mL
1 1/4 cups	all-purpose flour	300 mL
1 1/2 tsp	ginger	7 mL
1/2 tsp	cinnamon	2 mL
1/8 tsp	cloves	0.5 mL
1 tsp	granulated sugar	5 mL

In small saucepan, melt margarine; add molasses and bring to boil, stirring constantly. Remove from heat; let cool for 15 minutes.

In small dish, combine baking soda and water; stir into molasses mixture.

In mixing bowl, sift 1 cup (250 mL) of the flour, ginger, cinnamon and cloves. Stir in molasses mixture until well combined. Add enough of the remaining flour to make dough that is easy to roll. Chill dough in refrigerator for 20 minutes.

On unfloured surface and using unfloured rolling pin, roll dough out to about 1/8 inch (3 mm) thickness. Cut into 2-inch (5 cm) rounds. Sprinkle with sugar. Bake on ungreased baking sheet in 375°F (190°C) oven for 5 to 8 minutes or until set.

Makes 4 dozen cookies.

PER COOKIE

Calories		29
g	total fat	1
g	saturated fat	**trace**
g	fibre	**trace**
g	protein	**trace**
g	carbohydrate	5
mg	cholesterol	0
mg	sodium	23
mg	potassium	41

HERMITS

These old-fashioned favorites are made healthier by using whole wheat flour and reducing the sugar and fat. Use only chopped dates or any combination of dried fruits, such as apricots, raisins or figs.

1/3 cup	soft margarine	75 mL
2/3 cup	packed brown sugar	150 mL
1	egg, lightly beaten	1
	Grated rind of 1 lemon	
3/4 cup	all-purpose flour	175 mL
2/3 cup	whole wheat flour	150 mL
1 1/2 tsp	baking powder	7 mL
1/2 tsp	each allspice and cinnamon	2 mL
1/4 tsp	each cloves and nutmeg	1 mL
1 cup	chopped dried fruit	250 mL
1/4 cup	low-fat milk	50 mL

In large bowl and with electric mixer, cream margarine; gradually add sugar, beating at medium speed until light and fluffy. Beat in egg and lemon rind.

In separate bowl, combine all-purpose flour, whole wheat flour, baking powder, allspice, cinnamon, cloves and nutmeg; mix well. Stir in dried fruit. Alternately add to creamed mixture along with milk, beginning and ending with flour mixture and mixing well after each addition.

Drop by spoonfuls onto lightly greased baking sheets. Bake in 325°F (160°C) oven for 15 minutes or until golden. Let cool slightly before removing from baking sheet.

Makes 30 cookies.

PER COOKIE		
Calories		71
g	total fat	2
g	saturated fat	1
g	fibre	1
g	protein	1
g	carbohydrate	12
mg	cholesterol	7
mg	sodium	37
mg	potassium	83

CORNMEAL PEACH PANCAKES

These are delicious thin pancakes: the peaches add juicy flavor; the cornmeal adds color and crunch. If you like thick pancakes add 1/4 cup (50 mL) all-purpose flour.

3/4 cup	cornmeal	175 mL
3/4 cup	all-purpose flour	175 mL
1/2 cup	whole wheat flour	125 mL
2 tbsp	granulated sugar	25 mL
1 tbsp	baking powder	15 mL
1/2 tsp	baking soda	2 mL
2	eggs	2
2 cups	low-fat milk	500 mL
2 tbsp	vegetable oil	25 mL
1 1/2 cups	chopped peaches (fresh OR canned)	375 mL
1 tsp	soft margarine	5 mL

Top pancakes with maple syrup or fresh fruit or a mixture of either with yogurt — you'll never miss the butter or margarine.

In large bowl, mix cornmeal, all-purpose flour, whole wheat flour, sugar, baking powder and baking soda.

In medium bowl, beat eggs until light; stir in milk and oil. Pour into flour mixture. Add peaches; stir until dry ingredients are wet. (Don't worry about a few lumps.)

Heat nonstick skillet over medium heat until hot. Add margarine to lightly grease. Drop large spoonfuls of batter into skillet to form rounds; cook until bubbles form on surface and underside is golden brown. Turn pancakes and cook just until bottom is lightly browned.

Makes 6 servings of three 5-inch (12 cm) pancakes each.

Variations: Add blueberries or finely diced apple instead of peaches.

PER SERVING	
Calories	**301**
g total fat	**9**
g saturated fat	**2**
g fibre	**3**

GOOD: Thiamin, Niacin, Riboflavin, Calcium

g	protein	**9**
g	carbohydrate	**46**
mg	cholesterol	**78**
mg	sodium	**306**
mg	potassium	**310**

DESSERTS

Ricotta Lemon Cheesecake
with Blueberries

Strawberry Pavlova with
Lemon Cream

Fruit with Quick Marmalade
Sauce

Lemon Cream Sauce

Heather Epp's Fresh Fruit
Tart

Pastry

Berry Bread Pudding

Lighthearted Strawberry
Shortcake

Three Berry Sauce

Peach Shortcake

Frozen Raspberry Yogurt

Frozen Apricot Yogurt

Frozen Vanilla Yogurt

Raspberry Yogurt Kuchen

Chris Klugman's Orange
Yogurt Bavarian

Prune Whip

Quick Lemon Yogurt Sauce

Apple Streusel Pie

Lime Meringue Pie

Lemon/Lime Pudding Cake
with Berries

Plum and Nectarine Cobbler

Rhubarb Strawberry Cobbler

Rhubarb Apple Crisp

Baked Apples with Maple
Yogurt Sauce

No Need to Skip Dessert

As a general rule, I consider a dessert healthy if it is relatively low in fat and calories (less than 10 g fat per serving) and has some nutrients other than the core ones of carbohydrates, protein and fat—for example, vitamin C, calcium or fibre. What I try to avoid—or eat less often—are desserts made with whipping cream, sour cream, cream cheese, chocolate, butter or margarine. Yogurt or ricotta cheese can often make perfect substitutes for some of these high-fat ingredients.

For those times when you really want a treat, here are charts to help you make wise choices when buying ice cream and frozen desserts.

ICE CREAM: THE FAT FACTS

Ice cream's the ultimate dessert — cool, satisfying and ready in an instant. But some ice creams have a lot more butterfat than others. To keep fat to a minimum, choose a lower-fat ice cream, ice milk or sherbet, or eat just a tiny portion of a high-fat ice cream if you simply can't resist. Most ice cream labels don't say how much fat is in the product, so here's the scoop.

Calories and fat in 1/2 cup (125 mL) vanilla ice cream

Product	Calories	Fat (g)
Haagen-Dazs	283	18.0
Neilson All Natural	190	10.8
Mövenpick	160	10.3
Neilson Famous	148	8.1
Vanilla Ice Cream (10% b.f.)	142	8.0
Home Scoop	123	6.8
Neilson Dietetic Delight (no sugar)	116	4.1
Light 'n' Lively Ice Milk (Neapolitan)	108	2.4

Calories and fat in 1/2 cup (125 mL) frozen yogurt, sherbet and Tofutti

Tofutti Wildberry Supreme	196	10.4
Fruit Fantasy Frozen Strawberry Whipped Yogurt	94	2.0
Frozen Vanilla Yogurt (recipe page 221)	181	1.9
Yogurty's Frozen Yogurt	120	1.7
Neilson Lime Sherbet	118	1.0
Tofutti Lite	95	0.6

Calories and fat in frozen dessert bars

Richard D Bar (110 mL)	360	27.2
Haagen-Dazs Vanilla Sundae Cup (110 mL)	248	17.0
Neilson Sweet Marie Bar (75 mL)	179	12.6
Oreo Cookies n' Cream Stick Bar (75 mL)	171	11.5
Neilson Ice Cream Sandwich (100 mL)	156	6.0
Fruit Fantasy Frozen Yogurt and Fruit Bar (75 mL)—Mixed Berries	71	1.5
Dole Fruit and Cream Bar (75 mL)	90	1.0
Dole Fruit and Juice Bar (75 mL)		
banana	80	trace
pineapple, strawberry	70	trace
Fruit Fantasy Fruit in Nectar Bar (75 mL)	72	0

Ricotta Lemon Cheesecake with Blueberries

I have always liked a cheesecake made with ricotta rather than cream cheese — even before I became concerned about using so much fat. However, this marvellous cheesecake recipe is much lower in fat than any other because of the small amount of fat in the crust. Using a combination of whole eggs and whites instead of using only whole eggs also reduces fat.

3 cups	low-fat ricotta cheese	750 mL
2	large eggs	2
1/2 cup	granulated sugar	125 mL
1/2 cup	low-fat yogurt	125 mL
1/4 cup	lemon juice	50 mL
	Grated rind of 2 lemons	
2 tbsp	all-purpose flour	25 mL
2 tsp	vanilla	10 mL
2	egg whites	2
1/2 cup	light sour cream	125 mL
2 cups	fresh blueberries	500 mL

Crust:

1 1/2 cups	graham wafer crumbs	375 mL
2 tbsp	granulated sugar	25 mL
1 tsp	cinnamon	5 mL
1 tbsp	soft margarine, melted	15 mL
1	egg white	1

Crust: In bowl, combine crumbs, sugar, cinnamon and margarine. Whisk egg white until frothy; stir into crumb mixture. Press into bottom of 9-inch (2.5 L) springform pan. Bake in 375°F (190°C) oven for 7 to 10 minutes or until lightly browned. Let cool.

In food processor (or using electric mixer), process ricotta cheese and whole eggs until smooth. In bowl, combine cheese mixture, sugar, yogurt, lemon juice and rind, flour and vanilla; beat until well mixed. Beat egg whites until soft peaks form; fold into cheese mixture. Spread over crust.

Bake in 375°F (190°C) oven for 50 to 55 minutes or until centre of cake is firm to touch. Run knife around edge of cake to loosen; let cool. Remove side of pan; cover cheesecake and refrigerate until chilled, at least 2 hours or up to 1 day.

Just before serving, spread top with sour cream, then cover with fresh blueberries.

Makes 10 servings.

PER SERVING	
Calories	**288**
g total fat	**11**
g saturated fat	**5**
g fibre	**1**

GOOD: Riboflavin, Calcium

g	protein	**13**
g	carbohydrate	**36**
mg	cholesterol	**67**
mg	sodium	**246**
mg	potassium	**246**

STRAWBERRY PAVLOVA WITH LEMON CREAM

Pavlova is one of my all-time favorite desserts to make. I use strawberries, raspberries, peaches, blueberries or a combination. I used to make it with whipping cream but now use a yogurt-based lemon sauce, which is fabulous. If you are making it in advance, use the Lemon Cream Sauce on facing page. If preparing it at the last minute, you can also use a double recipe of the Quick Lemon Yogurt Sauce on page 224.

3	egg whites (at room temperature)	3
Pinch	cream of tartar	Pinch
3/4 cup	granulated sugar	175 mL
1 tsp	vanilla	5 mL
2 cups	Lemon Cream Sauce (facing page)	500 mL
4 cups	strawberries, raspberries, peaches OR blueberries	1 L

In large bowl, beat egg whites with cream of tartar until soft peaks form. Beat in sugar 1 tbsp (15 mL) at a time until stiff glossy peaks form. Beat in vanilla.

On foil-lined baking sheet, spread meringue into 10-inch (25 cm) circle, pushing up edge to form ring. Bake in 275°F (140°C) oven for 1 1/2 hours or until firm to the touch. Turn off oven and leave meringue in oven to dry. Remove foil, then let cool and place meringue on serving platter.

Prepare fruit, slicing strawberries or peaches. Just before serving, spread Lemon Cream Sauce over meringue; cover with fruit. Cut into wedges to serve.

Makes 8 servings.

Meringue Shells: Prepare meringue as above. Spoon onto foil-lined baking sheet in bite-sized or 4- to 5-inch (10 to 12 cm) rounds. Using back of spoon, press down to indent and form shells. Bake and fill as above.

PER SERVING	
Calories	224
g total fat	2
g saturated fat	1
g fibre	2

GOOD: Vitamin C, Riboflavin, Calcium

g	protein	8
g	carbohydrate	44
mg	cholesterol	7
mg	sodium	106
mg	potassium	423

Fruit with Quick Marmalade Sauce

Make this with any combination of fresh fruit or berries and serve over Frozen Vanilla Yogurt (page 221) or with Pineapple Carrot Bars (page 204).

1/2 cup	marmalade	125 mL
1/4 cup	orange juice	50 mL
1 tbsp	lemon juice	15 mL
1/2 tsp	each grated lemon and orange rind	2 mL
5 cups	sliced fruit or berries	1250 mL
2 tbsp	Cointreau OR orange liqueur (optional)	25 mL

In bowl, mix marmalade, orange and lemon juice and rind. Add sliced fruit or berries; gently stir to mix well. Cover and let stand for up to 4 hours. Just before serving, stir in Cointreau (if using).

Makes 6 servings.

PER SERVING
(based on sliced peaches and plums)

Calories		102
g	total fat	trace
g	saturated fat	0
g	fibre	2
g	protein	1
g	carbohydrate	27
mg	cholesterol	0
mg	sodium	4
mg	potassium	138

Lemon Cream Sauce

I use this great-tasting sauce instead of whipped cream in many desserts such as cobblers or Pavlova. The fresh flavor pairs beautifully with fresh fruit, too—strawberries, blueberries, peaches or a combination of all three.

4 cups	low-fat yogurt* (no gelatin)	1 L
1/3 cup	granulated sugar	75 mL
2 tbsp	lemon juice	25 mL
	Grated rind of 1 lemon	

In cheesecloth-lined sieve set over bowl, cover yogurt and let drain in refrigerator for at least 4 hours or overnight or until yogurt is about 2 cups (500 mL) or less. Discard liquid.

In bowl, stir together drained yogurt, sugar, lemon juice and rind. Refrigerate for up to 2 days.

Makes 2 cups (500 mL).

*Be sure to use a natural yogurt without gelatin. One yogurt I used didn't drain.

Compare 1/4 cup (50 mL) of this lemon cream sauce with the same amount of unsweetened whipped cream:

This sauce: 2 g fat
Whipped cream: 10 g fat

PER 2 TBSP (25 ML)

Calories		55
g	total fat	1
g	saturated fat	1
g	fibre	0
g	protein	3
g	carbohydrate	9
mg	cholesterol	4
mg	sodium	43
mg	potassium	145

HEATHER EPP'S FRESH FRUIT TART

Heather Epp, a talented young chef, developed this wonderful pie. Combinations of other fruit — raspberries and blueberries, or peaches and plums, or kiwifruit and banana — look colorful and attractive, too. (Pictured opposite page 218.)

1	baked 9-inch (23 cm) pie shell (recipe follows)	1

Filling:

8 oz	dry curd no fat cottage cheese	250 g
1/4 cup	granulated sugar	50 mL
1	lemon, grated rind and juice	1

Topping:

3 cups	halved strawberries	750 mL
1 tbsp	currant jelly, melted (optional)	15 mL

Filling: In food processor or bowl, combine cottage cheese, sugar, lemon rind and juice; process or beat with electric mixer until smooth. Spread evenly in pie shell.

Topping: Arrange strawberries over filling. Brush strawberries with melted jelly (if using). Serve or refrigerate for up to 8 hours.

Makes 6 servings.

PER SERVING	
Calories	169
g total fat	4
g saturated fat	2
g fibre	2

EXCELLENT: Vitamin C

g	protein	8
g	carbohydrate	25
mg	cholesterol	13
mg	sodium	133
mg	potassium	160

PASTRY

This rich-tasting pastry makes a very thin crust so you might have to patch a little when you put it in the pie plate. Patches or not, it tastes wonderful and has half the fat of standard pastry. This recipe makes enough for one 8- or 9-inch (20 to 23 cm) single-crust pie shell.

2/3 cup	cake-and-pastry flour	150 mL
1/4 tsp	salt	1 mL
2 tbsp	hard margarine OR butter	25 mL
5 tsp	cold water	25 mL

In bowl, combine flour and salt. With pastry blender or fingertips, cut or rub in margarine until mixture is size of crumbs. Sprinkle with cold water, tossing with fork to mix. Gather dough together and form into ball. Wrap in plastic wrap and refrigerate for at least 1 hour or up to 24 hours.

On lightly floured surface, roll out pastry into round shape. Loosely roll around rolling pin and transfer to 8- or 9-inch (20 to 23 cm) pie plate without stretching pastry. Trim and flute edge.

To bake pie shell before filling, prick pastry all over with fork. To prevent pastry from becoming uneven and sides collapsing, line pie shell with large piece of foil and fill evenly with dried peas, beans or rice. Bake in 400°F (200°C) oven for 10 minutes. Remove beans and foil (these can be used again). Bake for 6 to 8 minutes longer or until golden brown. Let cool before filling.

Makes 1 pie shell.

BERRY BREAD PUDDING

I like this dessert because it isn't too sweet or rich but has fabulous flavor from the raspberries and strawberries. Top each serving with a spoonful of Quick Lemon Yogurt Sauce (page 224).

Half	large loaf French bread	Half
1 1/2 cups	low-fat milk	375 mL
1/2 cup	granulated sugar	125 mL
2 tsp	vanilla	10 mL
1/2 tsp	each nutmeg and cinnamon	2 mL
1 cup	chopped strawberries	250 mL
1 cup	raspberries	250 mL
2	eggs, beaten	2
1 tbsp	soft margarine	15 mL

Tear bread into 1-inch (2.5 cm) pieces to make 6 cups (1.5 L). In bowl, combine milk, sugar, vanilla, nutmeg and cinnamon; stir in bread and let stand for 10 minutes. Stir in strawberries, raspberries and eggs.

Meanwhile, in 8-inch (2 L) square baking dish, melt margarine in 350°F (180°C) oven; swirl to cover bottom of pan. Pour in batter. Bake for 40 minutes or until puffed and browned. Serve warm.

Makes 6 servings.

Amount of fruit will vary slightly depending on size of cake. A cake made from a mix will be the largest; it will serve about 10 people and need about 5 to 6 cups (1.25 to 1.5 L) fruit.

Blueberry-Strawberry Shortcake
Make Lighthearted Strawberry Shortcake and add 2 cups (500 mL) blueberries. Arrange with strawberries.

PER SERVING	
Calories	**167**
g total fat	**trace**
g saturated fat	**trace**
g fibre	**1**

EXCELLENT: Vitamin C

g	protein	**8**
g	carbohydrate	**34**
mg	cholesterol	**2**
mg	sodium	**65**
mg	potassium	**145**

LIGHTHEARTED STRAWBERRY SHORTCAKE

The lemon, yogurt and pressed cottage cheese in this wonderful dessert combine to make a refreshing, low-fat alternative to whipped cream.

8 oz	dry curd no fat cottage cheese	250 g
1/4 cup	low-fat yogurt	50 mL
1/4 cup	granulated sugar	50 mL
	Grated rind of 1 lemon	
1	angel cake*	1
3 cups	sliced fresh strawberries	750 mL

In bowl or food processor combine cottage cheese, yogurt, sugar and lemon rind; process or beat with electric mixer until smooth.

Cut cake horizontally into 3 layers. Spread one third of cheese mixture over first layer; arrange one third of berries on top. Repeat with remaining cake, cheese and berries to make 3 layers. Refrigerate up to 8 hours or until needed.

Makes 8 servings.

*Prepare angel cake from a mix or your favorite recipe or use Sweet Biscuits from Peach Shortcake (page 219).

Compare one serving of this shortcake to the traditional recipe:		
This recipe	76 calories	0.4 g fat
Strawberry shortcake made with 1 cup (250 mL) whipping cream and angel cake	237 calories	10.7 g fat

THREE BERRY SAUCE

Spoon this over angel cake, Frozen Vanilla Yogurt (page 221) or into meringue shells (see Strawberry Pavlova, page 214).

3 cups	sliced strawberries	750 mL
1 cup	blueberries	250 mL
1 cup	raspberries	250 mL
1/4 cup	granulated sugar	50 mL
2 tsp	cornstarch	10 mL
1/2 cup	water	125 mL

Wash and drain berries; place in bowl.

In small saucepan, combine sugar and cornstarch; add water. Cook, stirring, over medium heat until mixture comes to boil; boil for 1 minute. Pour over berries; stir well. Refrigerate for at least 1 hour or up to 24 hours.

Makes 6 servings.

PER SERVING	
Calories	**82**
g total fat	**trace**
g saturated fat	**0**
g fibre	**3**

EXCELLENT: Vitamin C

g	protein	**1**
g	carbohydrate	**20**
mg	cholesterol	**0**
mg	sodium	**3**
mg	potassium	**177**

PEACH SHORTCAKE

Make this delicious dessert in peach season when they're ripe and juicy. At other times, use any fruit in this old-fashioned classic. When I'm in a hurry, I mix the biscuit dough in the food processor, then just pat the dough on the counter and cut it into rounds.

10	peaches, peeled and sliced	10
2 tbsp	granulated sugar	25 mL
1 1/2 cups	Lemon Cream Sauce (page 215) OR Quick Lemon Yogurt Sauce (page 224)	375 mL

Sweet Biscuits:

2 cups	all-purpose flour	500 mL
2 tbsp	granulated sugar	25 mL
1 tbsp	baking powder	15 mL
1/4 tsp	salt	1 mL
5 tbsp	soft margarine	75 mL
3/4 cup	low-fat milk	175 mL

Sweet Biscuits: In bowl, combine flour, sugar, baking powder and salt. Using 2 knives, cut in margarine until mixture resembles coarse crumbs. Stir in milk, mixing just until moistened. Gather mixture into ball; knead for 30 seconds and pat onto lightly floured surface to about 3/4-inch (2 cm) thick.

Using 3-inch (8 cm) round cookie cutter or glass, cut out 10 rounds and place on baking sheet. Bake in 450°F (230°C) oven for 12 to 15 minutes or until golden.

In bowl, toss peaches with sugar. Split each biscuit in half and place bottoms on individual plates. Spoon some peaches on biscuit; cover with top biscuit. Spoon a few peach slices on top and pour Lemon Sauce over.

Makes 10 servings.

PER SERVING
(with Lemon Cream Sauce)

Calories	**275**
g total fat	**7**
g saturated fat	**2**
g fibre	**2**

GOOD: Riboflavin, Calcium

g protein	**8**
g carbohydrate	**45**
mg cholesterol	**6**
mg sodium	**245**
mg potassium	**403**

Compare one serving of this shortcake to the traditional recipe:

Recipe	Calories	Total Fat	Saturated Fat	Cholesterol
Peach Shortcake with Quick Lemon Yogurt Sauce	252	7 g	2 g	4 mg
Shortcake made with sweet biscuits, 1/2 cup (125 mL) butter, 3/4 cup (175 mL) table cream (18% b.f.) and 1 cup (250 mL) whipping cream	340	21 g	13 g	66 mg
Shortcake, as above, but with 2 cups (500 mL) whipping cream	419	29 g	18 g	97 mg

Whole Wheat Blueberry Biscuits (p. 203), Leslie's Muesli (p. 187)

Frozen Raspberry Yogurt

This creamy frozen yogurt is packed with fresh raspberry flavor.

1	package (10 oz/300 g) frozen unsweetened raspberries, thawed	1
1 1/2 cups	low-fat yogurt	375 mL
1/3 cup	granulated sugar	75 mL

In food processor or blender or using sieve or food mill, purée raspberries. Add yogurt and sugar; process or stir until sugar is dissolved.

Freeze according to directions on opposite page.

Makes 6 servings, about 1/2 cup (125 mL) each.

<table>
<tr><td colspan="3">PER SERVING</td></tr>
<tr><td></td><td>Calories</td><td>104</td></tr>
<tr><td>g</td><td>total fat</td><td>1</td></tr>
<tr><td>g</td><td>saturated fat</td><td>1</td></tr>
<tr><td>g</td><td>fibre</td><td>2</td></tr>
<tr><td>g</td><td>protein</td><td>4</td></tr>
<tr><td>g</td><td>carbohydrate</td><td>21</td></tr>
<tr><td>mg</td><td>cholesterol</td><td>4</td></tr>
<tr><td>mg</td><td>sodium</td><td>43</td></tr>
<tr><td>mg</td><td>potassium</td><td>215</td></tr>
</table>

Frozen Apricot Yogurt

Frozen yogurt made with a low-fat — 2% butterfat (b.f.) or less — yogurt has much less fat than ice cream. But even better news is that yogurt tastes just as good, if not better than the old-fashioned favorite. Serve with fresh fruit or berries or garnish with fresh mint leaf.

1 1/2 cups	dried apricots	375 mL
1 1/2 cups	orange juice	375 mL
3 cups	low-fat yogurt	750 mL
1 tsp	grated orange rind	5 mL

In small saucepan or microwaveable dish, combine apricots with orange juice; bring to boil. Cover and simmer over medium heat for 10 to 12 minutes, or cover and microwave at High power for 7 minutes, or until apricots are softened. Purée in food processor or blender or pass through food mill; let cool.

Combine apricot mixture, yogurt and orange rind; mix well. Freeze according to directions on opposite page.

Makes 8 servings.

<table>
<tr><td colspan="3">PER SERVING</td></tr>
<tr><td></td><td>Calories</td><td>137</td></tr>
<tr><td>g</td><td>total fat</td><td>2</td></tr>
<tr><td>g</td><td>saturated fat</td><td>1</td></tr>
<tr><td>g</td><td>fibre</td><td>2</td></tr>
<tr><td colspan="3">GOOD: Vitamins A and C, Riboflavin, Calcium</td></tr>
<tr><td>g</td><td>protein</td><td>6</td></tr>
<tr><td>g</td><td>carbohydrate</td><td>27</td></tr>
<tr><td>mg</td><td>cholesterol</td><td>6</td></tr>
<tr><td>mg</td><td>sodium</td><td>67</td></tr>
<tr><td>mg</td><td>potassium</td><td>639</td></tr>
</table>

FROZEN VANILLA YOGURT

Serve this frozen yogurt instead of ice cream. For a creamier frozen yogurt, drain the yogurt first.

2 cups	plain, natural 2% yogurt OR drained yogurt*	500 mL
1/2 cup	granulated sugar	125 mL
2 tsp	pure vanilla extract	10 mL

In bowl, combine yogurt, sugar and vanilla, stirring to dissolve sugar. Pour into pan or ice-cream machine and freeze according to instructions below.

Makes 4 servings, 1/2 cup (125 mL) each.

*To drain yogurt, place 4 cups (1 L) yogurt (made without gelatin) in cheesecloth-lined sieve set over bowl. Refrigerate for 3 to 4 hours or until volume of yogurt is about 2 cups (500 mL).

Compare 1/2 cup (125 mL) of this frozen dessert to some others:		
Dessert	*Calories*	*Fat*
This recipe	181	1.9 g
Haagen-Dazs ice cream	283	18 g
Ice cream (10% b.f.)	142	8 g
Light 'n' Lively ice milk	108	2.4 g

The phrase "calorie reduced" means that the product must contain at least 25% fewer calories than the food in its usual form. The fat content may or may not be adjusted. For more labelling information, see page 240.

FREEZING AND SERVING INSTRUCTIONS FOR YOGURTS AND SORBETS

Transfer to an ice-cream machine and freeze according to manufacturer's instructions. Or, transfer to shallow metal cake pan; freeze until almost solid. Break into big chunks and beat with electric mixer or whirl in food processor until smooth. Transfer to airtight container and freeze until firm (about 30 minutes to 1 hour). Let stand in refrigerator for 15 to 30 minutes or until softened before serving.

RASPBERRY YOGURT KUCHEN

This easy-to-make cheesecake-type dessert is a family favorite. For such a rich-tasting finale, it is low in fat and calories.

1 1/2 cups	all-purpose flour	375 mL
1/2 cup	granulated sugar	125 mL
1 1/2 tsp	baking powder	7 mL
1/3 cup	soft margarine	75 mL
2	egg whites	2
1 tsp	vanilla	5 mL
3 cups	fresh raspberries OR 1 package (10 oz) individually frozen (not thawed)	750 mL

Topping:

2 tbsp	all-purpose flour	25 mL
2 cups	low-fat yogurt	500 mL
1	egg, lightly beaten	1
2/3 cup	granulated sugar	150 mL
2 tsp	grated lemon rind	10 mL
1 tsp	vanilla	5 mL

In food processor or mixing bowl, combine flour, sugar, baking powder, margarine, egg whites and vanilla; mix well. Press onto bottom of 10-inch (3 L) square cake pan or springform or flan pan; sprinkle with raspberries.

   Topping: In bowl, sprinkle flour over yogurt. Add egg, sugar, lemon rind and vanilla; mix until smooth. Pour over berries.

   Bake in 350°F (180°C) oven for 70 minutes or until golden. Serve warm or cold.

Makes 12 servings.

Pear Yogurt Kuchen
Prepare Raspberry Yogurt Kuchen, but substitute 5 peeled, thinly sliced small pears for raspberries. Substitute 1 tsp (5 mL) almond extract for vanilla.

PER SERVING

Calories		**235**
g	total fat	**6**
g	saturated fat	**2**
g	fibre	**2**
g	protein	**5**
g	carbohydrate	**39**
mg	cholesterol	**20**
mg	sodium	**122**
mg	potassium	**174**

Chris Klugman's Orange Yogurt Bavarian

Chris Klugman, talented Canadian chef, makes a variation of this lovely, light dessert.

1	envelope gelatin	1
1 cup	orange juice	250 mL
1/2 cup	low-fat yogurt	125 mL
	Grated rind of 1 orange	
2	egg whites	2
1/2 cup	granulated sugar	125 mL
1/4 cup	no fat milk	50 mL

In bowl, sprinkle gelatin over orange juice; let stand for 5 minutes to soften. Heat over simmering water until gelatin dissolves. Refrigerate until syrupy; stir in yogurt and orange rind until smooth.

In separate bowl, beat egg whites until soft peaks form; gradually beat in sugar until stiff peaks form. In another bowl, beat skim milk until frothy and tripled in volume.

Fold beaten whites, then whipped milk into orange mixture. Spoon into individual ramekins or serving dishes. Refrigerate until set, about 2 hours. (Bavarians can be prepared a day in advance.)

Makes 8 servings, 1/2 cup (125 mL) each.

PER SERVING		
Calories		87
g	total fat	trace
g	saturated fat	trace
g	fibre	trace
g	protein	3
g	carbohydrate	18
mg	cholesterol	1
mg	sodium	32
mg	potassium	138

PRUNE WHIP

For years my husband, Bob, had been telling me about this wonderful dessert that his mother used to make. I finally made it and now I agree with him — it does taste delicious. Serve with Gingersnaps (page 208) or Lemon Sugar Cookies (page 207).

1 cup	prunes	250 mL
3	egg whites	3
1/2 cup	granulated sugar	125 mL
2 tbsp	lemon juice	25 mL
1 tsp	grated lemon rind	5 mL
Pinch	salt	Pinch

In small saucepan, cover prunes with water and bring to boil; reduce heat, cover and simmer for 15 minutes. Drain prunes, saving 3 tbsp (45 mL) juice. Pit and chop prunes to make 1/2 cup (125 mL). Set aside.

In top of double boiler or heatproof bowl, combine egg whites, sugar, reserved prune juice, lemon juice, rind and salt. Place over hot simmering water and using electric mixer, beat for 5 to 7 minutes or until stiff peaks form. Remove from heat. Lightly fold in prunes. Spoon into individual stemmed sherbet glasses or dishes. Chill for 2 hours or up to 8 hours.

Makes 6 servings.

PER SERVING	
Calories	**138**
g total fat	**trace**
g saturated fat	**0**
g fibre	**2**
g protein	**2**
g carbohydrate	**34**
mg cholesterol	**0**
mg sodium	**26**
mg potassium	**230**

Orange Yogurt Sauce
Substitute grated orange rind for lemon rind.

PER 2 TBSP (25 ML)	
Calories	**36**
g total fat	**trace**
g saturated fat	**trace**
g fibre	**trace**
g protein	**2**
g carbohydrate	**6**
mg cholesterol	**2**
mg sodium	**21**
mg potassium	**73**

QUICK LEMON YOGURT SAUCE

Serve this delicious, easy sauce over fresh fruit or with baked desserts instead of whipped cream or ice cream.

3/4 cup	low-fat yogurt	175 mL
2 tbsp	granulated sugar	25 mL
	Grated rind of 1 lemon	

In small bowl, combine yogurt, sugar and lemon rind. Cover and refrigerate for up to 3 days.

Makes 3/4 cup (175 mL).

APPLE STREUSEL PIE

This old-fashioned dessert will always be a favorite in our house. Depending on the sweetness of the apples, you might want to reduce the sugar.

5 cups	thinly sliced peeled apple	1.25 L
2 tsp	lemon juice	10 mL
1/2 cup	granulated sugar	125 mL
3 tbsp	all-purpose flour	45 mL
1 tsp	grated lemon rind	5 mL
1 tsp	cinnamon	5 mL
1/4 tsp	nutmeg	1 mL
1	unbaked 9-inch (23 cm) pie shell (page 216)	1

Topping:

1/3 cup	packed brown sugar	75 mL
3 tbsp	rolled oats	45 mL
3 tbsp	whole wheat flour	45 mL
1 tsp	cinnamon	5 mL
1 tbsp	soft margarine	15 mL

In bowl, toss apples with lemon juice. In another bowl, combine sugar, flour, lemon rind, cinnamon and nutmeg; sprinkle over apples and stir until apples are well coated. Spoon into pie shell.

Topping: In bowl, combine brown sugar, rolled oats, flour and cinnamon. With two knives cut in margarine until mixture is crumbly; sprinkle over filling. Bake in 425°F (220°C) oven for 40 minutes or until top is golden and apples are tender.

Makes 8 servings.

PER SERVING	
Calories	**217**
g total fat	**5**
g saturated fat	**3**
g fibre	**2**
g protein	**2**
g carbohydrate	**43**
mg cholesterol	**12**
mg sodium	**114**
mg potassium	**125**

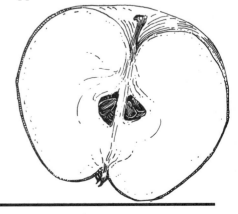

LIME MERINGUE PIE

A meringue crust with a tangy lime chiffon filling makes this a light and luscious dessert. This can be prepared early in the day or a day in advance.

Meringue Crust:

2	egg whites	2
1/4 tsp	cream of tartar	1 mL
1/2 cup	granulated sugar	125 mL

Lime Chiffon Filling:

2	eggs, separated	2
2	egg whites	2
3/4 cup	water	175 mL
2/3 cup	granulated sugar	150 mL
1 tbsp	grated lime rind	15 mL
1	envelope unflavored gelatin	1
1/3 cup	lime juice (about 2 large limes)	75 mL

Meringue Crust: In bowl and using electric mixer, beat egg whites with cream of tartar until soft peaks form. Beating constantly, gradually add sugar, a tablespoon (15 mL) at a time, and beat until stiff, glossy peaks form.

Spread meringue in foil-lined 9-inch (23 cm) pie plate, pushing mixture at sides to come about 1 inch (2.5 cm) above edge of plate. Bake in 275°F (140°C) oven for about 65 minutes or until lightly golden and dry to the touch. Carefully remove foil, then let cool on rack.

Filling: In nonaluminum saucepan, whisk egg yolks lightly; add water, half of the sugar and lime rind. Cook over low heat, stirring constantly, for 10 to 15 minutes or until mixture thickens slightly and coats metal spoon. Remove from heat.

Sprinkle gelatin over lime juice; let stand for 2 minutes to soften. Stir into yolk mixture until gelatin dissolves. Cover and refrigerate for about 10 minutes or until thickened slightly.

Meanwhile, in large bowl, beat the 4 egg whites until soft peaks form. Beating constantly, gradually add remaining sugar and beat until stiff peaks form. Fold into lime mixture. Spoon into meringue shell and refrigerate for about 3 hours or until set.

Makes 8 Servings

*** Lemon Meringue Pie***

Make Lime Meringue Pie, but substitute 1 tbsp (15 mL) grated lemon rind for lime rind and 1/3 cup (75 mL) lemon juice for lime juice.

PER SERVING	
Calories	**146**
g total fat	**1**
g saturated fat	**trace**
g fibre	**trace**
g protein	**4**
g carbohydrate	**31**
mg cholesterol	**54**
mg sodium	**43**
mg potassium	**51**

Lemon/Lime Pudding Cake with Berries

This old-fashioned dessert is really delicious. Bake it in eight individual (1/2 cup/125 mL size) ramekins, or one large (6 cup/1.5 L) baking dish. Serve topped with any kind of fruit or on its own sprinkled with icing sugar.

3/4 cup	granulated sugar	175 mL
2 tbsp	soft margarine	25 mL
	Grated rind of 3 limes OR 2 lemons	
2	eggs, separated	2
1/3 cup	lime OR lemon juice	75 mL
1/4 cup	all-purpose flour	50 mL
1 cup	low-fat milk	250 mL
2 cups	strawberries OR blueberries	500 mL

In mixing bowl, beat together sugar, margarine and lime or lemon rind. Beat in egg yolks, one at a time, beating well after each addition. Beat in lime or lemon juice, then flour and milk.

In separate bowl, beat egg whites until soft peaks form; fold into batter; pour into 6-cup (1.5 L) baking dish. Place in larger pan and pour in boiling water to come about 1 inch (2.5 cm) up sides of pan. Bake in 350°F (180°C) oven for 40 minutes. Spoon berries over top. Serve warm or cold.

Makes 6 servings.

PER SERVING		
Calories		221
g	total fat	6
g	saturated fat	2
g	fibre	1

GOOD: Vitamin C

g	protein	4
g	carbohydrate	38
mg	cholesterol	75
mg	sodium	77
mg	potassium	172

PLUM AND NECTARINE COBBLER

I used to make this dessert for Sunday-night dinners but thought it wasn't fancy enough for entertaining. Since I now think any home-made dessert is a treat, especially the comforting old-fashioned ones (with the sugar cut down), I served this at a dinner party and everyone asked for the recipe. Serve with Lemon Cream Sauce on page 215. (Pictured opposite page 187.)

1 cup	granulated sugar	250 mL
3 tbsp	all-purpose flour	45 mL
2 tsp	finely grated orange rind	10 mL
2 tsp	cinnamon	10 mL
5 cups	chopped plums	1.25 L
5 cups	chopped nectarines	1.25 L

Topping:

2 cups	all-purpose flour	500 mL
1/4 cup	granulated sugar	50 mL
2 tsp	baking powder	10 mL
1/2 tsp	baking soda	2 mL
1/2 tsp	salt	2 mL
1/3 cup	soft margarine, in bits	75 mL
1 1/3 cups	low-fat buttermilk	325 mL

Diet or calorie-reduced margarines are not recommended for baking.

In large bowl, combine sugar, flour, orange rind and cinnamon. Add plums and nectarines; toss to combine. Spread mixture in shallow glass 13- × 9-inch (3.5 L) baking dish; bake in 400°F (200°C) oven for 10 minutes.

Topping: Meanwhile, in large bowl, stir together flour, sugar, baking powder, baking soda and salt. Using fingers, rub in margarine until mixture is size of small peas. Make well in centre; pour in buttermilk. With fork, stir just until soft dough forms.

Drop dough by large spoonfuls in 12 evenly spaced mounds on hot fruit. Bake in 400°F (200°C) oven for 25 minutes or until top is golden.

Makes 12 servings.

PER SERVING	
Calories	**287**
g total fat	**6**
g saturated fat	**1**
g fibre	**3**
g protein	**4**
g carbohydrate	**55**
mg cholesterol	**1**
mg sodium	**273**
mg potassium	**308**

RHUBARB STRAWBERRY COBBLER

I like to make this for Sunday family suppers or a dinner party. Tangy rhubarb mixed with sweet strawberries is a great flavor combination. Serve with Quick Lemon Yogurt Sauce (page 224).

3/4 cup	granulated sugar	175 mL
2 tbsp	all-purpose flour	25 mL
1 tsp	cinnamon	5 mL
1 tsp	finely grated orange rind	5 mL
4 cups	coarsely chopped (3/4-inch/2 cm pieces) rhubarb	1 L
2 cups	sliced strawberries	500 mL

Topping:

1 cup	all-purpose flour	250 mL
2 tbsp	granulated sugar	25 mL
1 tsp	baking powder	5 mL
1/4 tsp	baking soda	1 mL
1/4 tsp	salt	1 mL
2 tbsp	margarine, chilled and cut in bits	25 mL
2/3 cup	low-fat buttermilk	150 mL

In bowl, combine sugar, flour, cinnamon and orange rind. Add rhubarb and strawberries; toss to mix. Spread mixture in 8-cup (2 L) shallow glass baking dish; bake in 400°F (200°C) oven for 10 minutes.

Topping: In large bowl, mix flour, sugar, baking powder, baking soda and salt. Using fingers or two knives, cut in margarine until mixture is size of small peas.

With fork, stir in buttermilk until mixture is moistened and soft dough forms. Drop by spoonfuls in 6 evenly spaced mounds on hot fruit. Bake in 400°F (200°C) oven for 25 minutes or until top is golden.

Makes 6 servings.

In the past, overly sweet desserts needed ice cream or whipped cream to balance the sweetness. When you cut down on the sugar in pies, cobblers and other desserts you will find that they don't need ice cream and are quite delicious on their own.

PER SERVING	
Calories	276
g total fat	5
g saturated fat	1
g fibre	3

GOOD: Vitamin C	
g protein	4
g carbohydrate	56
mg cholesterol	1
mg sodium	241
mg potassium	354

RHUBARB APPLE CRISP

The delicious flavor combination of apple and rhubarb is accented with a touch of lemon rind and cinnamon. This crisp has less fat than most recipes (2 tablespoons/25 mL rather than 1/2 cup/125 mL), and soft margarine is used rather than butter because it is lower in saturated fat. Traditional recipes call for the butter or margarine to be cut in. Here, it is melted and tossed with the topping ingredients, which makes it seem to go farther.

To peel or not to peel?

I always wonder if I should peel apples (or other fruits) in desserts. It mainly depends on the condition of the skin and the type of dessert. In a crisp, as long as the skin is free of blemishes, looks tender and isn't waxed, I don't peel the apples. The thinner you slice the apples the less you will notice the peel; as a bonus you will have more nutrients and fibre.

Filling:

2/3 cup	granulated sugar	150 mL
3 tbsp	all-purpose flour	45 mL
1 tsp	grated lemon rind	5 mL
3 cups	fresh OR frozen (thawed) rhubarb, cut in 1/2-inch (1 cm) pieces	750 mL
3 cups	sliced apples	750 mL

Topping:

1/3 cup	packed brown sugar	75 mL
1/3 cup	rolled oats	75 mL
3 tbsp	whole wheat flour	45 mL
1 tsp	cinnamon	5 mL
2 tbsp	soft margarine, melted	25 mL

Filling: In bowl, combine sugar, flour and lemon rind; mix well. Add rhubarb and apple; stir to mix. Spoon into 8-cup (2 L) baking dish.

Topping: In bowl, combine sugar, rolled oats, flour and cinnamon. Add melted margarine and stir to mix; sprinkle over filling.

Bake in 375°F (190°C) oven for 40 to 50 minutes, until filling is bubbly and topping is brown. Serve warm or at room temperature.

Microwave Method: Prepare as above. Microwave, uncovered, at High power for 9 minutes, or until fruit is tender.

Makes 6 servings.

PER SERVING		
Calories		**248**
g	total fat	**4**
g	saturated fat	**1**
g	fibre	**3**
g	protein	**2**
g	carbohydrate	**52**
mg	cholesterol	**0**
mg	sodium	**39**
mg	potassium	**123**

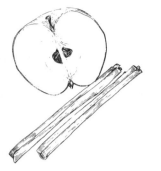

BAKED APPLES WITH MAPLE YOGURT SAUCE

When choosing apples for baking, look for a large, firm, tart apple such as the Ida Red or the Northern Spy. For a juicier apple, the Mutsu also makes an excellent baked apple. If choosing a medium-sized apple, the tender, sweet McIntosh requires a shorter cooking time and only 1/4 cup (50 mL) sugar.

4	apples	4
1/3 cup	packed brown sugar	75 mL
1/4 cup	raisins	50 mL
2 tsp	cinnamon	10 mL
1/2 tsp	nutmeg	2 mL

Maple Yogurt Sauce:

3/4 cup	low-fat yogurt	175 mL
1/4 cup	maple syrup	50 mL

Core apples; remove top inch (2.5 cm) of peel. Make a shallow cut through skin around centre of each apple to prevent skin from bursting. Place apples upright in baking dish or pie plate.

In small bowl, combine brown sugar, raisins, cinnamon and nutmeg; spoon into centres of each apple. Add water to cover bottom of dish. Bake, uncovered, in 375°F (190°C) oven for 25 to 30 minutes for less firm apples, and up to 50 minutes for firm varieties, or until apples are tender when pierced with toothpick.

Maple Yogurt Sauce: In bowl, combine yogurt and maple syrup. Pour over baked apples.

Microwave Method: Apples baked in the microwave have tougher skins than oven baked. Prepare as directed in recipe. Pierce skin in several places with toothpick to prevent skin from bursting. Cover with waxed paper; microwave at High power for 6 to 9 minutes or until apples are almost tender. Let stand for 5 minutes. Serve with Maple Yogurt Sauce.

Makes 4 servings.

PER SERVING	
Calories	252
g total fat	1
g saturated fat	1
g fibre	4
g protein	3
g carbohydrate	61
mg cholesterol	3
mg sodium	40
mg potassium	421

LIGHTHEARTED EVERYDAY MENUS

Seasonal Family Dinners (in 30 minutes or less)

Spring

Linguine with Asparagus and Red Pepper (page 150)
French Bread
Stewed Rhubarb

Microwave Sole with Mushrooms and Ginger (page 100)
Rice and Snow Peas OR Green Beans
Strawberries

Microwave Mustard Herb Chicken (page 85)
Orange Sherbet and Cookies

Salmon and Spinach Gratin (page 107)
Cherry Tomatoes and Toasted Whole Wheat English Muffins
Sliced Melon

Easy Everyday Chicken Stir-Fry (page 93)
Rice
Oranges and Bananas

Beef 'n' Bean Minestrone (page 53)
Quick Spinach Salad with Sprouts (page 78)
Toasted Pita Bread
Strawberries

Summer

Barbecued Salmon Fillets (page 63) OR Flank Steak with Citrus and Pepper Marinade (page 122)
New Little Potatoes with Fresh Dill
Corn-on-the-cob and Sliced Tomatoes
Blueberries

Burgers with Coriander-Yogurt Sauce (page 116)
Greek Salad (page 69)
Frozen Yogurt and Berries

Grilled Lemon Chicken with Rosemary (page 90)
Thai Noodle Salad (page 63)
Sliced Cucumbers

Indonesian Fried Rice (optional use of any leftover barbecued meats or chicken) (page 181)
Tossed Green Salad

Oriental Chicken Pasta Salad (page 68)
Sliced Tomatoes, Cucumbers, Leaf Lettuce
French Bread

Bean and Vegetable Burritos (page 174)
Melon with Blueberries

Fall

Penne with Tomato, Black Olive and Feta (page 154)
Tossed Green Salad with Creamy Garlic Dressing (page 80)
Sliced Peaches
Harvest Vegetable Curry (page 171) over Couscous or Rice
Sliced Tomatoes with Fresh Herbs
Fresh Pears

Beef and Pepper Stir-Fry (page 118)
OR Chicken Kabobs with Peppers and Zucchini (page 87)
Rice or Pasta
Fresh Plums

Pilaf Supper for One (page 129)
Tossed Green Salad with Creamy Garlic Dressing (page 80)

Pasta with Sweet Peppers, Cheese and Basil (page 161)
Green Beans and Whole Wheat Bread

Wild Rice and Bulgur Salad in Pita (page 74)
Sliced Tomatoes
Baked Apples with Maple Yogurt Sauce (Microwave) (page 231)

Winter

Favorite Spaghetti (page 164)
Quick Spinach Salad with Sprouts (page 78)
Orange Sherbet and Cookies

Easy Veal Cutlets with Tarragon Sauce
(page 131)
Steamed Squash and Microwave Baked
Potatoes
Low-Cal Coleslaw (page 72)

Chinese Noodles with Mushrooms and Pork
(page 166)
Frozen Peas
Baked Apples with Maple-Yogurt Sauce
(page 231)

Pork with Broccoli Stir-Fry (page 125)
Noodles OR Rice
Tossed Salad

Hearty Salmon Chowder (page 51)
Buttermilk Oatmeal Raisin Scones (page 201)
Bananas and Yogurt with Cinnamon

Penne with Italian Sausage, Tomato and Herbs
(page 155)
Raw Carrots, Green Pepper Strips
French Bread
Mandarin Oranges

15-Minute Dinners — any time of the year

Desserts: fruit, frozen yogurt or sherbet,
cookies

Instant salad: Use packaged or pre-washed
salad greens plus alfalfa sprouts, and
previously prepared salad dressing (page
79, 80 or 81) or a dash each of olive oil and
rice vinegar or balsamic vinegar.

Speedy Lentil and Bean Casserole (page 172)
Raw Carrots and Green Pepper Strips
Whole Wheat Toast

———————

Microwave Leek and Mushroom Flan
(page 188)
Frozen Peas and Sliced Tomatoes
Whole Wheat Buns

Spanish Omelette (page 189)
Tossed Green Salad and Whole Wheat Toast

———————

Sweet Pepper and Mushroom Pizza
(page 190)
OR Quick Tomato, Broccoli and Red Onion
Pizza (page 40)
Raw Vegetables

———————

Easy Fish and Tomato Stew (page 109) with
Couscous (page 176)
Pumpernickel Bread

———————

Teriyaki Orange Fish Fillets (page 106)
OR Pacific Snapper Fillets with Herbs
(page 102)
OR Microwave Sole with Mushrooms and
Ginger (page 100)
Asparagus OR Broccoli OR Frozen Peas
Creamed Corn OR Microwave Baked Potatoes

———————

Lamb Chops Dijon (page 128)
Broiled Tomato Half OR Cherry Tomatoes
Sesame Broccoli (page 145) OR Green Beans
Crusty Rolls

———————

Spicy Beef Chow Mein (page 119)
Green Salad (to make within 15 minutes, use
prepared salad greens and have dressing
made in advance)

———————

Pork with Broccoli Stir-Fry (page 125)
Chinese Vermicelli Noodles

———————

Microwave Mustard Herb Chicken (page 85)
Sesame Broccoli (page 145) OR Peas
Couscous

———————

Sliced cold meat (turkey, chicken) OR prepared
soup
Red Bean Salad with Feta and Pepper
(page 65)
Pita Bread

———————

Jiffy Bean, Broccoli and Tomato Chowder
(page 59)
Toasted Bagel with Light Cream Cheese

———————

Chinese Noodle and Mushroom Soup
(page 58)
Tomato Slices with Chevre and Basil (page 78)
Whole Wheat Pita Bread

Tarragon-Orange Grilled Turkey (page 97)
Microwave Baked Potatoes
Tossed Green Salad (prepackaged or pre-
washed greens)

Barbecued Salmon Fillets (page 103)
Boiled New Potatoes with Fresh Dill
Asparagus OR Broccoli

Easy Everyday Chicken Stir-Fry (page 93)
(to save time use pre-cut vegetables)
Chinese Rice Noodles

Burgers with Coriander-Yogurt Sauce
(page 116)
Coleslaw OR Sliced Tomatoes and Cucumbers

Lentil Spinach Soup with Curried Yogurt
(page 47)
Raw Vegetable Platter
Whole Grain Bread

Lighthearted Fettuccine Alfredo (page 165)
OR Kids' Easy Macaroni and Cheese with
Vegetables (page 162)
Sliced Tomatoes OR Frozen Peas

Quick and Easy One-Dish Dinners
*Serve with whole grain bread, raw carrots or
sliced tomatoes or cucumbers or green salad.*

Chinese Rice and Vegetable Stir-Fry
(page 182)
Spicy Thai Noodles with Vegetables
(page 156)
Kids' Easy Macaroni and Cheese with
Vegetables (page 162)
Tomato Ham Pasta Dinner for One (page 163)
Pasta with Tuna Cream Sauce (page 152)
Easy Linguine with Scallops and Spinach
(page 151)

Pasta with Sweet Peppers, Cheese and Basil
(page 161)
Lighthearted Fettuccine Alfredo (page 165)
Favorite Spaghetti (page 164)
Penne with Tomato, Black Olive and Feta
(page 154)
Penne with Italian Sausage, Tomato and Herbs
(page 155)
Linguine with Asparagus and Red Pepper
(page 150)
Jiffy Bean, Broccoli and Tomato Chowder
(page 59)
Quick and Easy Fish Chowder (page 50)
El Paso Pilaf (page 178)
Sweet Pepper and Mushroom Pizza
(page 190)
Bean and Vegetable Burritos (page 174)
Turkey and Potato Hash (page 98)
Indonesian Fried Rice with Chicken (page 181)
Harvest Vegetable Curry (page 171)
Steamed Mussels with Tomato and Fennel
(page 111)
Easy Fish and Tomato Stew (page 109)
Pilaf Supper for One (page 129)
Chinese Noodles with Mushrooms and Pork
(page 166)
Spicy Beef Chow Mein (page 166)
Hamburger and Noodle Skillet Supper
(page 117)
Pork with Broccoli Stir-Fry (page 125)
Speedy Lentil and Bean Casserole (page 172)
Oriental Chicken Pasta Salad (page 68)
Curried Rice and Salmon Salad (page 64)

Make-Ahead One-Dish Dinners
*Depending on the season, serve with sliced
tomatoes or raw vegetables or green salad and
whole grain bread.*

Family Favorite Lasagna (page 160)
Pasta e Fagioli (page 149)

Favorite Spaghetti (page 164)

Mediterranean Barley and Brown Rice Bake (page 183)

Black Bean and Ham Soup (page 49)

Old-Fashioned Quebec Pea Soup (page 44)

Hearty Salmon Chowder (page 51)

Smoky Sausage Lentil Soup (page 49)

Old-Fashioned Mushroom Barley Soup (page 56)

Beef 'n' Bean Minestrone (page 53)

French Onion Soup (page 57)

Old-Fashioned Baked Beans (page 175)

Lamb Shank and Vegetable Stew (page 130)

Beef and Vegetable Chili OR Vegetarian Chili (page 114)

Beef and Vegetable Stew (page 120)

Moroccan Chicken Stew with Couscous (page 95)

Simmered Chicken Dinner (page 86)

Curried Chicken and Shrimp (page 110)

Oriental Chicken Pasta Salad (page 68)

Make-Ahead Turkey Divan (page 96)

Hamburger and Noodle Skillet Supper (page 117)

Easy Fish and Tomato Stew (page 109)

Harvest Vegetable Curry (page 171)

Make-Ahead Risotto with Fresh Basil and Radicchio (page 179)

Italian Sausage (page 158) OR Vegetarian Lasagna (page 160)

Mushroom and Sweet Pepper Lasagna (page 158)

Eggplant-Tomato Gratin (page 142)

Kids' Easy Macaroni and Cheese with Vegetables (page 162)

Emergency Shelf Dinners From the Pantry and/or Freezer

Sometimes I get so busy I don't have time to grocery shop and my refrigerator is bare. Instead of ordering pizza or rushing out to pick up chicken, I think it's just as easy to have a few staples in the freezer or pantry so you can make a quick meal. Try to have the following basics on hand: onions, garlic, gingerroot, reduced-sodium soy sauce, rice vinegar, sesame oil, herbs and spices. Consider the following possibilities:

If you have canned tomatoes and frozen fish fillets you can make Easy Fish and Tomato Stew (page 109).

If you have frozen fish fillets, yogurt or orange, frozen peas, couscous or rice on hand you can make Teriyaki Orange Fish Fillets (page 106) OR Pacific Snapper Fillets with Herbs (page 102) with Frozen Peas, Couscous OR Rice.

Ground beef, peas and corn from the freezer and tomato sauce and noodles from the cupboard will make Hamburger and Noodle Skillet Supper (page 117).

Frozen ground beef, canned tomatoes and beans can be made into Beef and Vegetable Chili (page 114).

Ground pork, beef or turkey or shrimp from the freezer, dried mushrooms and Chinese vermicelli can be made into Chinese Noodles with Mushrooms and Pork (page 166).

Frozen ground beef, tomato paste, canned tomatoes and spaghetti will provide a meal of Favorite Spaghetti (page 164).

If you have frozen sausage, canned tomatoes and pasta you can make Penne with Italian Sausage, Tomato and Herbs (page 155).

Canned kidney beans, lentils and tomatoes will combine for Speedy Lentil and Bean Casserole (page 172).

Special Dinners

Saturday Night Dinner Party for Eight

Crudités with Spinach and Artichoke Dip (page 26)

Summer Tomato and Green Bean Soup (page 45)
OR Purée of Carrot and Parsnip (page 54)

Pasta with Shrimp, Zucchini and Mushrooms (page 153)
Arugula and Boston Lettuce Salad with Walnut Oil Vinaigrette (page 82)

Raspberry Yogurt Kuchen (page 222)

Buffet Dinner for Twelve

Endive Spears with Chevre and Shrimp (page 31)
Light and Easy Guacamole (page 32)

Lemon Ginger Pork Loin with Mango Salsa (page 123)
Grilled Sweet Peppers and Leeks (page 135) OR Sesame Broccoli (page 145)
Make-Ahead Risotto with Fresh Basil and Radicchio (page 179)

Plum and Nectarine Cobbler with Lemon Cream Sauce (page 228 and page 215)
OR Lime Meringue Pie (page 226)

Dinner Party in an Hour

Tomato Slices with Chevre and Basil (page 78)

Baked Salmon Trout with Papaya-Cucumber Salsa (page 104)
Rose Murray's Baked Asparagus (page 141)
Couscous with Lemon and Fresh Basil (page 177)

Lime Pudding Cake (page 227) OR Fresh Berries

Buffet Dinner for A Crowd

Moroccan Chicken Stew with Couscous (page 95) OR Rice
Rose Murray's Baked Asparagus (page 141) OR Green Beans
Orange and Fennel Salad (page 77)
OR Arugula and Boston Lettuce Salad with Walnut Oil Vinaigrette (page 82)

Strawberry Pavlova with Lemon Cream Sauce (page 214)
OR Chris Klugman's Orange Yogurt Bavarian (page 223)
and Lemon Sugar Cookies (page 207)

Compare the fat and calorie counts for a traditional turkey dinner and a lighthearted one:

Holiday Turkey Dinner

	g total fat	g saturated fat	calories
Eggnog (1 drink): 4 oz/115 mL eggnog and 1 1/2 oz/ 20 mL rum	9.5	5.6	264
Chicken liver pâté: 4 tbsp/60 mL pâté on 4 Ritz crackers	10.3	2.1	176
Raw vegetables with 2 tbsp/30 mL dip (made with mayonnaise)	16.0	1.5	146
Turkey: 6 oz/170 g dark meat with skin	19.6	5.9	376
Stuffing: 1/2 cup/125 mL made with added fat	5.0	1.0	96
Gravy: 1/4 cup/50 mL	1.3	.4	31
Mashed potatoes			
1/2 cup/125 mL	0.1	.0	67
with 2 tsp/10 mL butter	7.7	4.8	68
and 2 tsp/10 mL 18% cream	1.8	1.1	18
Turnips			
1/2 cup/125 mL	.2	.0	42
with 1 tsp/5 mL butter	3.7	2.3	33
Jellied salad	.1	.0	37
with 2 tsp/10 mL mayonnaise	7.3	.7	66
Mincemeat pie	18.1	4.7	427
with 2 tbsp/30 mL hard sauce (made with butter)	11.4	7.1	101
12 oz/375 mL white wine	0	0	255
TOTALS	112.1	37.2	2,203 (45% of calories from fat)

Lighthearted Holiday Turkey Dinner

	g total fat	g saturated fat	calories
White wine spritzer: 3 oz/90 mL wine + soda	0	0	58
Skewered Tortellini, 2 (page 25)	4.1	1.1	150
Spinach and Artichoke Dip: 2 tbsp/25 mL (page 26)	1.7	.2	27
Vegetables plus 2 tbsp/25 mL dip made with 2% cottage cheese	.5	.3	44
Turkey: 4 oz/115 g white meat, no skin	.8	.3	153
Stuffing: 1/2 cup/125 mL moistened with stock or water, not added fat	1.0	0	60
Cranberry sauce: 2 tbsp/25 mL	.1	0	53
Gravy: 2 tbsp/25 mL	.6	.2	15
Mashed potatoes: 1/2 cup/125 mL made with 1 tbsp/15 mL 2% milk	.4	.2	75
Turnips mashed with carrots and orange juice	.2	.0	54
Jellied salad or green salad with 1 tbsp/15 mL Creamy Garlic Dressing (page 80)	1.2	.1	54
Frozen Vanilla Yogurt (page 221)	1.9	1.2	181
with 1/4 cup/50 mL mincemeat sauce	.7	0	92
6 oz/175 mL white wine	0	0	119
TOTAL	13.2	3.6	1,135 (10% of calo- ries from fat)

APPENDICES

Hints for People on Therapeutic Diets

This book is written for the average, healthy person to reduce his or her risk of cancer and other chronic diseases. However, many families have a member who has elevated blood cholesterol or high blood pressure or are on a very low-fat diet under the care of a doctor or dietitian. This book is also for them; however, they have to be even more careful about their diet. Here are a few suggestions:

For high blood pressure:

Follow the suggestions "How to Cut Down on Salt" on page 241. When cooking recipes from this book you can reduce the sodium further:

- Use homemade meat or vegetable stocks or water or low-sodium stocks. Most canned stocks or stocks made from a cube are high in sodium.
- Use low-sodium canned tomatoes or freeze your own tomatoes.
- Instead of salt, add flavor with herbs and spices, lemon juice, mustard, garlic, onions, hot pepper flakes or hot pepper sauce.
- Rinse canned beans or lentils under cold water, then drain before using.
- Don't add salt to water when cooking vegetables, pasta or rice.
- Choose frozen vegetables over canned.

Cutting down on sodium

Sodium content of tomato products

Per cup/250 mL	mg sodium
Tomato sauce, canned	1,476
Spaghetti sauce, canned	1,238
Stewed tomatoes, canned	646
Whole tomatoes, canned	390
Tomato paste: 1/3 cup/75 mL*	56
Ripe, raw tomatoes	14

*Mix 1/3 cup tomato paste with 2/3 cup (150 mL) water and use instead of tomato sauce.

Seasonings and sodium content

Per tbsp/15 mL	mg sodium
Table salt	6,975
Bouillon cube	1,440
Soy sauce, regular	830
Soy sauce, sodium-reduced	484
Hoisin sauce	346
Chili sauce, bottled	225
Mustard, prepared yellow	200
Tomato ketchup, bottled	175
Worcestershire sauce	147
Cranberry sauce	5
Vinegars	0

For high blood cholesterol:

If you have an elevated blood cholesterol you need to limit the fat in your diet even more. Here are a few suggestions:

- Use no-fat milk.
- If you need to use a spread, use a diet or fat-reduced soft margarine, however these are not recommended for baking.
- Instead of 1 egg, use 2 egg whites in most recipes in this book. Don't worry about throwing out the egg yolks, it is still cheaper than buying egg substitutes. (You can always mix yolks with water and use to water plants.)
- Follow the recipes in this book and, except for recipes for baked goods, try to reduce the fat in most recipes by half.
- Limit your use of foods high in cholesterol: egg yolks, caviar, organ meats, shrimp, crab or lobster.

CUTTING DOWN ON DIETARY FAT

Choose fats that are lowest in saturated fat

The most important and easiest way to reduce the amount of fat consumed is to use less fat while preparing food—from what is put on toast in the morning to how the fish is cooked at night—use as little fat as possible. Whenever fat is used, try to use ones that are lowest in saturated fat. Butter, lard and shortening are all higher in saturated fat than most soft tub margarines.

The oil with the least amount of saturated fat is Canola oil. Other oils low in saturated fat (in order of least amount of saturated fat) are safflower, sunflower, corn, olive and peanut.

The margarines with the least amount of saturated fat (including the least amount of hydrogenation and trans fatty acids) *are soft tub margarines*, the ones with the nutrition information printed on the label are usually the best.

Diet or calorie reduced margarines are even lower in total and saturated fat and are fine as a spread but not recommended for baking. Read the label for margarine substitutes or imitation margarines. *All margarines made from vegetable oils are cholesterol free.*

Fat Content of Dairy Products

Per 1 cup/250 mL	g total fat	g saturated fat
Milk		
whole	8.2	5
2% b.f.	4.7	3
1% b.f.	2.2	1.6
buttermilk	2.0	1
skim	0.4	0.3
condensed, sweetened, canned	28	18
evaporated, whole, 7.6% b.f. (undiluted)	20	12
evaporated, 2% b.f. (undiluted)	5	3
Commercial eggnog	20	12
Cream		
whipping, 35% b.f.	88	55
table, 18% b.f.	46	28
half and half, 12% b.f.	31	19
Sour cream 14% b.f.	46	28
Ice cream		
vanilla, 16% b.f.	24	16
vanilla, 10% b.f.	16	10
vanilla, soft	8	4
Yogurt (3/4 cup/175 mL)		
fruit bottom, 3.6% b.f.	6.5	4.2
plain, 3.2% b.f.	5.9	3.8
plain, 1.5% b.f.	2.8	1.8
plain, 0.2% b.f.	0.3	0.2

*Fat and Calorie Content of Cheese (per 1 oz/25 g *)*

Type	g total fat	calories
Cottage cheese; 2% m.f.	0.6	26
Cottage cheese; 4% m.f.	1.3	30
Ricotta, 12% m.f.	3.7	50
Mozzarella, part skim; 15% m.f.	4.5	74
Cheese slices; 23% m.f.	7.0	94
Process cheese spread (jar); 24% m.f.	7.2	92
Brie; 26% m.f.	7.9	95
Blue cheese; 27% m.f.	8.2	101
Mozzarella; 28% m.f.	8.4	108
Parmesan, grated; 28% m.f.	8.6	130

Processed Cheddar; 29% m.f.	8.9	107
Colby; 30% m.f.	9.2	112
Cream cheese; 31% m.f.	9.4	100
Cheddar; 32% m.f.	9.7	120

*1/4 cup (50 mL) grated hard cheese or 2 tbsp (25 mL) cream or cottage cheese.

NO-FAT AND REDUCED-FAT CHEESES

Today there is a growing availability of no-fat and reduced-fat cheeses that offer a good way to get the nutritional benefits of dairy products without all the dietary fat of regular cheeses. In the past, some brands of no-fat and reduced-fat cheeses seemed a little rubbery, had a bland taste, or did a poor job of melting when used in cooking. Today, however, there have been many improvements and many brands are now excellent. Most regular hard cheeses, such as Cheddar and Swiss, contain about 8 to 9 grams of fat per ounce. You'll find that reduced-fat cheeses contain only about 3 to 5 grams of fat per ounce.

Try several different brands to find one whose taste and texture you enjoy. While most no-fat cheeses don't melt very well in cooking, most reduced-fat cheeses melt just fine. For best results when using a reduced-fat cheese as a topping on a baked dish, add it near the end of the baking and heat it just until it melts.

Remember that in recipes that call for grated, chopped or crumbled Cheddar or other hard cheese, 1 oz (25 g) of solid cheese equals about 1/4 cup (50 mL) of grated cheese.

Coffee Whiteners

If you drink 3 or 4 cups of coffee or tea a day and add a whitener, you can save up to 9 grams of fat a day by switching to 2% milk.

Per tablespoon (15 mL)	g total fat	g saturated fat
Table (coffee) cream 18%	2.7	1.7
Coffee whitener powder	2.1	1.9
Half and half cream (10%)	1.5	0.9
Coffee whitener liquid	1.5	0.3
Whole milk	0.5	0.3
2% milk	0.3	0.2

LABELLING

Claims you might see on labels and their meaning:
Low fat: 3 grams or less fat per serving
Low saturated fat: 1 gram or less saturated fat per serving and no more than 15% of calories from saturated fat
Low cholesterol: 20 milligrams or less cholesterol per serving and 2 grams or less saturated fat per serving
Low sodium: 140 milligrams or less sodium per serving
Reduced sodium: at least 25% less sodium when compared with a similar food
Light in sodium: 50% less sodium per serving: restricted to foods with more than 40 calories per serving or more than 3 grams fat per serving
Light; Lite: one-third fewer calories or 50% less fat per serving. If more than half the calories are from fat, fat content must be reduced by 50% or more.

How to Cut Down on Salt

- Try to prepare more foods from scratch instead of relying on packaged convenience foods. Frozen meals and entrees, flavored rice mixes, casserole and dinner helper mixes, cake mixes and pudding mixes all contain more salt than similar foods made at home from basic ingredients.

- Also watch out for the more processed foods since processing generally results in the use of more salt. For instance, slices of roast meat are lower in salt than processed meat like bologna and salami; fresh potatoes don't contain as much salt as instant potatoes or frozen, stuffed potatoes; processed cheese food has more salt than regular cheese.

- Watch your consumption of fast food: hamburgers, chicken sandwiches, fish and chips, pizza. These foods are often high in salt.

- Eat fewer snacks like potato and taco chips, as well as regular crackers, which can be very high in salt.

- Cut out, or cut by half, the salt called for in recipes.

- Don't add salt to cooking water when cooking vegetables and pastas.

- Use pure seasonings like onion and garlic powder rather than onion and garlic salts for flavoring meats, fish, poultry and vegetables.

- Remove the salt shaker from the table but leave the pepper. A sprinkle of pepper or any favorite spice helps to perk up a food that's crying out for seasoning.

Packed Lunches and Snacks

The planning for packed lunches and snacks is no different from planning for a regular meal at home. You're aiming to make the lunch or snack with a variety of nutritious foods. The one thing you want to be more careful about is the amount of sugar in these meals and snacks because chances are teeth won't be brushed after eating.

Lunches to Go

- Nothing invented to date can match the convenience of a sandwich. Use whole grain bread or rolls but alternate kinds to add variety. Go light on sandwich fillings and butter/margarine if you use either at all. Pack lettuce and sliced cucumbers or tomatoes separately to be added to the sandwich at lunchtime.

- Pack extra veggies or fruit to go with a sandwich.

- If you get tired of sandwiches, there's nothing wrong with alternatives like these:
—muffins/yogurt/vegetable sticks
—crackers/cheese/apple
—cottage cheese/sliced pineapple/slice of rye bread
—pasta salad/milk/peaches
—slice of pizza/orange

- Keep foods like these on hand for easy add-ins:
—snack pack cheese or peanut butter/crackers
—whole grain, lower-fat crackers
—juice boxes/cans
—individual-sized servings of fruit, yogurt, pudding[1]
—different breads and rolls; pita bread, bagels, bread pretzels
—low-fat cookies like social teas, fig bars, sultana raisin cookies, ginger snaps
—muffins
—portable fruit like bananas, oranges, grapes, apples, pears

- Children are often under a lot of pressure to bring "goodies" in their lunch. Pretzels, home-made popcorn that isn't highly buttered, and peanuts once in a while are good substitutes for chips; cookies that are low in fat are okay as well.

Snacks

Snacks should be viewed as just small meals covered by the same principles of healthy eating as regular meals. The food given should be nutritious and safe for teeth. Healthy snacking is particularly important for young children who often get a significant proportion of their day's food from snacks. Here are some suggestions for good snacks:

- low-fat milk, unsweetened fruit juice, vegetable juice
- non-sugar-coated cereals, preferably whole grain
- whole grain crackers with reduced-fat cheese or peanut butter
- bran muffin or whole grain muffin, not too sweet
- low-fat yogurt
- milk pudding
- fruit — fresh, or canned in fruit juice, not syrup
- vegetable sticks or rounds
- bread sticks
- a sandwich
- half bagel with cheese
- slice of pizza
- popcorn or nuts for older children who are less likely to choke on them

Taco and potato chips, candy, sweet baked goods, fruit leathers, pop, sugared cereals and dried fruits like raisins are not good snacks because they are either non-nutritious or their sugar content makes them a poor choice for teeth.

[1]Individually packaged foods, while convenient, add to the growing problem of garbage disposal and are not considered environment friendly. To be sensitive to environmental issues, consider buying a thermos for each family member and stocking up on a variety of reusable plastic containers to pack lunches in.

Eating Out the Healthy Way

Eating out, especially if it's three or four times a week, can take its toll on an otherwise healthy diet. Restaurant meals tend to be larger, higher in calories, fat and sodium, and lower in dietary fibre than meals you eat at home. But there's good news too! Now, more than ever before.

Here are some tips to help you take advantage of this trend whether you're grabbing a bite on the run or dining out at a five-star restaurant.

- Go to restaurants, buffets and cafeterias where there is a large and varied menu. When there are lots of different dishes to choose from, you're bound to find some healthy choices.

- Learn to *ask* for what you want: fish that is broiled or baked instead of pan fried; milk for coffee instead of cream; low-fat salad dressings and sauces served on the side so you can control the amount that goes on the food.

- Order a broth-based soup like chicken noodle instead of a cream soup.

- Enjoy the fresh bread or rolls without butter or margarine. Always ask for whole wheat rolls, bread and toast.

- For a main entree, choose low-fat items like a half chicken breast, baked fish, or pasta with a tomato sauce, or a small grilled steak. Old-time favorites like lasagna, quiche, ribs and macaroni and cheese are okay once in a while but are too high in calories, fat and sodium to choose often.

- Order lower-fat, fibre-rich items like bean-based chili, split pea or minestrone soup; add a whole wheat roll and a glass of low fat milk to complete the meal.

- Watch out for some salads! A salad of garden greens and veggies with a low-fat dressing is a good choice. But salads like potato, pasta, Caesar and julienne are quite high in calories and fat.

- Choose plain rice or baked potato instead of french fries. Flavor the baked potato with some low-calorie salad dressing or a sprinkling of pepper, but don't put butter or sour cream on it.

- Try stir-fry meals where you get mostly low-fat rice or pasta, lots of vegetables and little meat. Ask the chef to go light on the oil and stir-fry sauce.

- When portions are large, don't feel that you have to clean your plate if you've had enough.

- Dessert, if eaten at all, should be simple: a fresh fruit cup, sherbet or frozen yogurt.

Fast Foods: How to Get the Best and Leave the Rest

Contrary to popular belief, not all fast-food meals are a nutritional disaster. It depends on what you choose.

Fast foods are notoriously high in calories and fat. Deep-fat frying, special sauces and doubling up on cheese and meat are mostly to blame.

HOW TO CUT DOWN ON CALORIES AND FAT

- Always choose the smallest portion size.

- Choose basic menu items like a regular hamburger instead of a deluxe burger, a fried chicken or fish sandwich; a regular pizza instead of one with double cheese and extra bacon.

- Order milk or juice instead of a milkshake or pop.

- Ask for a low-calorie salad dressing to go with salad.

- Beware of breakfast items. An English muffin or croissant with egg, bacon and cheese is a high-fat way to start your day. Try the hot cakes or pancakes instead. Leave off the butter and use a little syrup.

- Give your business to the places that offer healthier menu items: salads, whole wheat bread products, roast beef sandwiches, baked or grilled chicken, chili, bean-based Mexican food.

Fast Food Check

The values for calories and fat are average values for typical fast-food menu items. They are used here to point out that even at fast-food restaurants your choice of foods can make a difference.

FAST FOOD ITEM	CALORIES	FAT (g)
Regular hamburger	260	11
Deluxe burger — 2 patties, cheese, sauce	950	60
Chicken sandwich	596	33
Fish sandwich	437	26
Bowl of chili	230	9
Taco	195	11
Garden salad with:		
—packet light dressing	105	5
—packet regular dressing	262	21
Breakfast sandwich	435	30
Hot cakes breakfast		
—butter and syrup	359	8
—no butter, syrup only	290	1

Sodium

It's just about impossible to escape high levels of sodium in most fast-food meals. Healthy people should try to offset this sodium load at other meals; those on sodium-restricted diets should not eat fast foods too often.

Fibre

Dietary fibre is not abundant in most fast-food meals. There are a few fibre-rich items but for the most part, you're going to have to make up for the lack of fibre at other times during the day.

Fibre Finds in Fast Foods

- Salads — Use a low-calorie, low-fat dressing.
- Baked potatoes — Top with something low in calories and fat like chili or salsa instead of bacon and cheese.
- Chili — The more beans, the better.
- Bean-based Mexican food.
- Whole wheat rolls.
- Fruit salad.

—Denise Beatty, R.D., Consulting Nutritionist

INDEX